Advance Praise

Dr. Tyner offers us a thoughtful and enlightened view of the role of the lawyer as agent of social change. Focusing on four lawyer-leaders who have inspired change and inspired others to work for change, she shows us an optimistic way for lawyers to lead in their service as the gatekeepers of social justice. Acknowledging the depth and breadth of society's problems, she advocates for lawyers to be trained to be leaders and to lead in the resolution of issues that otherwise seem intractable.

Sarah Redfield
Professor of Law

This work is a significant contribution to the education of lawyers as leaders of change for social justice. Building on the principles of authentic and shared leadership, the book highlights the importance of lawyers fulfilling their ethical responsibility, leading from wherever and whoever they are. Similar to what is happening in the engineering profession, this work is at the forefront in filling a gap in leadership development for lawyers that is timely and crucial to the responsibilities of the profession.

Ronald J. Bennett, PhD
Founding Dean & Professor Emeritus of Engineering, University of St. Thomas

Artika Tyner's book is a call to action. The action she seeks is a fresh, rethinking of legal training. Tyner describes a "New Social Justice Lawyering," which articulates a vision of legal education that recognizes a primary role for leadership development in law school curriculum. The kind of leadership she describes empowers people in our communities whose voices go unheard. Empowering marginalized people requires community organizing skills, and the kind of communication skills that can discover community

I

wisdom, and mobilize the community's assets in support of positive social change. This book provides guidance for developing these and other critical skills in lawyers dedicated to social justice.

If we want to live out the greatest promises of democracy, then our definition of leadership must transcend the limiting notion that it is just positional, or that it is part of some zero-sum equation where some people are leaders, and others are not. Because attorneys practice their craft within "the system," it is often difficult to think of them as change agents whose skills and talents can be dedicated to *dismantling* systems. The re-imagining of institutions requires collaborative leadership skills, not just technical knowledge used to assist clients when they need to "lawyer up." *Lawyer as Leader* recognizes this, and offers a good roadmap for legal education for those who want to be involved in creating transformative change in the world.

John Hamerlinck
Associate Director at Minnesota Campus Compact

This book speaks to lawyers whose passion for social justice will be ignited so that they can be true leaders of social change. Professor Tyner not only gives us the vision for becoming effective social justice leaders but speaks to our souls to empower us to take those first steps to serve and transform communities.

H. Wesley Sunu
Attorney at Law, Tribler Orpett & Meyer P.C.

The Lawyer as Leader: How to Use Your Legal Skills to Plant People and Grow Justice is a young lawyer's practical vision for empowering lawyers to stand in the great legal traditions of Gandhi and Mandela to motivate systematic change. It is a passionate call for the development of coursework in law schools and continuing education curriculum to train lawyers on the fundamentals of leadership that will target critical issues of justice. Dr. Tyner's work is foundational and necessary—not only for the practice of law but that of a more just society.

Kao Kalia Yang
Author, *The Latehomecomer: A Hmong Family Memoir*

The law is often viewed as an obstacle to justice by change agents and activists. In this groundbreaking book Dr. Artika Tyner argues that this need not be the case and that lawyers are often leaders of social movements. Through profiles of four social justice lawyers Dr. Tyner explores how insights from leadership theory can help us envision the practice of social justice lawyering. This is a crucially important book that will be welcomed by change agents and educators everywhere.

Stephen Brookfield
John Ireland Endowed Chair, University of St. Thomas, Minneapolis-St. Paul, Co-author *Learning as a Way of Leading: Lessons from the Struggle for Social Justice*

The Lawyer as Leader: How to Use Your Legal Skills to Plant People and Grow Justice is a very powerful read—inspiring, empowering, motivating, immediately useful and applicable across business sectors and professions. This book addresses what leaders today and in the future can employ to develop others as well as develop his/her self. A must-read for anyone passionate about promoting social change!

Debra A. Lindh, Ed.D,
President and Founder, Mindful Effect, LLC

When leadership, a passion for service and a passion for justice intersect, there exists a potential for great things to happen. That intersection is far from unique in the legal profession, but in Dr. Artika Tyner there is clear evidence of the extraordinary. Her book speaks truth as Dr. Tyner speaks in life—with careful deliberation, thorough preparation, and quiet power. A valuable resource for young lawyers seeking to make a difference.

Bill Woodson
Assistant Dean, Opus College of Business The University of St. Thomas

Dr. Tyner's special new book is a fresh reminder to all of us in the legal community that ours is one of the healing professions, and that some of our most important professional obligations are to help heal the wounds of social injustice, and to help advance the opportunity for all of our citizens to enjoy 'life, liberty and the pursuit of happiness' fully and fairly. That requires both commitment and work, and Dr. Tyner's book—her "guide"—helps point the way. It won't happen on its own. As Dr. King reassured us: " The arc of the moral universe is long, but it bends toward justice." President Obama has rightly reminded us, though, that "the arc of the moral universe may bend toward justice, but it doesn't bend on its own." Each of us, in our own way, given the many ways of serving in our profession, can and should put our hand on that arc and help bend it toward justice, sooner instead of later. Dr. Tyner's book provides both inspirational examples and practical tools for doing just that, and for that we should be thankful as well as newly challenged.

Tom Nelson, Partner
Stinson Leonard Street

Dr. Tyner challenges lawyers to answer the call to lead for justice. This book offers current and aspiring lawyers the inspiration and tools to stay true to that vision and nurture the seeds of change in their communities.

Vina Kay, Interim Executive Director/Director of Research and
Policy, Organizing Apprenticeship Project

Dr. Artika Tyner's empirical work illuminates for us the pivotal role that lawyers have in promoting justice and social change. It serves as a beacon to inspire and empowering lawyers and students to serve and lead the change they wish to see in the world. Its insightful profiles of four innovators of "social justice lawyering" draw the reader in and does not let go.

Yvette L. Pye, Ph. D.
Saint Mary's University of Minnesota

Bearing in mind Justice Oliver Wendell Holmes Jr.'s famous admonition of the importance of "experience," Prof. Tyner is providing a critically important and timely primer for lawyers as conscientious counselors to community by rolling back our sleeves and getting to work as leaders in our increasingly diverse society.

Steve Hunegs
Executive Director
Jewish Community Relations Council of Minnesota and the Dakotas (JCRC)

In *The Lawyer as Leader: How to Use Your Legal Skills to Plant People and Grow Justice,* Dr. Artika Tyner gives a timely and bold case for a new model of law founded on social justice lawyering, leadership, and public policy change. Tyner's concept of new social justice lawyering provides a roadmap for the legal profession to better meet the justice needs of all members of society, including the poor and the disenfranchised. *The Lawyer as Leader* is an important contribution to the scholarly literature on leadership in legal education, offering a framework for fostering social justice change as well as effective, ethical professional practice within all areas of law.

Verna Monson, PhD
Principal, Fifth Wave Evaluation Consulting

This book is a hard-hitting directive and a manual on how to become a leader and practice social justice lawyering. Dr. Tyner charges lawyers, always recognized as the gatekeepers of justice, to step up to their responsibility, get involved, build community and coalitions, and lead the way to a better tomorrow where the previously voiceless will have gained equity, access and equality. It is a thought-provoking book and uses fascinating heroes of our past to illustrate her points.

Patti Weber
Retired CIA Senior Executive
President, The Woman's Club of Minneapolis
Pierce-Weber Partnership, LLC

Tyner provides not just a crucial vision of lawyers as leaders of social justice causes, but practical pathways for making that vision reality. Read it as a call to action for what the law can do in changing what must change in society.

Jane Kise, Ed.D., author of *Intentional Leadership*

Dr. Tyner encapsulates the roles of humanist, activist and gardener, in her quest to invoke awareness, sensitivity and action in individuals, organizations and systems. Her book is a must read that delivers a provoking outcry to transform (or abolish) the persistent inequities of our society. It provides a challenging guide for anyone committed to leading the charge in addressing the social injustices of the ostracized, less privileged and the powerless. Students from cultures around the world will be inspired to advocate for those without a voice or choice for justice.

Cheryl Chatman, Ed. D.
Executive Vice President and Dean of Diversity
Concordia University

Tyner's ideas in this book give a clarion call for law schools to realize what they've always done. Law schools train leaders, but as lawyers with technical legal problem solving skills. Intentionally including leadership curriculum in legal education truly connects the missing links. I see lawyers working as international development professionals, human rights advocates, political and social policy entrepreneurs. In *The Lawyer as Leader: How to Use Your Legal Skills to Plant People and Grow Justice*, Tyner calls for creating the linkages that will truly position lawyers as leaders with a Social Justice frame.

Ahmed Sirleaf, International Development Professional, Lecturer at the Kofi Annan School at the University of Liberia in Leadership and International Relations

This book by Dr. Artika Tyner which is aimed at reinventing social justice lawyering and justice education in general is quite inspiring. It will be an important tool beyond the United States; particularly for us in Africa where the reforms in legal education have embraced social justice and public interest lawyering through clinical legal education.

Olugbenga Oke-Samuel Senior lecturer & Coordinator Clinical Legal Education Program Faculty of Law, Adekunle Ajasin University, Akungba-Akoko, Nigeria

An important and necessary book for all legal scholars and practitioners to read. Professor Tyner, using real life examples, reminds us that law is always a language of power. And that the fluency and literacy of the legal practitioner is enhanced only when their practice is not only informed, but led by community.

Amalia Deloney, Senior Policy Director, Center for Media Justice

Dr. Tyner's book argues for a vision of "new social justice lawyering." The book is grounded in civil rights history and explores many related theories of lawyering and organizing. At the core is a model of social justice lawyers collaborating with and learning from communities as community leadership capacity grows. Social change and movement toward justice can only happen with engaged communities, and Dr. Tyner's vision sees lawyers as part of those communities, not as isolated experts. I have admired Dr. Tyner's personal role in this area, and this very helpful book will help spread the model.

Mary Keefe, Executive Director, Hope Community, Minneapolis

Dr. Artika Tyner is a rising star as a writer and educator on the compelling and most important subject of leadership and diversity. Tyner takes what we know now and leads us into what we need to know to carve a new path for the future where cooperative living and racial integration is no longer something we give lip service to but something we actually live out in real time. Dr. Tyner's passion to express these innovative strategies and principles is exciting. Her flawless research combined with her passion to lead us into greater knowledge make this a must read for anyone involved in leadership who wants to learn how to do it better.

Melanie Bragg, Author, Speaker, Coach

Artika Tyner has outlined what amounts to a useful manual for the preparation, inspiration and participation from the standpoint lawyer/activism. What the writer calls social justice lawyering is clearly conceptualized as the three pillars of social justice lawyering: 1) Advocacy, public and private, 2) leadership and 3) giving access to the legal system to clients. Further, the model encompasses being a champion for voices not traditionally heard like children, women, migrant workers, communities of color, and the elderly, etc. This sentiment represents a powerful moral overtone, which should not be divorced from "just the facts" as the truth.

By citing key pioneers in the evolution of social justice lawyering and organized community action Tyner gives due recognition to likes of revolutionary thinkers such as Charles Hamilton Houston, the father of social engineering at Howard University and Myles Horton, of the Highlander Folk School with its ingenious tactics of community organization. Tyner gives due homage to history and history makers. All ideas evolve via the historical process.

Over the past half-century a plethora of ideas and action around the American system, its practitioners from judges, celebrated clients, seriously impacted how lawyers in particular functioned. The rise and influence of the Black civil rights movement on the American legal system cannot be over stated. This movement has been the major transformative engine for most of what has happened in our era. Happily, Artika Tyner has a handle on this phenomenon. "The drum major instinct" of Dr. Martin Luther King, his style and spirit of servant driven leadership, has given a generation of marching feet. King's interpretation of Christian moral principles is a direct challenge to the mind, i.e. "Any law that degrades human personality is unjust. We have a moral obligation to disobey unjust laws."

Dr. Mahmoud El-Kati
Professor Emeritus of history at Macalester College

In *The Lawyer as Leader: How to Use Your Legal Skills to Plant People and Grow Justice*, Dr. Tyner sets out a bold challenge to the field of law and education of lawyers: use your power for good. This type of change can only come from within, and Dr. Tyner has a clearly articulated set of ideas and plans to do just that. It is exhilarating to read a new voice taking on the most venerable of our institutions.

Charlotte Landreau
International Baccalaureate Coordinator and Teacher,
Highland Park Senior High School

I agree with Dr. Tyner's vision for the future of social justice lawyering: attorneys have capacity and great power to wield their sword in one direction or the other, to fight the good fight for truth, justice, and social change.

D.A. Pridgen, Girl Scouts USA

This is a breakthrough book! As a leader, I found myself being deeply influenced, motivated, and even inspired.

Cyrus Batheja, MBA, PHN, BSN, ASN, RN

Dr. Tyner makes a new and wonderfully engaging contribution to the message that lawyers who help to preserve justice and fairness for others follow a noble, and vitally important calling. Her writing style pulls you in and you don't want to stop reading because the content is both educational and heartwarming. I believe Dr. Tyner's book is perfect as a legal text and as a story about lawyers as heroes making a much needed difference for local and national communities. This book exemplifies the ABA message of standing for Liberty and Justice in day-to-day practice. I am reminded of the ABA coming to help preserve the judicial infrastructure when Haiti was hit by a devastating tsunami that destroyed and damaged the buildings that were part of that Country's judicial underpinnings. I believe Dr. Tyner's book also serves as an inspiration for all who read its pages to be vigilant and remain an active participant in underpinning our most precious goal of making sure everyone has access to fair treatment under our laws.

David King Keller, PhD
Best-selling ABA author
Founder, Keller Business Development Advisory Group
Member, Corporate Minority Counsel Program
CLE Instructor on Ethics and Eliminating Bias In Attorney-Client Relationships

Highly recommended. The author is a wise and experienced change agent.

Thomas E. Holloran
Holloran Center for Ethical Leadership in the Professions,
University of St. Thomas School of Law; Former President, Medtronic, Inc.

The Lawyer as Leader effectively argues that all lawyers can be leaders influencing the process of justice. The book provides an outstanding toolbox for every lawyer who wants to make a difference for social justice.

Neil Hamilton
Professor of Law
Director of the Holloran Center for Ethical Leadership in the Professions

How to Plant People
and Grow Justice

THE LAWYER
AS LEADER

DR. ARTIKA R. TYNER

Foreword by Marian Wright Edelman

Printed in the United States of America.

18 17 16 15 14 5 4 3 2 1

Library of Congress Cataloging-in-Publication data on file.

Discounts are available for books ordered in bulk. Special consideration is given to state bars, CLE programs, and other bar-related organizations. Inquire at Book Publishing, ABA Publishing, American Bar Association, 321 N. Clark Street, Chicago, Illinois 60654-7598.

www.ShopABA.org

This book is dedicated to the memory of my grandparents (Nellie Light-foot, Nadine Tyner, and Joseph Buckhalton Sr.), who fostered my love for learning and taught me the importance of love for God, service to others, and the courage to lead.

Foreword

Lawyers must be visionaries in our society. We must be the nation's legal architects who renovate the place of justice and redesign the landscape of opportunity in our nation. The policy choices that lawyers promote will have far more significance for our children and our grandchildren than will the credentials that we wield as we confront the intricacies of government and private enterprise.
—Judge A. Leon Higginbotham, Jr., speaking at the 100th anniversary celebration of the *Harvard Law Review* in 1987

In his final book, Dr. Martin Luther King, Jr. asked us a critical question: "Where do we go from here: chaos or community?" The same question looms in our nation today as we continue to see the challenges facing children and all those living at the margins of society. We must make a conscious choice to strengthen our communities. This goal has inspired the work of the Children's Defense Fund and the life calling of the lawyers featured in this book.

The Children's Defense Fund was founded forty years ago to ensure that no child is left behind and create a level playing field for all children. This vision of hope for the future is shared by Dr. Tyner and the four lawyers profiled here, each of whom has taken a courageous stand to reset our nation's moral compass. These lawyers demonstrate ways to wield the transformative power which lies in each of our hands.

We *can and must* chart a new course for America's future if it is ever to live up to its promise. This fair and hopeful future is within our reach with tenacious advocacy and determined wills. We can end child poverty in the richest nation on earth. All in America can have access to affordable health care. Communities can be freed from the blight of gun violence. A quality education can be guaranteed every child. *The Lawyer as Leader* offers a new definition of leadership focused on collective engagement and a moral imperative to serve. Although this book is a particular call to action for lawyers, everyone can and must play their part in making America into the America of our ideals by addressing the indefensible social and economic inequalities of our time. All caring citizens must choose community over chaos by garnering the moral courage to stand up for all those who share our nation. These four civil rights attorneys provide a fine example for all lawyers and all of us.

Marian Wright Edelman
Founder, Children's Defense Fund

Contents

Preface

Lawyers are the gatekeepers of justice. History demonstrates the important role that lawyers have played in promoting justice and social change. Whether it be protecting the rights of children (Marian Wright Edelman), promoting equal access to a quality education for all children (Charles Hamilton Houston and Justice Thurgood Marshall), or advocating for the human rights of marginalized communities (Mohandas Gandhi), for decades, lawyers have been at the forefront of social change movements. Lawyers have played a key role in protecting the rights of the voiceless by serving as engineers of social change. This exercise of one's technical training coupled with a courageous commitment to the cause of justice is demonstrative of leadership.

Leadership is an individual's ability to exercise influence by organizing others around a shared vision. It focuses on making this vision become a reality in partnership with other collaborators and allies. Leadership is also about motivating and inspiring others to lead. In the process of social change, the leader focuses on empowering others to lead and sustaining the momentum of change movements. A leader recognizes that each person has a unique leadership role to play in influencing the process of justice. A leader also acknowledges that leadership is not hierarchical or positional but instead it is a shared a responsibility to create stronger communities and collectively effect change. This is a new definition of leadership that focuses on what the collective can build together since we are stronger together than apart. How can we lead together in the fight for justice?

This book examines the role of lawyers as leaders in the promotion of social justice initiatives, explores the history of social justice lawyering, and introduces key tools for promoting social change. I introduce the conceptual framework of "new social justice lawyering" in order to critically examine the phenomenon of lawyers playing an active role in promoting social change.

New social justice lawyering is a method of lawyering that draws upon leadership principles, public policy advocacy, and notions of social justice lawyering in order to work in partnership with communities to foster and support social change.

Lawyers are commissioned to protect the rights of the citizenry. "A lawyer is the key to access to the legal system, and without such access few rights are granted and none is secure."[1] In order to fulfill this fiduciary duty, lawyers must gain an understanding of the challenges experienced by those living at the margins of society and recognize the lawyer's power to effect meaningful social change in partnership with marginalized populations and other key allies and supporters. This is a call to action for lawyers to actively pursue the cause of justice. *This is a call to leadership.*

The Lawyer's Call: The New Social Justice Lawyer

This book will aid lawyers in heeding the call to leadership by assisting in the development of their core leadership competencies and establishing the key dispositions of "new social justice lawyering." According to the sage wisdom of Alexander Solzhenitsyn, "[j]ustice is conscience, not a personal conscience but the conscience of the whole of humanity,"[2] and therefore we have a responsibility to lead in an authentic manner. Justice is defined in the *American Heritage Dictionary* as "the conformity to moral rightness in action or attitude." In preparation to assume this important leadership role, lawyers must gain new skills and tools that are needed to uphold the foundational precepts of justice. My research and experience in the leadership field have provided me with key insights related to identifying and employing these new tools. Sound lawyering skills (analytical, critical thinking, research, and writing skills) are the foundational tools. However, additional tools are needed to promote justice, fairness, and equality.

---

1. Southern Minnesota Regional Legal Services, Free Legal Assistance for Low Income People on Critical Legal Problems (2010), http://www.smrls.org.

2. *Collected Quotes Pertaining to Equal Justice*, NATIONAL LEGAL AID & DEFENDER ASSOCIATION, http://www.nlada.org/News/Equal_Justice_Quotes (last visited Apr. 18, 2014).

These other tools move beyond engaging in social justice lawyering alone to building the leadership capacity of others. This allows leaders to build people power in order to transform systems that create inequities and to advocate for policy reform. I refer to these tools as the three pillars of new social justice lawyering. The three core pillars are (1) social justice lawyering; (2) leadership; and (3) public policy advocacy. I have spent the past six years helping law students to build this particular type of multifunctional toolbox in order to leverage these tools for engaging in social justice–related work. My goal is to now share this toolbox with you and instruct you on how to maximize these tools.

The book will showcase the stories of four lawyers in order to provide you with key insights on how you can use the three pillars as tools to effect social change. These four profiled lawyers are (1) Bonnie Allen (Mississippi Center for Justice); (2) Edgar Cahn (TimeBanks USA, University of District of Columbia Law School); (3) Nekima Levy-Pounds (Community Justice Project); and (4) john a. powell (formerly of the Kirwan Institute). These lawyers embody the qualities of new social justice lawyers as transformative leaders, practitioner-scholars, community advocates, and policy entrepreneurs. They have employed their legal training as a tool for creating new inroads on the pathway to justice.

A Missing Link: Leadership Education and Law Schools

In order to address the social justice challenges of our time, lawyers must be equipped to exercise leadership as an indispensable tool. Law schools play a crucial role in preparing law students to become lawyers. These institutions should also serve as learning laboratories for developing core legal competencies and establishing a firm foundation of professionalism. Leadership development serves as a bridge at the intersection of these goals. Unfortunately, leadership development is conspicuously missing from the traditional law school curriculum.

Further, an explicit focus on leadership development in the law school curriculum is consistent with the learning objectives outlined in "Educating Lawyers: Preparation for the Profession of Law," published by the Carnegie

Foundation.[3] These goals focus on preparing law students to exercise servant leadership by ministering to the needs of those they are pledged to serve and recognizing that the practice of law is a public service calling. It also is consistent with the core competencies of effective law practice as described in an article by Shultz and Zedeck titled "Predicting Lawyer Effectiveness: Broadening the Basis for Law School Admissions Decision": creativity/ innovation, strategic planning, community involvement and service, and the ability to see the world through the eyes of others.[4] Further, best practices in legal education published by Stuckey identified that the primary goal of legal education should be to develop competence in resolving legal problems effectively and responsibly.[5] Leadership education would fulfill this goal by aiding future lawyers in developing core competencies in understanding the intersection of law and policy, analyzing the dynamics of organizational leadership, developing effective client counseling skills, strengthening interpersonal communication, and exercising a range of problem-solving skills—to name a few. This type of training and skills development would be beneficial in all sectors whether a lawyer is serving as general counsel or as a county lawyer.

Other professional schools (e.g., business, engineering, and medical) have recognized the importance of leadership development training. These schools teach leadership skills through case studies, ethical dilemma simulations, and reflective exercises. However, the vast majority of law schools have failed to take intentional steps to provide leadership development training in order to raise the next generation of lawyer-leaders. This book can serve as a guide on how to incorporate leadership principles into the law school curriculum. Law schools are increasingly tailoring their curricula toward the practical aspects of lawyering, including more opportunities for preparing law students to become "practice ready" by offering courses that focus on experiential learning (e.g., clinic, externship, and practicum). These courses provide students with the opportunity to gain hands-on experience before

---

3. MARJORIE M. SHULTZ & SHELDON ZEDECK, FINAL REPORT: IDENTIFICATION, DEVELOPMENT & VALIDATION OF PREDICTORS FOR SUCCESSFUL LAWYERING (Sept. 2008).

4. Marjorie M. Shultz & Sheldon Zedeck, *Predicting Lawyer Effectiveness: Broadening the Basis for Law School Admissions Decisions*, 36 LAW & SOC. INQUIRY 620 (2011).

5. ROY STUCKEY, BEST PRACTICES FOR LEGAL EDUCATION: A VISION AND A ROAD MAP (2007).

joining the legal profession. Because law schools are already moving in this direction, now is the perfect time to advocate for meaningful leadership training and to adopt a comprehensive leadership curriculum.

A focus on leadership development should not be limited only to law school classrooms but should also extend to ongoing professional development for lawyers. Lawyers are endowed with a mantle of leadership; however, far too many lawyers have not been given the opportunity to develop and hone their leadership skills. Instead, it is assumed that lawyers are leaders, and so no one provides them with the tools to effectively lead. Therefore, leadership development should also be adopted as an integral part of continuing legal education offerings.

Acknowledgments

This journey of discovery was a divine appointment. It was a process of exploration that nourished my soul, encouraged my spirit, and motivated me to lead within my sphere of influence. I express my heartfelt gratitude to the profiled lawyers who served as my guides on this journey: Professor Bonnie Allen (Mississippi Center for Justice), Dr. Edgar Cahn (TimeBanks USA), Professor Nekima Levy-Pounds (Community Justice Project), and Professor john a. powell (formerly of the Kirwan Institute). They are truly ambassadors of justice who have been commissioned to uphold the precepts of justice, democracy, and freedom.

Thank you to my mother (Jacklyn Milton), aunt Geneva Kirtley, grandmama Rosie Jiles, and Bishop Dr. Dorothy Blaylark-Hill who encouraged me to embark on this journey and provided daily encouragement. I am indebted to the many family members and friends who offered ongoing support, read drafts, and shared ideas. A special thanks to Judge Larry Cohen, Father Dennis Dease, Marian Wright Edelman of the Children's Defense Fund, Dr. Mahmoud El-Kati, Jackie Grossklaus, Dr. John Holst, Mr. Nathaniel Khaliq, Dr. Bruce Kramer, Judge LaJune Lange of the International Leadership Institute, Dr. Stacey Larsen, Cindy Lavorato, Todd Phelps of Leonard, Street, and Deinard, Justice Alan C. Page of Page Education Foundation, and Dean Robert Vischer of the University of St. Thomas School of Law for helping to make this dream a reality. My graduate assistants, Maria Bazakos and Hannah Tekhaar. I also would like to express my sincere gratitude to Melanie Bragg, Timothy Brandhorst, Kevin Cummins, Kelly Keane, Richard Paszkiet, and the ABA Solo, Small Firm and General Practice Division Publications Board for helping to bring my vision to fruition.

Introduction

If your vision is for a year, plant wheat. If your vision is for ten years, plant trees. If your vision is for a lifetime, plant people.
—Chinese Proverb

The title of this book was inspired by the idea of planting people with the goal in mind of furthering the cause of justice. Imagine if lawyers across the world began planting seeds of social change, justice, and freedom. Could you be the one who plants the seeds for the promotion of access to affordable housing, fair sentencing, educational equity, or racial justice? This is your beckoning to lead—will you answer the call?

The social justice challenges of our time call for the need for lawyers to seek the promotion of justice, exercise leadership, and facilitate the process of policy change/reform. Presently, U.S. communities are facing great social challenges as evidenced by the economic crisis and widening justice gap. In this time of social crisis and when there is a pressing need for social change, these "great necessities call forth great leaders."[1]

Social justice–oriented lawyers are being called upon to lead. They are needed to bridge the gap in serving the needs of impoverished clients and in continuing antipoverty reform efforts. The demand for legal services and social change continues to grow. Currently, 46 million people, or one in seven residents, live in poverty in the United States; this creates a barrier to accessing the legal system and to exercising political power.[2] "The income-level disparity in this country is now wider than at any point since

---

1. E.L. Walker, Transcending Moments in the Lives of Leaders 3 (2009) (unpublished dissertation) (available via ProQuest Digital Dissertations at AAT 2400217).
2. KATHLEEN SHORT, SUPPLEMENTAL POVERTY MEASURE: 2011 (U.S. Department of Commerce, Census Bureau, 2012), http://www.census.gov/hhes/povmeas/methodology/supplemental /research/Short_ResearchSPM2011.pdf.

the Great Depression."[3] The poor are often marginalized, feel excluded from the rule-making/public policy process, and lack the allies needed to facilitate change in political agendas and budgetary allocations that affect their social and legal needs.[4] "Needed now are theories and practices that support liberty and opportunity for the poor and disenfranchised, in their contests with the rich and super-franchised."[5]

Further, 80 percent of the civil needs of poor people are not being met because of "chronically and grossly" underfunded legal services and pro bono programs.[6] In 2009, Legal Services Corporation demonstrated an imminent need for lawyers to assume leadership in protecting justice for all through the development of programs and initiatives that address this gap in much-needed services. The legal needs of low-income persons are basic to their survival and ability to thrive in a society. Fundamental legal rights need to be enforced as they relate to such basic necessities as nutrition, health, shelter, income, education, and protection from violent physical abuse, in order to uphold the foundational tenets of social justice.[7]

These particular statistics illustrate only one dimension of the challenge in pursuit of justice: equal access to legal services. More specifically, the challenge is to dismantle the systems that maintain and uphold discrimination, disparate outcomes, and subordination based upon one's social identity (characterized by race, gender, and socioeconomic class). Hence, there is a call to action for lawyers to engage in work that will lead to meaningful changes in the administration of justice.

The lawyers profiled in this book have heeded this call by working collaboratively with allies and communities to effect change. These lawyers demonstrate leadership and a commitment to the cause of justice.

---

3. P. EDELMAN, SO RICH, SO POOR (2012).

4. B.L. Bezdek, *To Forge New Hammers of Justice: Deep Six the Doing-Teaching Dichotomy and Embrace the Dialect of "Doing Theory,* 4 U. MD. L.J. RACE, RELIGION, GENDER & CLASS 301 (2004).

5. *Id.*

6. LEGAL SERVICES CORPORATION, DOCUMENTING THE JUSTICE GAP IN AMERICA: THE CURRENT UNMET CIVIL LEGAL NEEDS OF LOW-INCOME AMERICANS (2009), http://www.lsc.gov/pdfs/documenting_the_justice_gap_in_america_2009.pdf.

7. Southern Minnesota Regional Legal Services, Free Legal Assistance for Low Income People on Critical Legal Problems (2010), http://www.smrls.org.

Bonnie Allen was drawn to the Mississippi Delta to work for social change.

Allen advocates for a lawyering model that places people in the center of the advocacy efforts. More specifically, the ability to work with people to advocate for social change is what drew her to Mississippi and to the Mississippi Center for Justice. Upon her visit to Mississippi (following Hurricane Katrina), she described herself as being "hooked on the work and hooked on people."

Dr. Edgar Cahn acknowledges that community members are at the center of social change.

Cahn believes lawyers have a responsibility to use the law as a tool to build a shared vision of justice and equity. He describes lawyers as social architects whose "job in part is to structure the institutional vehicles into which and through which people can channel their energy and contribute in ways that are collectively more powerful."

These institutional vehicles provide opportunities for the community to become engaged in the process of social change. This framework moves beyond lawyering in a case-by-case format to lawyering in partnership with the community.

The experiences of the lawyers profiled in this book informed my theory of new social justice lawyering, which was developed as I explored this question: *What are the leadership characteristics of lawyers currently engaged in social justice efforts and what tools do they use to build and sustain social change?* The two key components of new social justice lawyering are planting people and growing justice. The new social justice lawyer builds and sustains social change through the exercise of the three pillars: (1) social justice lawyering, (2) leadership, and (3) public policy advocacy.

Planting People

The new social justice lawyer is a planter—a planter of ideas, seeds of change, and a vision for justice. His or her leadership capability is evaluated by raising the question: Do you grow the people that you lead? To answer this question in the affirmative, it is essential to exercise leadership. Leadership is a common theme that was evidenced through the profiled lawyers' actions, words, and publications. They also can be characterized metaphorically as *planters* based upon their commitment to inspire, motivate, and encourage others to lead. Planting people is an organic process that yields a great harvest over time. It starts from the ground up as a seed is planted until it takes root. This seed represents resistance against marginalization and oppression in order to further the cause of social justice. The seed also represents a partnership between lawyers and community stakeholders. Together, they are able to build a shared vision of a just society and engage in community-building. As the seed begins to germinate, community members start to view themselves as leaders with the capacity to address their own challenges and realize their power to resist oppression. This is an ongoing process of collective engagement, perseverance, teamwork, and diligence. The ultimate result is creating social change, which equates to reaping a harvest of justice, fairness, and equity.

Growing Justice

Social change is reflected in the image of the banyan tree. This particular tree represents the progression of social change as it moves from a vision to materialization. The banyan tree as a metaphor illuminates the image of the partnership between these *new social justice lawyers* and community members. Unique to this tree is its ability to grow upward since new roots are formed from the branches. Each community member represents a branch as his or her leadership voice begins to emerge. These branches grow upward together and are intertwined as they exercise their united power and utilize their voices to advocate for social change. Collectively, the stakeholders are able to create a shared vision of community-building

Figure 1
Banyan Tree

and establish the key steps for making this vision a reality. The branches are connecting, growing together, and supporting one another. They in turn create new roots that establish a firm foundation for the tree and extend to new growth. The process of social change, like the growth of the banyan tree, demonstrates the power of collective engagement.

Overview

This book explores the experiences of lawyers who are working at the forefront of social change initiatives ranging from addressing economic inequities to promoting juvenile justice reform. I will share their stories about their leadership journeys. My hope is that these stories will inspire you to ignite your passion for justice, build your leadership capacity, and equip you to take action.

This book includes seven chapters with reflection questions at the end of each chapter.

Chapter 1, "Pillar One: Social Justice Lawyering," defines social justice lawyering, discusses the obligations of lawyers to assist the disempowered and marginalized, and examines the theories of collaborative lawyering, change-oriented lawyering, rebellious lawyering, and social engineering.

Chapter 2, "Pillar Two: Lawyers and the Exercise of Leadership," introduces the principles of servant leadership and transformational leadership and discusses the connections between social justice lawyering, leadership, and the lawyer as a facilitator in the process of social change.

Chapter 3, "Pillar Three: Facilitating Social Change through Public Policy Advocacy," explores the role of the lawyer as a policy entrepreneur and coalition builder and examines how lawyers can establish community partnerships and engage in agenda setting and agenda advocacy.

Chapter 4, "Profiles of the New Social Justice Lawyer," profiles four lawyers who exemplify the qualities of new social justice lawyers. It describes how their passion for social justice has informed their professional formation and inspired their vocational journeys. It also provides an overview of their work, which includes organizing public policy campaigns, educating students, and empowering others to lead. Their work will serve as an example for you to explore your role in leading change.

Chapter 5, "Building Blocks of Leadership," will provide you with guidance on how to build a leadership platform. It focuses on how lawyers can utilize leadership skills to guide others, motivate them, and support their leadership development during the course of social change. This exercise of leadership provides a firm foundation for initiating and sustaining social change since it draws upon each contributor's assets. New social justice lawyers have the capacity to work in partnership with community members to reach their shared vision of justice and exercise the transformative power that initiates the process of social change. This is a new definition of leadership that is not positional or hierarchical (endowed by title), but instead focuses on what the collective can contribute—how they can lead together in the fight for justice.

Chapter 6, "Planting People, Growing Justice," explores principles of community empowerment and asset-based community organizing. The focal point is how to build the capacity of others to lead. Leadership development at the grassroots level is integral to the success of not only building but sustaining social change, since people are at the center of the process of social change. An ancient Chinese proverb provides the context for this creation of a shared vision of justice, valuing people, and working together in partnership to foster social change. The proverb provides: "If your vision is for a year, plant wheat. If your vision is for ten years, plant trees. If your vision is for a lifetime, plant people." In essence, a key perspective or frame of mind for the new social justice lawyer is *planting people*. This leadership is evaluated by raising the question: Do you grow the people that you lead? You will learn how to empower others to lead and how to work collaboratively to effect social change.

Chapter 7, "The New Social Justice Lawyer's Toolbox: Redefining Money, Power, and Lawyering," will provide you with practical tools for applying the techniques of new social justice lawyering. It focuses on developing a multifunctional toolbox that can be used to facilitate the process of social change. These tools include the following: engaging in coalition-building, mobilizing stakeholders through social media, and organizing policy campaigns. Model examples of how these tools can be applied will be provided.

As you read each chapter, take the opportunity to pause and reflect. This is the beginning of a new chapter of your growth and development as a leader.

Summary

The new social justice lawyer seeks to plant people and support the process of growing justice. This lawyer is a planter of people by promoting a vision of justice and effecting social change. In turn, this particular type of lawyer also focuses on growing justice by empowering others to lead.

Reflection Questions

The new social justice lawyer is drawn to promoting the cause of justice and builds a rapport with others who share the same passions. Allen's example of being "hooked on" the work and the people when she relocated to the South following Hurricane Katrina serves as an example of this point. Her love for the people and the pursuit of justice drew her to the Mississippi Delta to help protect the rights of the people after the devastation of the storm.

1. Social justice has been characterized as involving "the goals of equality, of access, opportunity, and outcome."[8] How do you define social justice?
2. What social justice issues are you passionate about (criminal justice, housing law, poverty law, education law)?
3. How are these issues affecting your community?
4. What groups or individuals are working to address these issues? How can you contribute to their efforts and aid in collaborative efforts?

---

8. M. Bok, Civil Rights and the Social Programs of the 1960s: The Social Justice Functions of Social Policy 15 (1992).

Chapter 1

Pillar One: Social Justice Lawyering

As a public citizen, a lawyer should seek improvement of the law, access to the legal system, the administration of justice, and the quality of service rendered by the legal profession.
—The American Bar Association Model Rules of Professional Conduct (2010)

Lawyers are called upon to serve as the gatekeepers of justice by upholding the rule of law, principles of democracy, and foundational tenets of justice. This role is fulfilled traditionally when a lawyer is called upon by a client to offer legal advice, provide access to the legal system, and aid in navigating the system. The client seeks a lawyer to address a legal issue and the lawyer crafts the legal arguments. Renowned social justice lawyer Gerald Lopez has characterized this traditional model as "regnant lawyering" when a lawyer is viewed as the primary actor in addressing a client's legal matter.[1] The lawyer is called upon to address a legal issue and offer solutions based upon his or her legal expertise.

Within this role, lawyers have created a model of technocracy in which lawyers are the problem solvers and they exercise their power based upon their professional credentials to resolve client legal matters.[2] The lawyer acts within his or her knowledge base of the functioning of the legal system

---

1. Gerald P. Lopez, *Critical Race Lawyering: Living and Lawyering Rebelliously*, 73 FORDHAM L. REV. 2027, 2041–54 (2005).
2. HARRY CHATTEN BOYTE, THE CITIZEN SOLUTION: HOW YOU CAN MAKE A DIFFERENCE (2008).

to achieve the client's desired goals and objectives through the utilization of legal skills such as fact investigation, case strategy development, and analytical perspectives.[3] Lawyers then translate a client's claim into a legal framework through legal research and analysis. In essence, the lawyer serves as a technical expert who is paid to reach the most favorable outcome for his or her client. Within this framework, at least in the case of subordinate clients or those who are not legally savvy, the clients are perceived as helpless dependents in need of rescue from the expert lawyer.[4] The theoretical framework that informs the work of the new social justice lawyer offers an alternative view. The new social justice lawyer focuses on how he or she can work in partnership with the community to eradicate systems of oppression and establish new inroads to the pathway of justice. The work of the new social justice lawyer is grounded on an assets-based, community empowerment model through the application of principles of social justice lawyering, leadership, and public advocacy (see Figure 1.1).

An Introduction to Social Justice Lawyering

The traditional role of lawyering falls short in addressing the needs of subordinate and oppressed groups and in creating social reform, thus obstructing access to justice, fairness, and equity.[5] Lawyers with a passion for social justice have expanded the traditional definition of lawyering by exploring the role of lawyers in social justice initiatives in pursuit of equal justice under the law. Social justice lawyering challenges lawyers to enlist in the furtherance of a particular social justice cause in partnership with the affected community. This lawyering for a cause occurs when a lawyer advocates for social justice through a variety of channels, such as litigation, community-organizing, public education/outreach, and legislative advocacy, in order "to advance a cause past its current legal limitations and boundaries."[6]

---

3. Ascanio Piomelli, *Foucault's Approach to Power: Its Allure and Limits for Collaborative Lawyering*, 24 UTAH L. REV. 395 (2004).
4. *Id.*
5. Gerald P. Lopez, *The Work We Know So Little About*, 42 STANFORD L. REV. 1, 13 (1989).
6. BLACK'S LAW DICTIONARY 251 (9th ed. 2009).

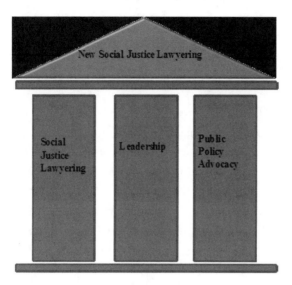

Figure 1.1
Three pillars of new social justice lawyering.

Empowerment focuses on enhancing the capacity of poor people to influence the state institutions that affect their lives by strengthening their participation in political processes and local decision making. And it means removing the barriers—political, legal, and social—that work against particular groups and building the assets of people to enable them to engage effectively in markets.[7]

While engaging in social justice lawyering, the lawyer aids in empowering clients and promoting their self-reliance.[8] Client-centeredness is also paramount with the goal in mind of facilitating client autonomy and empowering clients to engage in activism. This model focuses on giving voice to

---

7. World Development Report, Causes of Povery and a Framework for Action (2000), http://siteresources.worldbank.org/INTPOVERTY/Resources/WDR/English-full-text-Report/Ch2.pdf.

8. C. Shdmaimah, The Practice of Public Interest Law: Power, Professionalism, and the Pursuit of Social Justice (2005) (unpublished dissertation) (available via ProQuest Digital Dissertations at AAT 3172573).

the voiceless, providing power to the powerless, and aiding in overcoming subordination. For instance, it explores how procedural fairness is affected by social factors, such as race, class, or gender, and it challenges disparate outcomes. Another example of this empowerment model is examining how certain policies result in systemic disparities that have a negative impact on certain communities.

Furthermore, social justice lawyering also seeks to uphold the professional ethical aspirations of the legal bar. The American Bar Association Model Rules of Professional Conduct (2010) suggest: "As a public citizen, a lawyer should seek improvement of the law, access to the legal system, the administration of justice, and the quality of service rendered by the legal profession."[9]

Moreover, the body of research related to social justice lawyering has defined the role of the lawyer as a gatekeeper of justice; however this research has yet to explore the role of the lawyer as a leader or the full range of ways a lawyer can serve as a policy advocate.[10] Yet, one's legal training could serve as a vehicle for the effective exercise of leadership. Lawyers could exercise leadership by using writing as a form of advocacy, engaging in strategic planning, working with others to influence legal systems and policies, and serving as zealous advocates for reform efforts. Presently, there is a dearth of research related to leadership development for lawyers; only a few key empirical studies are available on this topic.[11]

9. ABA Model Rules Prof'l Conduct Preamble (2000).

10. *See, e.g.,* Gerald P. Lopez, *Critical Race Lawyering: Living and Lawyering Rebelliously*, 73 Fordham L. Rev. 2027, 2041–54 (2005); Genna Rae McNeil, Groundwork: Charles Hamilton Houston and the Struggle for Civil Rights (1983); Ascanio Piomelli, *Appreciating Collaborative Lawyering*, 6 Clinical L. Rev. 427, 516 (2000); Lucie E. White, *To Learn and Teach: Lessons from Driefontein on Lawyering and Power*, 1988 Wis. L. Rev. 699 (1988).

11. Judy Brown & Bonnie Allen, Leadership in the Legal Academy: Principles, Practices and Possibilities (2009), http://www.law.umaryland.edu/programs/initiatives/lead/docs/LeadershipLawSchoolRpt.pdf; Larry Richard, Herding Cats: The Lawyer Personality Revealed, Report to Legal Management 1 (Aug. 2002), http://www.managingpartnerforum.org/tasks/sites/mpf/assets/image/MPF%20%20WEBSITE%20%20ARTICLE%20-%20Herding%20Cats%20-%20Richards1.pdf; Roland Smith, *The Struggles of Lawyer Leaders: What They Need to Know*, NYSBA J. 38–40 (2009).

Theoretical Frameworks: Social Justice Lawyering

Social justice in action requires the lawyer to act with and on behalf of those who are experiencing suffering caused by social neglect, social decisions, or social structures and institutions.[12] The social justice lawyer is challenged to examine the root causes of injustice and their impacts on marginalized populations in order to effectuate change.[13] This work is drawn together as a part of a collective effort among lawyers and affected communities, groups, and individuals based upon solidarity, which "means together we search for a more just world and together we work for a more just world."[14] The essence of justice recognizes the lawyer's responsibility to contribute to the common good, create access to justice, and provide resources to the community in order to preserve the rights of the community.[15] Collectively, lawyers and community members can work together to realize their vision of change in the landscape of America's legal system.

A lawyer engaging in social justice lawyering critiques the laws by seeking out those whose voices are not traditionally heard, such as children, women, migrant workers, communities of color, and the elderly, and provides an opportunity for their voices to be heard.[16] William Quigley provided a framework for engaging in this process of critical reflection for lawyers.[17] This framework requires social justice–oriented lawyers to (a) engage in active listening to understand the cause of injustice; (b) analyze the power structures and identify who benefits from the injustice; (c) explore the evolution of the law; and (d) examine the structural challenges that affect those of a particular race, class, and gender.[18]

Through this process, relationships are built with people and organizations that are needed to challenge subordination and remedy injustices.

---

12. john a. powell, *Lessons from Suffering: How Social Justice Informs Spirituality*, 1 UNIV. ST. THOMAS L.J. 102, 127 (2003).

13. William Quigley, *Letter to a Student Interested in Social Justice*, 1 DEPAUL J. SOC. JUST. 7, 28 (2007).

14. *Id.* at 21.

15. JERRY WINDLEY-DAOUST, LIVING JUSTICE AND PEACE: CATHOLIC SOCIAL TEACHING IN PRACTICE (2008).

16. Quigley, *supra* note 13.

17. *Id.*

18. *Id.*

Additionally, opportunities for establishing solidarity and engaging in community-building emerge. Hence, the social justice lawyer carries out the role of knowing and interpreting the law and providing the means to protect the interests of the poor and marginalized.[19]

Over time, legal scholars have developed and introduced specific genres of social justice–oriented lawyering that challenge lawyers to reconstruct traditional norms related to the practice of law. These include collaborative lawyering,[20] change-oriented lawyering,[21] social engineering,[22] and rebellious lawyering.[23] These genres of social justice lawyering aid lawyers in establishing a new vision of lawyering that focuses on transforming systems, promoting equity, and establishing partnerships between lawyers and communities. Each of these theories shares the common goal of lawyers working in partnership with key allies to challenge injustice and establish equitable outcomes. However, each theoretical framework provides its own specific guidance on how to achieve this goal through the utilization of a range of strategies that include building a shared vision of justice, engaging in mutual learning, and conducting qualitative research.

Collaborative Lawyering

The collaborative lawyering theoretical framework establishes the importance of collective engagement in building a shared vision of justice through reflection, problem solving, and mutual learning processes. Collaborative lawyering extends beyond the traditional notion of lawyering, which explores how to solve a legal dilemma, and begins to examine the participatory and developmental democratic questions: "What shall we do together?" and "Who shall we become as a result?"[24] It is a joint partnership

---

19. Paul Finkelman, *Not Only the Judges' Robes Were Black: African-American Lawyers as Social Engineers*, 47 STANFORD L. REV. 161, 209 (1994).
20. Ascanio Piomelli, *Appreciating Collaborative Lawyering*, 6 CLINICAL L. REV. 427–516 (2000).
21. White, *supra* note 9.
22. GENNA RAE MCNEIL, GROUNDWORK: CHARLES HAMILTON HOUSTON AND THE STRUGGLE FOR CIVIL RIGHTS (1983).
23. Lopez, *supra* note 1.
24. Ascanio Piomelli, *The Democratic Roots of Collaborative Lawyering*, 12 CLINICAL L. REV. 541, 555 (2006).

with clients that can effectuate social change.[25] Collaborative lawyering promotes client autonomy, upholds respect, and fosters a sense of equality while furthering collaborative efforts.[26]

Collectively, clients and lawyers work together to change the world with the ultimate goal of lawyering against subordination. Subordination, in this context, refers to being under the authority or control of another, which restricts one's power to act. Both clients and lawyers recognize and unveil their power to act in partnership to solve current social justice problems faced by marginalized communities and populations.[27] The underlying theme is that the realization of the power to act focuses on building leadership capacity within communities and collaborating to challenge systems and polices that restrict their power unjustly. This is a learning process that focuses on reciprocal efforts in which everyone learns and everyone teaches.[28] All parties engage in active listening, challenge one another, and solve problems together.[29] The lawyer's role is not to merely work for an individual client but to work with community partners to reach a shared outcome and vision of justice.[30]

Both the collaborative lawyer and the community are learning from each other as they foster social change. On one hand, collaborative lawyers gain invaluable insights about the daily lives of community members, root causes of the issue, and how the issues affect individuals and communities. On the other hand, clients and communities share their problem-solving approaches, practical wisdom, and insights. Clients are viewed as assets who provide key insights and have the capability to engage in reform efforts as activists for change.[31] Interactions between clients and collaborative lawyers create a fertile ground for collective engagement. This process shares similarities with the qualitative methodology of ethnography since the lawyer plays a role similar to that of a participant observer.[32]

---

25. Piomelli, *supra* note 19; Piomelli, *supra* note 23.
26. Shdaimah, *supra* note 8.
27. Piomelli, *supra* note 3.
28. *Id.*; Piomelli, *supra* note 23.
29. Piomelli, *supra* note 3.
30. *Id.*
31. *Id.*
32. Robert K. Yin, Case Study Research: Design and Methods (6th ed. 2009).

Collaborative lawyers as participant observers seek to be immersed in the experiences of those surrounding them (community members, allies, opponents) and gain a deeper appreciation for their daily life experiences. The lawyer enters the community as a guest with the hopes of gaining knowledge through community engagement.[33] The collaborative lawyer partners with clients to reach a shared vision of social change. The client does not simply hand over a legal problem to a lawyer; instead, the collaborative lawyer utilizes his or her legal training to establish a coalition of support for reform. Collaborative lawyers "aim to join with clients, communities, and any allies they can enlist in collective efforts to change the world and through the process each other."[34] Together, the collaborative lawyer and key stakeholders engage in problem solving to address long-standing injustices.[35]

Further, the collaborative lawyer is a coequal and not a dominant decision maker.[36] The collaborative lawyer and community work together to frame, strategize, and implement the community's strategic plan.[37] Both clients and collaborative lawyers can discover a sense of renewed hope due to the recognition of the community's power to act. This recognizes the power of ordinary citizens to influence social change by engaging in participatory democracy.

The collaborative lawyer understands that power must be exercised in order to reach desired outcomes and transform systems. He or she recognizes that each individual has the capacity to utilize power effectively and can serve as a change agent. Power is characterized as dynamic and ever changing. It can be influenced through relationships; in essence, power is a mechanism that can be employed to initiate the community's collective action.[38] French philosopher Michel Foucault theorized power as a mechanism that yields productivity that can produce change in actions, beliefs,

---

33. N. Cook, *Looking for Justice on a Two-Way Street*, WASH. U. J. L. & POL'Y 20, 169–200.

34. Piomelli, *supra* note 37, at 559.

35. Bill Gates, *Bill Gates Sr. on Public Service Law: Reflections on the Value of Public Service by the Private Bar*, NEWSWEEK (2004), available at http://www.newsweek.com /bill-gates-sr-public_service-law-111947.

36. Piomelli, *supra* note 11.

37. Piomelli, *supra* note 37.

38. Piomelli, *supra* note 37.

perceptions, and rituals.[39] The collaborative lawyer encourages others to identify their power sources and utilize this power to initiate the process of social action. "Collaborative work often is required to create enough 'power with' to challenge 'power over.'"[40] The calculated exercise of "power with" lays the foundation for the process of social change.

Change-Oriented Lawyering

Change-oriented lawyering builds upon themes of collaboration by offering guidance for lawyers and community members acting together in furtherance of social change. The purpose of change-oriented lawyering is to facilitate social change within a given community. The focus is to address the impact of disempowerment on social groups and seek ways to empower communities to lead. White characterizes this theoretical framework as change-oriented lawyering that seeks to change the dynamics of power and subordination by drawing upon the strengths of the community served.[41] This differs from the traditional model of lawyering in which the community would be expected to allow the lawyer to solve its problems. In that framework, litigation is viewed as the most effective and best solution to all of the community's problems. However, the change-oriented lawyer works in partnership with the community to facilitate social change. The lawyer is sensitive to the needs of the community and seeks to empower the community. This process mirrors a shared-power model of leadership in which leaders are called upon to engage in joint problem solving and in which they share responsibility to engage in activism.[42]

This is a community-initiated process and it begins when the community extends an invitation to the lawyer to become a part of the struggle for resistance. The lawyer aids the community in fostering its strengths and developing ideas together. Also, the lawyer engages in an interprofessional

39. Piomelli, *supra* note 11; M. FOUCAULT & C. GORDON, POWER KNOWLEDGE: SELECTED INTERVIEWS AND OTHER WRITINGS, 1972–1977 (1980).

40. Marshall Ganz, *Leading Change: Leadership, Organization, and Social Movements, in* HANDBOOK OF LEADERSHIP THEORY AND PRACTICE 509, 535 (Nitin Nohria & Rakesh Khurana eds., 2010).

41. White, *supra* note 15.

42. BARBARA CROSBY & JOHN BRYSON, LEADERSHIP FOR THE COMMON GOOD: TACKLING PUBLIC PROBLEMS IN A SHARED-POWER WORLD (2d ed. 2005).

approach. In White's case study of the Driefontein in South Africa, an interprofessional model is utilized by the lawyer in conjunction with the organizer. These professionals, along with community members, used their imaginations to further social change efforts. The organizer aided the community in carrying out its ideas through implementation phases, which included the development of a community health clinic and legal clinic. This was a holistic approach that sought to address the root causes of the community's social problem.[43]

The change-oriented lawyer also seeks to empower the community in resisting oppression and subordination. White utilizes a three-tiered model to explore the multidimensional nature of subordination and offers possible legal responses.[44] The first dimension is the traditional case-by-case litigation. The main focus at this level is to obtain favorable results through litigation. It acknowledges that the foundation of the law is acceptable but questions its application. The second dimension is law as a public conversation. Law is viewed as a public conversation; therefore it creates opportunities for public policy reform.

The third and final dimension focuses on "lawyering together toward change," which is referred to as change-oriented lawyering. It is a dialectic process of reflection, which leads to action and promotes mutual learning. Both community members and lawyers participate in social justice education within an informal setting.

The goal of social justice education is to enable people to develop the critical analytical tools necessary to understand oppression and their own socialization within oppressive systems, and to develop a sense of agency and capacity to interrupt and change oppressive patterns and behaviors in themselves and in the institutions and communities of which they are a part.[45] This educational process serves as a mechanism of empowerment as communities and lawyers recognize the power within one's hands to challenge subordination, exercise power, and create systemic change.

---

43. *Id.*
44. *Id.*
45. MAURIANNE ADAMS, LEE ANNE BELL, & PAT GRIFFIN, TEACHING FOR DIVERSITY AND SOCIAL JUSTICE 2 (2d ed. 1997).

Within these three dimensions, power dynamics are at play. Professor Lani Gunier[46] has identified three dimensions of this community-led exercise of power. The dimensions are metaphorically contrasted with participating in a game. Within the first dimension, the conflict is manifested while the rules of game are manipulated for one's gain. The second dimension examines the intents and desires of the game designers and how they use their power to shape the rules.

Professor Gunier critiques that most social justice–oriented lawyers operate within this second dimension by seeking to rewrite the rules of the game; however social change occurs in the third dimension.[47] The third dimension seeks to understand the story of power, which explores why winners deserve to win and why losers continually lose. Within this dimension, the change-oriented lawyer deconstructs the power of those in authority. According to Foucault, this requires one to deconstruct how those in authority formulate the "subjugated knowledge" and control systems through the "regime of truth," which aids the change-oriented lawyer in increasing the capacity of community members to exercise their power in manifesting change.[48]

Most importantly, within this third dimension of lawyering together toward change the community is empowered to develop innovative and sustainable solutions to its own legal problems. Myles Horton,[49] a social reformer and cofounder of Highlander Folk School, encouraged community-based problem solving and collaborative processes when he stated: "Get the people together and trust that the solution will arise from them."[50] In the process of change-oriented lawyering, the people are drawn together to orchestrate change, engage in agenda setting, and challenge inequitable policies. The people, with the assistance of lawyers (who are committed to lawyering together toward change) exercise their power to facilitate mutual

---

46. Ashly Hinmon, *Achieving Justice through Rebellious Lawyering: Restructuring Systems of Law and Power for Social Change*, 6 MOD AM. 15–16 (2010).

47. *Id.*

48. FOUCAULT & GORDON, *supra* note 39; White, *supra* note 15.

49. MYLES HORTON, JUDITH KOHL & HERBERT KOHL, THE LONG HAUL: AN AUTOBIOGRAPHY (1991).

50. *Id.* at 98.

learning, initiate the process of social action, and exercise the power necessary to create systemic change.[51]

White's research links lawyering together toward change with community-building to create an image of community that is connected, restorative, and transformative.[52] This sense of connectedness is representative of a circle. "The circle is a sacred symbol of life . . . individual parts within the circle connect with every other; and what happens to one, or what one part does, affects all within the circle."[53] It also recognizes the transformative power of the community since "[i]n every community there is work to be done. In every nation, there are wounds to heal. In every heart there is the power to do it."[54] The lawyer plays a vital role in community-building through the exercise of legal skills to deconstruct current oppressive power structures and replace them with more just systems.

In essence, power is used to initiate social change and compel action. "The most powerful theory, in the end, may be our practice of deliberating together on our experience and our action."[55] The community then realizes that its strength lies in its capacity to deliberate together and take action.

Houston's Social Engineering

Social engineering is a theory of social justice lawyering espoused by the late Dean Charles Hamilton Houston of Howard Law School. It represents the initiation of action and implementation process required to foster social change efforts that sustain social justice movements through legal action. Lawyers can use their legal training to serve as social architects[56] and engineers of social change.[57] Houston characterized the role of the lawyer as a social engineer; he believed that a lawyer was "either a social engineer

---

51. White, *supra* note 15.

52. *Id.*

53. Sisters of St. Joseph http://brentwoodcsj.org/spirituality/daily-prayer/january-29.

54. Marianne Williamson, http://thinkexist.com/quotation/in_every_community-there_is
_work_to_be_done-in/216307.html.

55. White, *supra* note 9, at 769.

56. PETER G. NORTHOUSE, INTRODUCTION TO LEADERSHIP CONCEPTS AND PRACTICE (5th ed. 2010).

57. MCNEIL, *supra* note 22; Michael Wilson Reed, *The Contribution of Charles Hamilton Houston to American Jurisprudence*, 30 HOW. L.J. 1095 (1987).

or . . . a parasite on society."[58] A lawyer as a social engineer is "the mouthpiece of the weak and a sentinel guarding against wrong."[59] Houston's personal commitment to becoming a social engineer was influenced by his life experience in his adulthood, in particular serving in the military. Houston's experience of racism and discrimination in the military left a lasting impact. Following his military service, he later vowed to gain power by speaking with fluency the language of the law (i.e., the language of power). Houston's commitment to wage a relentless battle against injustice was manifested in these words:

> [I vowed] that I would never get caught again without knowing something about my rights; that if luck was with me, and I got through this war, I would study law and use my time fighting for men who could not strike back.[60]

Houston fulfilled his commitment and pursued a law degree with great vigor at Harvard Law School.

Houston later paved the road of freedom through the Civil Rights Movement in an effort to espouse his social justice mission to end racial injustice by burying Jim Crow. He was the first black lawyer to win a case before the United States Supreme Court.[61] He crafted a legal plan to end racial segregation nationwide in all public spaces (schools, buses, and trains).[62] He began this strategic plan by litigating cases related to equalization, particularly school integration cases, with an ultimate goal in mind of establishing the precedent that separate could never be equal.[63] He commissioned black lawyers to join in the fight against segregation in schools by warning, "We need to break this up or perish."[64] Dr. Martin Luther King Jr. acknowledged

---

58. McNeil, *supra* note 22, at 84.

59. Roger A. Fairfax, *Wielding the Double-Edged Sword: Charles Hamilton Houston and Judicial Activism in the Age of Legal Realism*, 14 Harv. Blackletter L.J. 17, 26 (1998).

60. Rawn James Jr., Root and Branch: Charles Hamilton Houston, Thurgood Marshall, and the Struggle to End Segregation 41 (2010).

61. Colin Evans, Super Lawyers: America's Courtroom Celebrities: 40 Top Lawyers and Cases That Made Them Famous (1998).

62. James, *supra* note 60.

63. *Id.*

64. McNeil, *supra* note 22, at 138.

Houston's work in social engineering and the contributions of others doing the same type of work during a speech to the Bar Association of the city of New York, when he stated:

> You should be aware, as indeed I am, that the *road to freedom* is now a highway because lawyers throughout the land, yesterday and today, have helped clear obstructions, have helped eliminate roadblocks, by their selfless, courageous espousal of difficult and unpopular causes.[65]

Houston also paved the "road to freedom" in his classroom. Houston not only demonstrated excellence in the practice of law but also developed a teaching pedagogy of social engineering. As a law professor, he passionately trained law students to use the law as a tool to change systems and establish civic engagement. "He understood that if it were not for teachers and scholars, the law might never be more than precedent-judgments confirming the correctness of earlier judgments."[66] Houston trained his students to think outside the box. Instead of merely looking to the precedent and black letter of the law, Houston taught his students to critically examine the spirit of the law and the very essence of justice. His teaching pedagogy went beyond the traditional case analysis methodology, the Langdell model, by training students to engage in systems reform by overturning *Plessy v. Ferguson* and burying Jim Crow once and for all.[67]

Houston instilled in his students a sense of determination and perseverance in fighting for justice. His most notable slogan was "no tea for the feeble, no crepe for the dead."[68] Houston's power to transform minds in the classroom and train social engineers is demonstrated through the success of students and protégés, like Spottswood Robinson III, Oliver Hill, William Bryant, and Justice Thurgood Marshall, who effectively used the law to better society.[69] The latter two achieved historical stature as federal jurists. These lawyers were instrumental in transforming the road to

---

65. *Id.* at xv.
66. *Id.* at 63.
67. JAMES, *supra* note 60; DIANA KLEBANOW & FRANKLIN L. JONAS, PEOPLE'S LAWYERS: CRUSADERS FOR JUSTICE IN AMERICAN HISTORY (2003); MCNEIL, *supra* note 22.
68. KLEBANOW & JONAS, *supra* note 67.
69. JAMES, *supra* note 60; MCNEIL, *supra* note 22.

freedom into a highway of justice. It has been duly noted that Houston either taught or mentored all of the black lawyers who participated in the Civil Rights Movement.[70]

Through his instructional pedagogy, Houston challenged law students to be leaders in paving a road to freedom that could not be destroyed. Houston's life journey demonstrates the courage needed to use the leadership characteristics of a social engineer. Houston characterized a social engineer as a "highly skilled, perceptive, sensitive lawyer who understood the Constitution of the United States and knew how to explore its uses in the solving of problems of local communities and in bettering conditions of the underprivileged citizens."[71] Social engineering required the following social obligations for lawyers:

(1) to pioneer the cause of group advancement; (2) to advocate for those in need of assistance and protection against moral injustice; (3) to work as peacemaker in the pursuit of social change; (4) to exploit the flexibility within the American legal regime and to use law as an instrument for social change; and (5) to advance a litigation strategy that establishes firm precedent while simultaneously generating favorable public opinion and grassroots support.[72]

Houston's process of social engineering provided a framework for building a social reform movement and initiating coalition-building. Houston aimed to strengthen and equip local communities to fight for their rights and derive model procedures from test cases that could be used in other jurisdictions.[73] The test cases began with equalization of state-sponsored graduate schools since these institutions would aid in preparing the next generation of black professionals who would lead and advocate for the advancement of their people.[74] Litigation related to equal pay for teachers was also a part of the series of test cases. These test cases were incremental

---

70. KLEBANOW & JONAS, *supra* note 67.
71. HOWARD UNIVERSITY SCHOOL OF LAW, HISTORY, http://www.law.howard.edu/19.
72. MCNEIL, *supra* note 22, at 217.
73. JAMES, *supra* note 60.
74. J. Clay Smith Jr., *Principles Supplementing the Houstonian School of Jurisprudence: Occasional Paper No. 1*, 32 HOW. L.J. 493 (1989).

steps in establishing the framework for *Brown v. Board of Education*,[75] which overturned the doctrine of separate but equal outlined in *Plessy v. Ferguson*.[76] Thus, Justice Marshall stated, "the school case was really Charles' victory. He just never got a chance to see it."[77] Moreover, Houston was able to engage in coalition-building since litigation attracted attention to the National Association for the Advancement of Colored People and aided in building notoriety, which in turn attracted the masses to join the NAACP. Houston also awakened the consciousness of the general public through his publications, which served as a call to action. Examples include "The Need for Negro Lawyers" (1935), "Don't Shout Too Soon" (1936), "Educational Inequalities Must Go" (1935), and "Cracking Closed University Doors" (1935).[78] These publications served as advocacy tools to ignite the passion of the masses to fight in the Civil Rights Movement. Houston was instrumental in establishing political power and civic engagement within the African American community. Through his legal advocacy in *Smith v. Allwright*,[79] Houston aided in the creation of equal access to the ballot box.[80]

Rebellious Lawyering

Rebellious lawyering provides a theoretical framework for action research and fostering cooperative, collaborative processes. Rebellious lawyers are inspired by a vision of social justice since they must be proactive in effectuating social change by reflecting and "usher[ing] in the world we hope to create."[81] In envisioning changing the world as we know it, one's imagination can be unleashed.[82] The rebellious vision supports a concerted organized

---

75. 347 U.S. 483 (1954).
76. 163 U.S. 537 (1896).
77. Klebanow & Jonas, *supra* note 67.
78. Charles H. Houston, *The Need for Negro Lawyers*, 4 J. Negro Educ. 49 (1935); Charles H. Houston, *Don't Shout Too Soon*, Crisis (Mar. 1936); Charles H. Houston, *Educational Inequalities Must Go*, Crisis (Oct. 1935); Charles H. Houston, *Cracking Closed University Doors*, Crisis (Dec. 1935).
79. 321 U.S. 649 (1944).
80. Evans, *supra* note 61.
81. Gerald P. Lopez, Rebellious Lawyering: One Chicano's Vision of Progressive Law Practice 382 (1992).
82. Lopez, *supra* note 1.

effort against subordination, based upon factors such as race, gender, socio-economic status, and age.[83] Rebellious lawyers work diligently to "dismantle those social structures that reinforce hierarchy and injustice."[84] This rebellious vision is "perceiving that the world we would like to see varies from the world as it is, we all find ourselves persistently trying to move the world in desired directions."[85] It recognizes the ability of the rebellious lawyer and the clients and communities being served to work together to realize a vision of equality and justice. This moves beyond working for a client to working collaboratively with a client and allies.[86]

The ideology of rebellious lawyering is based upon the premise of fostering cooperative and collaborative processes. Rebellious lawyers integrate themselves and their clients into "a large network of cooperating problem-solvers."[87] Traditionally, a lawyer is viewed as the sole problem solver who has the capacity and training to frame the issues and identify the legal problem. The lawyer serves as an expert who asks questions to confirm his or her course of action and maintain his or her power.[88] To that end, lawyering is nonparticipatory and isolated given that lawyers envision themselves as "self-perceived visionaries who make decisions exclusively."[89] Within this model of lawyering, community members and clients play a very limited role by simply allowing the lawyer to solely formulate solutions.

Contrary to the traditional role of lawyers as experts, Lopez envisions rebellious lawyering as collaboration between co-eminent institutions and individuals where each learns from each other.[90] Each participant in this process has the opportunity to learn and grow, and in addition may offer a unique, diverse perspective in the problem-solving process. The process of problem solving begins with storytelling since stories create a sense of a shared experience and enable us to live with a sense of solidarity. Stories are the framework for creating a social justice–oriented narrative since they aid

83. Gerald P. Lopez, *Shaping Community Problem Solving around Community Knowledge*, 79 N.Y.U. L. Rev. 59 (2004).

84. Hinmon, *supra* note 46, at 16.

85. Lopez, *supra* note 82, at 69.

86. Lopez, *supra* note 5.

87. Lopez, *supra* note 80, at 55.

88. Lopez, *supra* note 1.

89. Lopez, *supra* note 5, at 12.

90. Lopez, *supra* note 82.

in identifying the relevant audience, telling the story of a lived experience, and compelling others to act to bring forth the desired change.[91]

Through storytelling, the diverse experience of those experiencing subordination is shared to facilitate social change and create shared space for ongoing dialogue. By sharing these stories, the power of persuasion is manifested, which allows the lawyer and community partners to challenge others to change the world to mirror the world that they desire to see.[92]

> In this idea—what I call the rebellious idea of lawyering against subordination—lawyers must know how to work with (not just on behalf of) women, low-income people, people of color, gays and lesbians, the disabled, and the elderly. They must know how to collaborate with other professionals and lay allies rather than ignoring the help that these other problem-solvers may provide in a given situation. They must understand how to educate those with whom they work, particularly about law and professional lawyering, and, at the same time, they must open themselves up to being educated by all those with whom they come into contact, particularly about the traditions and experiences of life on the bottom and at the margins.[93]

This perspective acknowledges the role of lawyer as problem solver in partnership with communities to shape problem solving around the community's experiences and build shared knowledge.[94] It also recognizes the importance of working with other professionals to problem solve together and discover new ways for promoting social justice.

Additionally, rebellious lawyering initiates and compels action. Community members and the rebellious lawyer work together to realize their vision of social change. Collectively, they seek to " . . . make those communities we call our own."[95] This demonstrates a shared responsibility to create change

---

91. Gerald P. Lopez, *Lay Lawyering*, 32 UCLA L. REV. 1 (1984).
92. *Id.*
93. Lopez, *supra* note 81.
94. Lopez, *supra* note 82.
95. Lopez, *supra* note 5, at 13.

and enact ownership over the change process. Each is "standing shoulder to shoulder" while engaging in problem solving and community-building.[96]

Overall, the rebellious lawyer learns how to aid in building and sustaining social justice coalitions, help imagine and orchestrate strategies for pursuing desired goals, understand the theoretical political frameworks that they challenge and make concrete, and pursue visions of social justice.[97]

Based upon the principles of rebellious lawyering, Lopez developed the Center for Community Problem Solving (the Center) in 2003.[98] The Center partners with marginalized populations (immigrant, low-income of-color communities) to problem solve around issues with political, economic, social, health, and legal elements. The goal is to foster participatory democracy and equal citizenship. The Center draws together the strengths of problem solvers from all walks of life—business owners, service providers, teachers, artists, policy officials, lawyers, and doctors—to develop practical solutions for problems facing the communities. The Center has the following key fundamental values:

(a) The Center seeks to collaborate with those who live and work in low-income communities, communities of color, and immigrant communities in order to share knowledge of how to address present challenges, identify resources, and develop useful strategies for change.

(b) The Center connects those with problems with service providers who can help to address these problems.

(c) When problems remain unaddressed after making the requisite connections outlined above, the Center seeks additional resources to fill this void.

(d) The Center monitors and evaluates progress in the problem-solving phase.

(e) The Center shares information gathered from its program-evaluation processes to aid in developing more effective strategies for exercising collective problem solving.[99]

---

96. Lopez, *supra* note 1.
97. Lopez, *supra* note 5.
98. Lopez, *supra* note 1.
99. Lopez, *supra* note 1.

Lopez's rebellious lawyering theoretical framework challenges lawyers to engage in problem solving and foster community connections.[100] This will aid in remedying social problems facing the community.

Summary

Social justice lawyering offers a framework for the realization of equal justice under the law. The lawyer seeks to empower the community to lead their own change. Lawyers can draw upon the theoretical frameworks of collaborative lawyering, change-oriented lawyering, social engineering, and rebellious lawyering to develop social justice lawyering skills. These skills focus on promoting collective engagement (collaborative lawyering), leveraging transformative power (change-oriented lawyering), taking strategic legal action (social engineering), and becoming a cooperative problem solver (rebellious lawyering).

Reflection Questions

A lawyer engaging in social justice lawyering seeks to address the root causes of oppression and marginalization. In partnership with community stakeholders, the social justice lawyer develops a strategic plan of action and facilitates the process of social change.

PILLAR 1: Social Justice Lawyering.
1. What are some of the challenges facing members of your community?
2. Do these issues have a legal component? If so, how can you leverage your legal talent to aid in systemic reform and social change?

---

100. Lopez, *supra* note 81.

Chapter 2

Pillar Two: Lawyers and the Exercise of Leadership

There is a natural synergy between social justice lawyering and leadership. The two principles are interconnected since leaders seek to motivate, inspire, and engage community members to bring the shared vision of social justice to fruition. Further, the community is empowered to assume leadership roles in the future, in order to address inequities and overcome subordination. I intend to explore the natural connection between social justice lawyering and leadership by adding a new dimension of scholarly research for demonstrating definition and adding clarity for the role of lawyer as facilitator in the process of social change. Leadership in Law

Due to the societal reliance on lawyers to serve in leadership roles, lawyers are relied upon to exhibit the qualities of public servants (servant leadership) and social engineers (transformational leadership).[1] Over the years, lawyers have been called upon to serve a key role in creating access to justice and protecting the civil liberties of others and fostering a sense of community. Historically, lawyers have been influential in ensuring that the promise of justice is manifested. Notable examples of lawyers serving in a leadership role in furtherance of social change include predecessors like Justice Thurgood Marshall (U.S. Supreme Court Justice) and Robert Sengstacke Abbott (founder and chief editor of *The Chicago Defender*).

---

1. ROBERT K. GREENLEAF, THE SERVANT AS LEADER (2d ed. 1991); GENNA RAE MCNEIL, GROUNDWORK: CHARLES HAMILTON HOUSTON AND THE STRUGGLE FOR CIVIL RIGHTS (1983).

Both men exemplified the moral courage, strength, and passion for social justice consistent with principles of servant leadership and transformational leadership. They used their legal training to create societal reform, to positively influence others, and to exercise power in resisting subordination and oppression. This characterization of a lawyer's professional identity illustrates that inherently lawyers assume leadership roles.[2] Therefore, it is necessary to explore other disciplines (outside the field of law) that provide insight into the nexus between lawyers and leadership.

Theories from the Field of Leadership

Initially, leadership was viewed as an innate set of skills endowed to a limited few.[3] However, subsequent research has demonstrated that effective leadership skills can be taught and developed.[4] Currently, leadership is characterized as an influence process that occurs when a leader seeks to influence the goals of others and empower them to take action in order to reach their desired goals.[5] "Leadership is the ability and courage to create a vision that inspires others, the ability to communicate that vision and to engage all the talent in the organization to focus on the same goal."[6] Therefore, leadership is a process or activity that draws upon the strengths of the leader and followers. The leader teaches by example how to exercise influence. Sullivan characterizes this as a process of mutual influence during which leaders and followers combine their values, beliefs, and actions to achieve a shared purpose.[7] Further, one's ability to excel is based upon

---

2. Ben J. Heineman, *Lawyers as Leaders*, 116 YALE L.J. POCKET PART 266 (2007); HERB RUBENSTEIN, LEADERSHIP FOR LAWYERS (2d ed. 2008).

3. JOHN ADAIR, HOW TO GROW LEADERS: THE SEVEN KEY PRINCIPLES OF EFFECTIVE DEVELOPMENT (2005).

4. RICHARD HUGHES, ROBERT GINNETT & GORDON CURPHY, LEADERSHIP: ENHANCING THE LESSONS OF EXPERIENCE (4th ed. 2002) (supporting the notion that good leaders are made, not born).

5. KENNETH BLANCHARD & PHIL HODGES, SERVANT LEADER: TRANSFORMING YOUR HEART, HEAD, HANDS & HABITS (2003).

6. RONALD BENNETT & ELAINE MILLAM, LEADERSHIP FOR ENGINEERS: THE MAGIC OF MINDSET xvi (2012).

7. DEBRA REN-ETTA SULLIVAN, LEARNING TO LEAD: EFFECTIVE LEADERSHIP SKILLS FOR TEACHERS OF YOUNG CHILDREN (2003).

the nature of the relationship and transaction process that occurs between leaders and followers.[8] This is a process of dualism that affects the learning, growth, and development of both leaders and followers. Hence, a key characteristic of leadership is relationship-building, which contributes to an interactive process of collaboration.[9]

During this transaction process, a leader intentionally exercises his or her power to influence. Influence is one's ability to change or alter a situation based on one's resources, talent, position and power.[10] Dr. Martin Luther King described a leader's influencing capability when he stated, "I refuse to accept the idea that man cannot influence the unfolding events that surround him."[11] In addition to an exercise of influence, leadership happens within a group context and gives attention to common goals.[12] Leaders and followers have a mutual purpose and shared goal to reach. Groups are influenced by their leaders; accordingly, group involvement is paramount to leadership. This group effort can carry forward the vocation of justice.[13] Leaders and followers should work together strategically to develop a plan of action and devise implementation processes. Thus, leadership combines a leader's ability to influence others, encourage group participation, and develop shared goals.

A range of leadership theoretical frameworks and classifications aid in exploring the nature of leadership and an individual's ability to influence and further a group's shared vision within a leadership capacity. There are 65 classifications systems that have been developed to define the multifaceted nature of leadership[14] and there are more than 100 definitions of leadership.[15] The *Encyclopedia of Leadership* provides 38 leadership theories and

---

8. PETER G. NORTHOUSE, LEADERSHIP: THEORY AND PRACTICE (5th ed.) (2010).

9. PETER G. NORTHOUSE, INTRODUCTION TO LEADERSHIP: CONCEPTS AND PRACTICE (2009).

10. AMERICAN HERITAGE DICTIONARY 660 (1985).

11. Nobelprize.org, 2011.

12. NORTHOUSE, *supra* note 9.

13. JERRY WINDLEY-DAOUST, LIVING JUSTICE AND PEACE: CATHOLIC SOCIAL TEACHING IN PRACTICE 93 (2008).

14. Edwin A. Fleishman, Michael D. Mumford, Stephen J. Zaccaro, Kerry Y. Levin, Arthur Korotkin, & Michael Hein, *Taxonomic Efforts in the Description of Leader Behavior: A Synthesis and Functional Interpretation*, 2 LEADERSHIP Q. 245 (1991).

15. JOSEPH ROST, LEADERSHIP FOR THE TWENTY-FIRST CENTURY (1991).

identifies 17 leadership styles.[16] Northouse has compiled these leadership themes into five categories, namely, leadership as (1) a trait, (2) an ability, (3) a skill, (4) a behavior, and (5) a relationship.[17] Leadership combines components of each of these frameworks, classifications, and categories.

The themes of leadership as a behavior and leadership exercised within relationships are evidenced in the theoretical perspectives of servant leadership and transformational leadership. More specifically, the theories of servant leadership and transformational leadership are representative of the organic leadership category in which "the leader is part of a collective that through dialogue crafts a vision to challenge dominant ideologies, structures, and practices."[18] These theoretical frameworks share a commitment to furthering a moral imperative by seeking to promote the common good and shared values.

Servant Leadership

The premise of servant leadership emerged in response to a loss of community, human connections, and stagnation of one's moral imagination.[19] Servant leadership provides a theoretical framework of service that inspires each individual to serve and lead. "It begins with the natural feeling that one wants to serve, to serve first. Then conscious choice brings one to aspire to lead."[20] It requires a leader to heed the call of servanthood.[21] The leader's primary purpose is to serve others and promote the common good.[22] According to Adair, "Democracy needs experts, representatives, and leaders, but it needs them as servants and not as masters."[23] The servant leader utilizes his or her professional training as a tool to serve the needs of others.

---

16. GEORGE GOETHALS, GEORGIA SORENSON & JAMES MACGREGOR BURNS, ENCYCLOPEDIA OF LEADERSHIP (2004).

17. NORTHOUSE, *supra* note 9.

18. STEPHEN BROOKFIELD & STEPHEN PRESKILL, LEARNING AS A WAY OF LEADING: LESSONS FROM THE STRUGGLE FOR SOCIAL JUSTICE ix (2009).

19. ANN MCGEE-COOPER & GARY LOOPER, THE ESSENTIALS OF SERVANT LEADERSHIP: PRINCIPLES IN PRACTICE (2001).

20. GREENLEAF, *supra* note 1, at 7.

21. JAMES A. AUTRY, THE SERVANT LEADER: HOW TO BUILD A CREATIVE TEAM, DEVELOP GREAT MORALE, AND IMPROVE BOTTOM-LINE PERFORMANCE (2004).

22. BILL GEORGE, AUTHENTIC LEADERSHIP: REDISCOVERING THE SECRETS TO CREATING LASTING VALUE (2003).

23. ADAIR, *supra* note 4, at 124.

The foundation of servant leadership is a shared vision that inspires followers and empowers others through a moral commitment to serve and aid fellow community members in reaching their full potential.[24] According to Northouse, vision has five identifiers: picture (image of a better future), change (in the way of doing things), embodiment (in values), map (providing direction and a purpose), and challenge (to create change).[25] The servant leader is called upon to cultivate each of these key characteristics by supporting the community's vision of the future.

A servant leader's true motivation is to inspire others to lead and cultivate their leadership strengths.[26] The servant leader recognizes that he or she is not a sole actor but must foster collective engagement to realize the common vision.[27] During this process connectedness and interdependence are fostered while stronger communities are built. In essence, the progress of a servant leader is evaluated by raising the question "Do you grow the people you lead?"[28] Servant leadership, coined by Robert Greenleaf, is a facilitative approach that supports growth and development during which the traditional roles of leader and followers are transcended.[29]

Servant leadership is manifested through the leader's exercise of influence. Greenleaf warns of the importance of recognizing the impact of influence on one's self and others, since net effect (of an exercise of influence) can be beneficial, enriching, or depleting.[30] This self-awareness reminds servant leaders that they have influence, thus they must be wise stewards of this influence. In the face of injustice, the servant leader is called upon to eradicate social injustices and facilitate social change.[31] Servant leadership is community-focused as it seeks to shift leadership authority and power to each member of the community as he or she emerges from follower to

---

24. AUTRY, *supra* note 22; L.R. Hammargren, *Servant Leadership and Women in the Law: A New Nexus of Women, Leadership and the Legal Profession*, 4 U. ST. THOMAS L. J. 624–43 (2007).
25. NORTHOUSE, *supra* note 10.
26. MCGEE-COOPER & LOOPER, *supra* note 20.
27. NORTHOUSE, *supra* note 10.
28. MCGEE-COOPER & LOOPER, *supra* note 20.
29. BROOKFIELD & PRESKILL, *supra* note 19.
30. MCGEE-COOPER & LOOPER, *supra* note 20.
31. Jill W. Graham, *Servant-Leadership in Organizations: Inspirational and Moral*, 2 LEADERSHIP Q. 105 (1991).

leader. This process aids in the development of the leadership potential of every individual involved.

Servant leaders also recognize that service is paramount to community-building and they deem service a moral imperative. Through serving, everyone can contribute to the growth and development of a strong community. Dr. King described the significance of service in his speech titled "The Drum Major Instinct."[32] The drum major instinct refers to one's innate desire to seek recognition and promote self-indulgence. By contrast, King draws upon themes of servant leadership by challenging his audience to become drum majors for justice by seeking to promote the common good, justice, and servanthood. In this speech, given exactly two months before Dr. King's assassination, he deconstructed the notion of individualism and self-centeredness within communities, while offering an alternative paradigm of service and interrelatedness. This new paradigm empowers each individual to become a servant leader. He stated: "If you want to be important—wonderful. If you want to be recognized—wonderful. If you want to be great—wonderful. But recognize that he who is greatest among you shall be your servant. That's the new definition of greatness."[33] He concludes the speech with a vision for his own eulogy in which he requested to be remembered as one who "tried to give his life serving others."[34]

King's definition of greatness is portrayed in Greenleaf's scholarly research through the characterization of Leo.[35] The character of Leo is drawn from Herman Hesse's *Journey to the East*.[36] Leo accompanies a group of men on a mythical journey as the servant who performs routine menial tasks. Leo remains on the journey as a servant while uplifting the men and guiding the journey. One day, Leo disappears and is found by one of the men many years later. It is then discovered that Leo is also a great leader and a noble guiding spirit, in addition to being an indispensable resource to the group of men. Leo's inner strengths as a motivator and giver empowered him to serve in a merged role as both a servant and a leader. Greenleaf

32. Dr. Martin Luther King, Jr., The Drum Major Instinct (Feb. 4, 1968).
33. *Id.*
34. *Id.*
35. GREENLEAF, *supra* note 1.
36. HERMAN HESSE, THE JOURNEY TO THE EAST (1956).

characterizes Leo's servant leadership qualities as "the real person, not bestowed, not assumed, and not to be taken away."[37] This serves as an example of a servant leader's ability to uplift and motivate others through random acts of kindness.

Servanthood is also a moral imperative that compels one to serve others as an exercise of ethical leadership. Service has been characterized as "the rent we pay to be living. It is the very purpose of life and not something that you do in your spare time."[38] This is recognition that service is a part of the essence of living and being a part of the human family. Each person has the power and capacity to serve in a leadership capacity and make a difference. The endowment of this capacity creates a responsibility for each individual to act in creating a shared vision of social change.

The key qualities embodied by a servant leader are effective listening, perceptiveness, creativity, and empathy.[39] As a reflective listener, a servant leader is always searching, listening, and expecting that there are ways to foster change. For instance, the leader is listening to understand how to serve the community better or how to motivate the next generations of leaders. Servant leaders listen to gain a deeper understanding of the experiences of others. They exemplify the eagerness to maintain a relational perspective, which is highlighted in the prayer to St. Francis of Assisi: "Lord grant that I may not seek so much to be understood as to understand."[40]

A servant leader is perceptive and remains in tune with the rhythm of the community that he or she is serving. The servant leader is required to have a wide span of awareness in order to see the full picture of his or her surroundings. Further, servant leaders are attentive to the needs of the community since they are followed because they are trusted. The servant leader is "closer to the ground—he hears things, sees things, and his intuitive insight is exceptional."[41]

---

37. GREENLEAF, *supra* note 1, at 9.
38. Marian Wright Edelman, http://www.goodreads.com/author/quotes/73926.Marian _Wright_Edelman.
39. John E. Barbuto & Daniel Wheeler, *Scale Development and Construct Clarification of Servant Leadership*, 31 GROUP ORGANIZATIONAL MGMT. 300 (2006); GREENLEAF, *supra* note 1, at 10, 32.
40. GREENLEAF, *supra* note 1, at 10.
41. *Id.* at 32.

Additionally, the servant leader works collaboratively with others in the community to promote the furtherance of social justice initiatives. Greenleaf contrasts this collaborative process metaphorically with a dove, which offers a gentle stirring of life and hope that inspires others to serve in the community and work together to transform society.[42]

In addition, the servant leader exhibits the quality of creativity, which aids in creative problem-solving techniques and bridges the gap of intuition. Further, the servant leader is empathetic and demonstrates a strong sense of compassion for others. The servant leader focuses primarily on the needs and goals of others.[43] Researchers have also identified additional characteristics of servant leaders that include calling, healing, persuasion, conceptualization, foresight, stewardship, growth, and community-building.[44] The culmination of these characteristics provides the servant leader with the skills to think critically and act ethically. "A leader is at any moment a historian, contemporary analyst, and prophet" who combines knowledge of how the past and present influence the unfolding events of the future.[45] These skills enable the servant leader to demonstrate foresight and adaptability when challenges arise.

There are key steps required for fostering a commitment to servant leadership within a community, which requires one to listen without judgment (practice reflective listening), exhibit authenticity, build community, and share power.[46] Further, Autry posits that a servant leader is authentic, vulnerable, accepting, present, and useful.[47] Each of these steps aligns with demonstrating qualities consistent with the ethic of caring, which builds community connections and supports collaboration.

If lawyers engage in these steps, they will cultivate their own leadership skills and empower others in the community to fight for justice "that those alone may be servants of the law who labor with learning, courage, and

---

42. *Id.*
43. SULLIVAN, *supra* note 8.
44. Barbuto & Wheeler, *supra* note 40.
45. GREENLEAF, *supra* note 1, at 17.
46. McGEE-COOPER & LOOPER, *supra* note 20.
47. AUTRY, *supra* note 22.

devotion to preserve liberty and promote justice."[48] This differs from the traditional model of lawyering, which focuses on exerting power through the utilization of one's legal training. A lawyer who practices principles of servant leadership begins by serving first and then leading by exercising reflective listening, fostering a sense of connectedness, empowering others, and establishing rapport.

Transformational Leadership

In addition to servant leadership, transformational leadership also provides a theoretical perspective that focuses on motivating and influencing followers to realize a common social justice vision. Three decades ago, the concept of transformational leadership was first explored by Downton.[49] It materialized as a theoretical framework through the research of James MacGregor Burns, who coined the term "transforming leadership."[50] Burns introduced the transformational leadership model, which was characterized as an ongoing process of reciprocity that linked leadership to followership.[51] Burns distinguishes between "transactional leadership" and "transformational leadership."[52] Transactional leadership focuses primarily on the interactions between leaders and followers. The leader "transacts" with the followers to complete a specified goal and to reward successful completion, therefore satisfying the self-interest of both parties.[53] Contrarily, transformational leadership focuses on the process of engagement that occurs between leaders and followers, which aids in raising standards of morality and upholding collective values.

---

48. *Law School Life: The Layout*, Virginia L. (Oct. 20, 2012), https://www.law.virginia.edu/html/insider/life_layout.htm.
49. James V. Downton, Rebel Leadership: Commitment and Charisma in the Revolutionary Process (1973).
50. Bangalee Trawally, Nelson Mandela the Transformational Leader: The Struggle for Justice, Equality and Democratic Change in South Africa (unpublished Master of Arts in Leadership thesis, Augsburg College, 2009).
51. James MacGregor Burns, Leadership (1978).
52. *Id.*
53. Goethals, Sorenson & Burns, *supra* note 16.

> Transformational leadership is the process whereby a person engages
> with others and creates a connection that raises the level of motivation
> and morality in both the leader and the follower (Northouse, 2010).

The motivation derived during this process serves as an act of reciprocity
that promotes mutual learning and empowerment.[54] Burns hypothesized that
this process would raise the awareness of followers and challenge them to
reach a higher level of motivation and morality.[55] He envisioned that leaders could mobilize groups, parties, public policy, and legislative processes.
Burns saw leaders as catalysts for social change who could transform the
very nature of social conditions by empowering followers to lead. Followers
are initially led by the transformational leader but are inspired to become
leaders themselves.

Transformational leaders exhibit the qualities of charisma and persuasion that compel others to lead and seek social change. Charisma is defined
as a special, innate gift attributed to certain persons who have the ability
to do extraordinary things and win the devotion of others.[56] Other characteristics of transformational leadership include the Four I's: idealized
influence charisma, inspirational motivation, intellectual stimulation, and
individualized consideration.[57]

Through the exercise of the leader's "idealized influence charisma," followers are motivated by the inspiration of transformational leaders' vision
and passion. This is a moral vision that challenges injustices and seeks to
promote equity and justice. Transformational leader Myles Horton characterized this moral vision when he stated, "You have to do the best you
can in an unjust society. Sometimes that means that the laws you go by are
moral laws instead of book laws."[58] Transformational leaders challenge
followers to reach a higher moral standard of a collective vision of change.

---

54. B.C. CROSBY & J.M. BRYSON, LEADERSHIP FOR THE COMMON GOOD: TACKLING PUB-
LIC PROBLEMS IN A SHARED-POWER WORLD (2005).

55. GOETHALS, SORENSON & BURNS, *supra* note 17; Trawally, *supra* note 50.

56. AMERICAN HERITAGE DICTIONARY, *supra* note 11, at 260; HUGHES, GINNETT & CUR-
PHY, *supra* note 4; NORTHOUSE, *supra* note 9.

57. NORTHOUSE, *supra* note 9.

58. MILES HORTON & PAOLO FREIRE, WE MAKE THE ROAD BY WALKING: CONVERSATIONS
ON EDUCATION AND SOCIAL CHANGE 7 (Brenda Bell & John Gaventa eds., 1990).

Also, their charisma tends to be transmissible since it inspires others to serve as change agents. Charisma emerges as "a result of a social crisis and charismatic leaders are those with extraordinary appeal who emerge with radically new visions that provide a solution to a crisis, attracting followers, who strongly identify with them."[59] Transformational leaders also embody strong values and ideals. They promote the intellectual stimulation of followers and encourage creativity. Overall, this promotes opportunities to develop new approaches and engage in creative problem solving.

"Inspirational leadership" is communicated by transformational leaders as they promote shared values and advance a shared vision. The transformational leader focuses on creating and communicating this shared vision in a range of forums.[60] Transformational leaders also promote intellectual stimulation. Followers are encouraged to be creative and innovative. This is a process of thinking outside the box and engaging in creative problem-solving processes. The follower is encouraged to explore and challenge personal beliefs and values while also critically examining the leader's moral compass. Transformational leadership also provides "individualized consideration" by listening to the needs of followers and aiding in the process of self-actualization. The key aspect of self-actualization is recognition of each follower's unique leadership capacity. According to Bass, the transformational leader must gain an understanding of the desires, strengths, and aspirations of followers.[61] In developing this understanding, the transformational leader discovers ways to motivate the followers to maximize their leadership potential.[62]

Additionally, transformational leaders are visionaries and exercise foresight, which motivates others to follow their vision.[63] They support a vision of transformation of social systems and they foster social change. This vision implies change and it challenges followers to move social change

---

59. PETER G. NORTHOUSE, INTRODUCTION TO LEADERSHIP CONCEPTS AND PRACTICE 137 (2d ed. 2001).
60. CROSBY & BRYSON, *supra* note 55.
61. BERNARD M. BASS, LEADERSHIP AND PERFORMANCE BEYOND EXPECTATIONS (1985).
62. JAMES M. KOUZES & BARRY Z. POSNER, THE FIVE PRACTICES OF EXEMPLARY LEADERSHIP (2d ed. 2011).
63. SULLIVAN, *supra* note 8.

initiatives forward.[64] Transformational leaders are able to link this vision with the values and beliefs of followers to create a shared vision of how the world should be and to identify the role of each individual in bringing this vision to fruition.

Followers are encouraged to think strategically, act wisely, reach self-actualization, and strengthen their individual leadership capacity. They are challenged to question authority, analyze cultural influences, and become politically engaged; they in turn discover their identity as transformational leaders.[65] One such example of the development of the leadership capacity of future transformation leaders is the work of prominent civil rights leaders like Dr. Martin Luther King Jr., Fannie Lou Hamer, Rosa Parks, and Septima Clark, who inspired masses of followers to take a leadership role in the struggle for justice. These leaders were empowered to take action in their communities and train others to lead by having the "phronesis" (the disposition to act truly and rightly) guide the "praxis" (informed actions).[66]

Kouzes and Posner offer further considerations of leadership qualities from a transformational leadership perspective.[67] After interviewing more than 1,300 managers (at the mid and senior level) in private and public sectors, Kouzes and Posner identified the following five leadership practices that enable leaders to achieve extraordinary success: modeling the way, inspiring a shared vision, challenging the process, enabling others to act, and encouraging the heart.[68] Further, a transformational leader is an authentic leader who leads change, upholds values, builds relationships, practices discipline, and leads with his or her heart.[69] Finally, the transformational leader exhibits enthusiasm due to the overall satisfaction in discovering the essence of his or her calling.

---

64. NORTHOUSE, *supra* note 10.
65. Joyce Duncan, Historical Study of the Highlander Method: Honing Leadership for Social Justice (2005) (East Tennessee State University).
66. *Id.*
67. KOUZES & POSNER, *supra* note 63.
68. *Id.*
69. GEORGE, *supra* note 23.

Summary

Leadership begins with a vision for social change. The leader is then inspired to make this vision a reality by connecting with others who share a similar passion. They are able to build a partnership based upon the shared values of unity, justice, and freedom. The theoretical frameworks of servant leadership and transformational leadership provide a template on how to create a vision and build strategic partnerships. Servant leadership focuses on one's ability to motivate and inspire the community. Transformational leadership provides an empowerment framework which challenges each individual to discover opportunities for promoting the common good.

Reflection Questions

Leadership is at the core of social change since it aids in creating a shared vision and building strategic coalition.

PILLAR 2: Leadership.
1. After learning about servant leadership and transformational leadership, which leadership qualities do you think you exhibit?
2. Are there new leadership skills that you would like to develop? Make a list of the qualities and explore the leadership development exercises outlined in the appendix.

Chapter 3

Pillar Three: Facilitating Social Change through Public Policy Advocacy

Social change movements influence the process of systemic change, since change begins with dismantling systems that create marginalization and subordination. Active engagement in policy reform and advocacy is an indispensable tool utilized by lawyers in this process. This focuses on engaging in agenda setting and establishing community partnerships. This new type of lawyering also requires advocacy to work in partnership with community. Within this role, the lawyer engages in citizen professionalism, which is characterized by working collaboratively with others to engage in creative problem solving and discover common ground.[1]

Kingdon's Policy Entrepreneurship

Inherently, lawyers serve as political actors either in an active capacity (confronting oppression) or a passive capacity (supporting oppression).[2] Lawyers engage in an active capacity by initiating policy reform efforts and

---

1. Harry Chatten Boyte, The Citizen Solution: How You Can Make a Difference (2008).
2. Catherine Marshall & Maricela Olivia, Leadership for Social Justice: Making Revolutions in Education (2005).

obtaining a working knowledge of how to navigate the terrain of policy change. Kingdon provides a framework for influencing public policy and engaging in agenda setting.[3] Policy is the result of (a) setting the agenda, (b) specifying alternatives, and (c) making an authoritative choice among alternatives.[4] Issues (social, political, and economic) are addressed when agenda setting occurs. The agenda-setting process is influenced by emerging issues affecting policy makers.

Engaging in Agenda Setting

The policy entrepreneur understands how to operate the levers that lead to policy reform and create social change. This process begins by engaging in agenda setting. According to Kingdon, issues influence agenda setting in three ways. The first is by having a change in a widely respected value pressed on the system due to a crisis, prominent event, or alternative circumstance.[5]

Second, an increase in knowledge may affect agenda setting. Within the context of cultivating the transformative power of lawyers, new knowledge emerges. Third, in order for policy issues to be addressed, "streams" must align.[6] These streams can be characterized as pressing social problems that create a "window of opportunity" to bring forth new ideas, support consensus-building, and create solutions.

Kingdon characterizes change as occurring as the result of action.[7] The way change happens is via an actor that he refers to as the policy entrepreneur.[8] He or she is continually engaging in a preparation process by mobilizing and educating community members to address a given social justice issue. Throughout this process, the policy entrepreneur stands ready to take action. He or she prepares for a window of opportunity to open in order to engage in reform efforts. When this window of opportunity is open, policy entrepreneurs are able to offer solutions for challenges presented. This moment of opportunity occurs when policy entrepreneurs can bring their research and passion for a particular issue to the forefront. These

---

3. John W. Kingdon, Agendas, Alternatives, and Public Policies (2d ed., 2002).
4. *Id.*
5. *Id.*
6. *Id.*
7. *Id.*
8. *Id.*

solutions can be proposed when the next window of opportunity opens. This gives policy makers a chance to act in social reform and it gives policy entrepreneurs the opportunity to offer possible solutions.[9]

The policy entrepreneur recognizes the limitations of the law in effectuating social change. He or she recognizes that the adoption of equitable policies can be used to promote social justice. When serving in the capacity of policy entrepreneur, the lawyer develops an understanding of how agenda setting occurs. The lawyer is skilled enough to know how to operate the levers of agenda setting by reframing emerging social justice issues. The lawyer as policy entrepreneur also is prepared for the opening of the window of opportunity by offering practical solutions for public policy reform. Hence, policy entrepreneurship serves as a key tool for advancing social justice by influencing agenda setting and transforming systems.

Stewart's Coalition-Building Framework

Stewart focused on policy streams and the significant role of community-centered advocacy coalitions.[10] The framework's central themes are (a) that changes in policy are the product of individuals acting rationally and strategically within an organization and (b) that changes occur as a result of competing coalitions that share belief systems acting together.[11] Stewart's analysis is explored through a historical case study of the desegregation laws, which sought to create equal educational opportunities. Throughout this case study, Stewart evaluates the effectiveness of these methods used by advocacy groups and offers a variety of policy solutions.[12]

Stewart utilizes the case of *Brown v. Board of Education* to teach public policy lessons and demonstrate the significant role of coalition-building in addressing the root causes of a social problem.[13] The first lesson learned from the pursuit of equal educational opportunities was not to limit the

---

9. *Id.*

10. Joseph Stewart, *Policy Models and Equal Educational Opportunity*, 24 POL. SCI. & POL. 167 (1991).

11. *Id.*

12. *Id.*

13. *Id.*

definition of the policy problem because this also limited the ability to create effective solutions. When the education problem was defined as racial segregation in schools, ending segregation quickly became the solution. This rationale was problematic since it was a short-term fix to a larger systemic problem.[14] In this context, the larger systemic challenges included institutionalized racism and the doctrine of white supremacy. This narrow definition could lead only to temporary remedies. "Subsequent experience shows dramatically that segregated schools were just the symptom, not the disease."[15]

Stewart outlines policy lessons that can be learned from policy advocacy coalitions like the NAACP National Defense and Educational Fund Inc. (Inc. Fund).[16] The Inc. Fund was created to collectively draw together resources that would maximize the likelihood of producing favorable policy changes in civil rights. The Inc. Fund used litigation as a tool for social change, since it was viewed as a way to test strategies and influence public opinion. The Inc. Fund focused on using courts as an alternative to legislative advocacy during its civil rights mobilization efforts. Similarly, the pursuit of a social justice–related cause of action affecting marginalized populations (i.e., police misconduct/brutality, inequitable educational opportunities, and racial disparities in the criminal/juvenile justice systems) offered the opportunity to change public policy and empower marginalized communities.

A key to the success of the Inc. Fund was the skill of the lawyers and active engagement of community members. The lawyers used the courts to shape public opinion related to civil rights in furtherance of social engineering to implement a comprehensive strategy for obtaining favorable court rulings and decisions. These cases addressed the need for racial equity in every area of life, which included civic engagement, education, and economic spheres. Lawyers like Charles Hamilton Houston, Oliver Hill, and Justice Thurgood Marshall developed their expertise in civil rights law and appellate advocacy. As a result, these lawyers emerged as transformational leaders and they used their legal expertise as a tool to manifest their personal passions and professional ambitions with the hopes of advancing

---

14. *Id.*
15. *Id.* at 169.
16. *Id.*

their vision of social justice.[17] Once again, public opinion could be shaped to focus on removing the barriers to access to justice, which are obstructed based upon class, race, and gender.

New Stories and New Public Narratives

Stewart's philosophy related to shaping public opinion can be implemented at the macro level by sharing new stories and establishing new public narratives. This is a process of organizing the community and mobilizing community efforts around common goals. During the process of shaping public opinion, a new story is told. This story is the foundation of a public narrative that uplifts values, compels action, and initiates purposeful action.[18] "Through public narrative, social movement leaders and participants can move to action by mobilizing sources of motivation, constructing new shared individual and collective identities, and finding the courage to act."[19]

During the Civil Rights Movement, the force needed for political and societal changes through community engagement and mobilization was established due to the work of policy advocacy groups. Community mobilization became a powerful tool for influencing public policy, since Congresspersons seek to avoid electoral sanctions. The judicial branch was also affected by the Inc. Fund's advocacy efforts. The precedent set forth by the United States Supreme Court (following the Inc. Fund's advocacy) led to the construction of a new definition of equality and equitable policies. Additionally, community engagement is essential for a paradigm shift in the justice systems. Policy advocacy groups should educate community members on current social justice issues and prepare them to engage in legislative advocacy. Hence, following the example of the Inc. Fund, policy advocacy groups (consisting of lawyers working in partnership with affected communities) have the power to construct a new vision of justice through collective efforts and community engagement.

---

17. *Id.*
18. Marshall Ganz, *Leading Change: Leadership, Organization, and Social Movements, in* HANDBOOK OF LEADERSHIP THEORY AND PRACTICE 509, 535 (Nitin Nohria & Rakesh Khurana eds., 2010).
19. *Id.* at 527.

This power derived from community-led action laid the foundation for social movements, as with the Civil Rights Movement. Social movements are vehicles for furthering social change initiatives.[20] Coalition-building is essential for sustaining and building social change that can be manifested in a collective social movement. Social movements have been seen throughout U.S. history, ranging from the establishment of voting rights for women to the abolishment of slavery, and they have left a lasting impact on law and policies. Within the movement, community members have varying levels of commitment and engagement that are deeply rooted in moral values.[21] Community members who are actively engaged in the social movement hold dearly the hope of asserting new shared values, creating new relationships rooted in those values, and mobilizing political action.[22] These movements can be characterized as collective, strategic, dynamic, participatory, and organized.[23]

The power of the people is essential for engaging in these reform efforts. This power is derived from alliances built with organizations, community members, and other interested individuals, collectively creating a united front on the fight for justice. Together they can address the interrelatedness of social justice issues like earning a livable wage, obtaining quality education, and protecting the self-worth of each individual. "These issues create a formidable knot of many tightly wound strands. Only when the knot itself is undone will the threads come free."[24] A strong coalition of advocacy groups and community members can undo this "knot" and prevent future knotting by exercising their political power and influencing public policy reform.

---

20. Marshall & Olivia, *supra* note 2.
21. *Id.*
22. Ganz, *supra* note 18.
23. *Id.*
24. Jean Anyon, Radical Possibilities 175 (2005).

Alinsky's Community-Organizing Approach

Community-organizing serves as an essential tool for this process by helping ordinary people to have their voices heard.[25] Alinsky's *Rules for Radicals* provides guidance on how to "fertilize social change" by organizing the masses and building mass power.[26] This text is a guidebook that provides instruction based upon Alinsky's personal philosophy, which is driven by optimism. He writes: "It must be, for optimism brings with it hope, a future with a purpose, and therefore, a will to fight for a better world."[27] The community organizer is guided by this sense of optimism for creating a better world by promoting the common good in partnership with the people.

The community organizer is committed to protecting the dignity of the individual. This protection respects the community's autonomy and guards people's fundamental democratic right to fully participate in creating solutions to their own problems.[28] Additionally, the community organizer believes that communication is essential for moving forward with progress. The art of communication aids the organizer in understanding what the community is trying to communicate and in listening attentively to its members' needs, since communication is a two-way process. Further, the community organizer is also an imaginative creator. Unlike leaders who traditionally desire to hold power, the community organizer seeks to create new ways to maximize power in order to bring forth social change. The community organizer's work is informed by the exercise of moral imagination in skillfully creating tactics. He or she focuses on creating a mass ego in which to motivate and inspire others to take action. "The organizer finds his goal in creation of power for others to use."[29] These leaders seek to serve not merely as organizers but as reorganizers of social systems.[30] Alinsky characterizes

---

25. NICHOLAS VON HOFFMAN, A PORTRAIT OF SAUL ALINSKY: RADICAL (2010).

26. SAUL D. ALINSKY, RULES FOR RADICALS: A PRAGMATIC PRIMER FOR REALISTIC RADICALS 7 (1971).

27. *Id.* at 21.

28. *Id.*

29. *Id.* at 80.

30. HOFFMAN, *supra* note 25, at 157.

this work as a radical, revolutionary movement; hence the job of the organizer is "to fan the embers of hopelessness into a flame to fight."[31]

The community organizer begins by organizing the unorganized. Organization starts with mobilizing the community, which is characterized as "an organized, communal life; people living in an organized fashion."[32] It moves beyond the notion of neighborhood or community shared by common physical space to the idea of a community of interests. People are organized first by their self-interest and then are connected with others to establish a community of interests. These interests inform the strategy of the community organizer and the development of a plan of action. The experiences of the community inform the strategy by providing the context and starting point of analysis with the acknowledgment that "this is the world as it is. This is where you start."[33] This is the vision that inspires the work of the organizer and motivates community members to get involved in building social change.

The vision is then coupled with the power to create change, and the metaphor of an army begins to emerge. Alinsky recognized the transformative nature of power. "Power is an essential life force always in operation, either changing the world or opposing change. Power, or organized energy, may be a man-killing explosive or life-saving drug."[34] When utilized as the latter, the community can reach its desired goals and create lasting social change. The momentum built through organizing continues to grow over time. "Once a people are organized they will keep moving from issue to issue. People power is the real objective."[35] Organized people gain power by developing a unified voice of the collective whole and taking action. Alinsky shared the potential of this power with new organizers when he stated that if 2 percent of the population were organized, their collective power could be used to overthrow the government.[36] This demonstrates the magnitude of "people power."

---

31. ALINSKY, *supra* note 26, at 194.
32. *Id.* at 116.
33. *Id.* at 14.
34. *Id.* at 51.
35. *Id.* at 181.
36. HOFFMAN, *supra* note 25.

The result of these organized efforts lays the foundation for building and sustaining social change. It is recognition of the fact that change comes through revolutionary action. A careful analysis of history demonstrates this point since significant changes in history have occurred as a result of revolutions. Revolutions require social action and a commitment to the greater good. "The price of democracy is the ongoing pursuit of the common good by all of the people."[37] Each person plays an integral role in this pursuit by becoming a part of the social change movement.

A notable example is President Barack Obama's early career during which he combined social justice lawyering, leadership, and community-organizing skills. He served as a community organizer in the Altgeld Gardens public housing projects during the 1980s. He worked diligently to facilitate social change and still today draws upon these skills (some characterize him as "Community Organizer in Chief"). Through the exercise of this community-organizing tool, lawyers are able to work with the community to exercise collective political power. Further, community-organizing approaches offer guidance for sustaining social change.

According to Alinsky, movement requires developing a "stable, disciplined, mass-based power organization."[38] The movement is initiated by empowering the people. This process of empowerment enhances each individual's capacity to change the systems that affect their daily lives by becoming involved in political processes and decision making. Alinsky recognized the need for empowerment and characterizes the lack thereof as a tragedy. Alinsky writes: "There can be no darker or more devastating tragedy than the death of man's faith in himself and in his power to direct his future."[39] Community-organizing approaches can breathe life into the community and the people. The community organizer is a facilitator in this process and the community is the driving force. "An organizer doesn't have an actual set of responsibilities save that of putting responsibility of self-determination where it belongs, on the people themselves."[40] The people should lead the

---

37. *Id.* at xxv.
38. *Id.* at 72.
39. *Id.* at xxvi.
40. *Id.* at 22.

process of social change by initiating their power to act and to own their shared destinies.

Alinsky offers a critique of the Civil Rights Movement that illustrates his premise of the need for building a mass-based power organization. Although the Civil Rights Movement claimed many victories, Alinsky posited that the movement lacked a powerful organizational base. Alinsky notes that the victories were won primarily based on external world political pressures and centralized around the efforts of a charismatic leader. He warned: "[B]ut the truth is that the civil rights organizations have always been minuscule in actual size and power. Periodic mass euphoria around a charismatic leader is not an organization."[41] According to Alinsky, without an organization and mass power, social change can begin but may fall short in transforming systems and its overall sustainability is threatened.[42]

The social justice challenges of our time create a need to apply innovative and creative approaches to the practice of lawyering. This moves beyond traditional notions of lawyering to the promotion of community empowerment. The introduction of the theory of new social justice lawyering provided a framework for lawyers to play an active role in the process of social change. It combined three theoretical frameworks—social justice lawyering, leadership, and public policy advocacy—to inform the work of lawyers who seek to build and sustain social change. The alignment of these theories or three pillars of new social justice lawyering provide practical tools for effectuating social change. The first pillar, social justice lawyering, focuses on using the law as a tool to dismantle systems of oppression and create equal justice under the law. The second pillar challenges lawyers to develop their leadership skills and strengthen the leadership capacity of others. Within the leadership capacity, lawyers can aid in empowering others. This moves beyond serving a particular client to acknowledging that each person can serve as an invaluable contributor in the process of social change. Lawyers are challenged to explore the question "Do you grow the people that you lead?" Finally, the third pillar is the foundation of systems change and policy reform. Public policy advocacy focuses on working with

---

41. *Id.* at 72.
42. Alinsky, *supra* note 26.

communities to organize and mobilize around social justice issues affecting their daily lives. This type of advocacy cultivates the transformational power of collective engagement with the goal in mind of fostering equitable policies. Through the application of principles of "new social justice lawyering," lawyers can work in collaboration with marginalized communities to realize a vision of justice and equity.

Case Study: The Three Pillars and Leadership Profiles of Mohandas Gandhi and Nelson Mandela

The cultivation of the core competencies of the "three pillars," extends lawyers beyond the traditional role of lawyering to serving as *new social justice lawyers*. The question for new social justice lawyers then becomes: "What is the next step in actually trying to live out what we dream for ourselves, for our families and friends, and for the world we aim to make a fundamentally better place?"[43] This notion is based upon the premise that lawyers who serve in the capacity of leaders can aid their clients and community in creating a more just and fair world.[44] This practice is the furtherance of true peace and preservation of justice, which Dr. Martin Luther King describes as "not merely the absence of tension; it is the presence of justice."[45] New social justice lawyers seek to effect social change in order to preserve the foundational precepts of justice in the world.

Through the process of leadership development, lawyers will have an opportunity to engage in critical self-reflection and self-awareness to understand their role as agents of change to promote the common good and uphold foundational tenets of justice. This is an evolution in professional development that begins with thinking like a lawyer then moves to thinking like a professional then progresses to the final destination of thinking like a new social justice lawyer. It recognizes the biblical adage that to whom

---

43. Gerald P. Lopez, *Critical Race Lawyering: Living and Lawyering Rebelliously*, 73 FORDHAM L. REV. 2027, 2053 (2005).

44. L.A. Kloppenberg, *Education Problem Solving Lawyers for Our Profession and Communities*, 61 RUTGERS L. REV. 1099–1114 (2009).

45. Hope Christian Church, Quotes from Stride toward Freedom: The Mongomery Story (2012), http://www.hopemn.com/MLK.htm.

much is given, much is expected. In this case, "much" equates to your legal training, which can be used to shape, change, and alter public policy in the pursuit of justice.

Examples of lawyers who embodied the charisma of new social justice lawyers are Mohandas Gandhi and Nelson Mandela. Gandhi inspired others to hope and believe in the process of social change and, in turn, he was transformed in the process.[46] Mandela was able to motivate the masses and teach them how to organize in order to secure their personal freedom and liberty.[47] Mandela espoused the values of freedom, liberty, and justice. He once stated that "mightier than men and arms dedicated to preventing change in an oppressed society are the values, ideals, and motives of those seeking freedom."[48] He inspired others to live out those values by leading from behind the scenes and exhibiting courage in the face of grave adversity.[49]

New social justice lawyers exhibit characteristics similar to those of Gandhi and Mandela. They act in an authentic manner by serving as wise stewards of their strengths and committing to make a difference in the lives of the communities being served.[50] They demonstrate the strengths of intuition and motivation by addressing the needs of leaders and followers.[51] Shdaimah (2005) identifies additional qualities that are exhibited by lawyers acting in the capacity of transformational leaders after conducting a qualitative study of lawyers who further social justice initiatives.[52] These qualities include the new social justice lawyer serving in a partnership capacity as collaborator, learner, educator, community partner, and reflective listener.

46. PETER G. NORTHOUSE, LEADERSHIP: THEORY AND PRACTICE (5th ed. 2010).

47. NELSON MANDELA, LONG WALK TO FREEDOM: THE AUTOBIOGRAPHY OF NELSON MANDELA (1994).

48. Bangalee Trawally, Nelson Mandela the Transformational Leader: The Struggle for Justice, Equality and Democratic Change in South Africa 12 (unpublished Master of Arts in Leadership thesis, Augsburg College, 2009).

49. R. Stengel, *Mandela: His 8 Lessons of Leadership*, TIME MAGAZINE (2008), http://www.time.com/time/magazine/article/0,9171,1821659,00.html.

50. B. GEORGE, AUTHENTIC LEADERSHIP: REDISCOVERING THE SECRETS TO CREATING LASTING VALUE (2003).

51. Trawally, *supra* note 48.

52. C. Shdaimah, The Practice of Public Interest Law: Power, Professionalism, and the Pursuit of Social Justice (2005) (unpublished dissertation) (available via ProQuest Digital Dissertations at AAT 3172573).

New social justice lawyers are also characterized as being critically conscious, reflective, strategic, and self-aware. Most notably, they are visionaries who dream about the future of social change since "for anything new to emerge there must first be a dream, an imaginative view of what might be."[53] The culmination of these qualities aids new social justice lawyers in furthering social justice initiatives and upholding the moral imperative of community-building. "The result of transforming leadership is a relationship of mutual stimulation and elevation that converts followers into leaders and may convert leaders into moral agents."[54] The new social justice lawyer also recognizes the need for empowering the followers to sustain social change by assuming a leadership role in the future.

Unique to the new social justice lawyer is his or her ability to use the law as a tool to achieve social change. The new social justice lawyer understands the power of legal strategy, knows when to exercise this power, and recognizes limitations of the law. This power can be exercised to wage battle more broadly against systems of oppression and instances of injustices. When limitations of traditional lawyering strategies emerge, the new social justice lawyer seeks to promote community engagement and organize policy reform advocacy efforts.

As evidenced above through the lives of Gandhi and Mandela, new social justice lawyers can create monumental changes at all levels from grassroots efforts to international contexts by exhibiting morals and values, and fostering a vision of a "just" society. The new social justice lawyer utilizes his or her legal training to aid the community in reaching its goal of social change by drawing upon shared values, framing the issues, and supporting the vision until its materialization. Further, the new social justice lawyer draws upon the characteristics of charismatic leadership by empowering others, being a role model, persuading others to act, and engaging in consensus-building.[55] In this sense, the new social justice lawyer is both a cultural broker and cultural interpreter who can build alliances from the grassroots level (micro

---

53. ROBERT K. GREENLEAF, THE SERVANT AS LEADER, 9 (1970).
54. J.M. BURNS, LEADERSHIP 4 (1978).
55. GEORGE GOETHALS, GEORGIA SORENSON & JAMES MACGREGOR BURNS, ENCYCLOPEDIA OF LEADERSHIP (2004).

level) to political arena (macro level) in order to establish legal precedent and develop a shared public narrative.

New Social Justice Lawyers and Social Change

New social justice lawyers redefine their professional role by serving as "allies" and "coproducers."[56] Within this role, new social justice lawyers participate in partnership with communities to transform systems (i.e., political structures and legal systems) in order to promote equity, ensure fairness, and create equal access to justice. New social justice lawyers believe that all people who participate in the struggle for justice and equality are leaders. They work to empower others to assume this leadership role. Therefore, the key focus of authentic transformational leadership is socialized leadership, which focuses on the collective good.[57]

The essence of the collective good is the recognition of the interrelatedness of the human experience since all life is interdependent. Dr. Martin Luther King Jr. (1965) wisely stated:

> We are all caught in an inescapable network of mutuality, tied into a single garment of destiny. Whatever affects one directly, affects all indirectly. We are made to live together because of the interrelated structure of reality.

Interrelatedness also draws upon the strength of the collective whole, which is illustrated through the Zulu maxim of "ubuntu; a person is a person through others."[58] Therefore, according to Nelson Mandela, ubuntu recognizes the inevitability of "mutual interdependence" in the human condition.[59]

---

56. L. White, *The Transformative Potential of Clinical Legal Education*, OSGOODE HALL L.J. 603–612 (1997); E. CAHN, NO MORE THROW-AWAY PEOPLE: THE CO-PRODUCTION IMPERATIVE (2004).

57. NORTHOUSE, *supra* note 46.

58. DESMOND TUTU, THE RAINBOW PEOPLE OF GOD: THE MAKING OF A PEACEFUL REVOLUTION (John Allen ed., 1994).

59. A. Hallengren, *Nelson Mandela and the Rainbow of Culture* (2001), http://www.nobelprize.org/nobel_prizes/peace/laureates/1993/mandela-article.html.

"Ubuntu draws upon a relational worldview by recognizing the universal bonds and sense of interrelatedness of humanity by challenging lawyers to use their legal skills to promote social good and further humanitarian goals."[60]

The new social justice lawyer acts in solidarity with the community to achieve a shared vision of social justice. Together, they can live out this vision and move closer to this vision becoming a tangible reality.[61] Through the furtherance of interrelatedness, transformation can emerge through the collaborative efforts of the new social justice lawyer and community members working together to fight for justice.

Summary

The three pillars of new social justice lawyering offer a framework for a lawyer to utilize for leading in the process of social change. The framework combines principles of social justice lawyering, leadership, and public advocacy to provide you with guidance on how to be proactive in the pursuit of justice.

Reflection Questions

The work of the new social justice lawyer focuses on promoting justice and fairness, empowering others to lead, and transforming systems. The following reflection questions will aid you in preparing to serve as a leader and change agent.

PILLAR 3: Public Policy Advocacy.
Social change is a byproduct of strategic action and collective engagement.

---

60. Nekima Levy-Pounds & Artika Tyner, *The Principles of Ubuntu: Using the Legal Clinical Model to Train Agents of Social Change*, 13 INT. J. CLINICAL LEGAL ED. 8 (2008).
61. JERRY WINDLEY-DAOUST, LIVING JUSTICE AND PEACE: CATHOLIC SOCIAL TEACHING IN PRACTICE 93 (2008).

1. What lessons have you learned from the policy entrepreneur related to agenda setting and opening the window of opportunity?
2. What role can you play in building coalitions related to the vision, issues, and values that you share with others?
3. Through community-organizing, how can you promote the common good in partnership with others in the global community?

Chapter 4

Profiles of the New Social Justice Lawyer

You can make a difference in the world. For generations, lawyers have made a lasting impact in our society in preserving the tenets of justice, fairness, and democracy, and in strengthening our communities. Consider the work of these great leaders and how their efforts transformed the world:

Robert Abbott	Justice Thurgood Marshall
Marian Wright Edelman	Saint Thomas More
Paulo Freire	Constance Baker Motley
Mohandas Gandhi	President Barack Obama
Judge William Hastie	Justice Alan C. Page
Oliver Hill	Charlotte E. Ray
Charles Hamilton Houston	Paul Robeson
Robert F. Kennedy	Spottswood Robinson
Judge LaJune Lange	Lena O. Smith
Abraham Lincoln	Justice Sonia Sotomayor
Nelson Mandela	George Washington Williams

These leaders share a common vocation—the practice of law; however, what distinguishes them from other lawyers is their commitment to use the law as a tool to make a difference in the world. They took heed to the call to lead through service to others. This is the very essence of lawyering, since lawyers are called to serve and lead in the global community. U.S. Supreme Court Justice Sonia Sotomayor wisely stated, "[L]awyering is the height of service and being involved in this profession is a gift."[1] These leaders have shared a gift with each of us by pursuing the promotion of civil rights and human rights.

Although your impact may not reach the same level as the above-referenced leaders, you can still play a meaningful role in fostering change and strengthening your community. My grandmother's pearl of wisdom comes to mind: "Start where you are." The truth of the matter is that we all can make a difference by exercising leadership within our respective spheres of influence, whether it be through service in a pro bono clinic or volunteering in a social justice–related advocacy campaign. This is the work of the new social justice lawyer. The new social justice lawyer focuses on using his or her legal training to promote access to justice, ensure fair administration of the law, and provide legal services to those in need. Further, the new social justice lawyer is compelled to lead based upon his or her personal convictions and passion for justice. The profiled lawyers exemplify the three pillars of new social justice lawyering as they seek to promote social change (Pillar 1), exercise influence and motivate others to lead (Pillar 2), and organize social change movements (Pillar 3).

Bonnie Allen—"The Guide"

A leader is one who knows the way, goes the way, and shows the way.
—John Maxwell

An effective leader guides others on the path to change and growth. The result of those efforts is transformation that occurs internally (as new leaders discover their leadership potential) and externally (as people organize and engage in collaborative efforts). Professor Bonnie Allen's leadership role focuses on the implementation of ideas and strategies for the furtherance of social change. She works in partnership with members of the Mississippi Center for Justice to implement social change strategies using

---

1. Paul Campos, *Sonia Sotomayor Debate: Should Unhappy Lawyers Blame Themselves?*, TIME.COM (Jan. 28, 2013), http://ideas.time.com/2013/01/28/sonia-sotomayor-debate-should-unhappy-lawyers-blame-themselves/.

an integrated approach that includes community-organizing and community engagement strategies. This is a people-centered approach to advocacy. Community members aid in setting the agenda and informing the strategy for seeking social change.

Allen is a clinical professor, a leader in the nonprofit law field, a consultant on racial justice issues, and a leadership development trainer. Allen has extensive experience in developing innovative clinical legal education programs and leadership development training for public interest lawyers. Through these experiences, she "hope(s) to contribute to making the case for how the law—when it operates justly—serves individuals, communities, institutions, and societies by helping them operate at their highest level to create the greatest good." This hope in the future has inspired others to lead in the process of social change.

Allen is an influential contributor to the legal profession and to society as a whole, which is evidenced by her leadership in many social justice initiatives. In partnership with the University of Maryland Francis King Carey School of Law, she established a Katrina Summer Clinic on the Mississippi Gulf Coast, taught in the ethics and professional responsibility clinic, and supported the launch of the Leadership, Ethics and Democracy Building Initiative. Over many years, Allen has been actively involved in building the leadership capacity of lawyers. Also, she has provided organizational leadership and leadership development training at a number of legal services providers. In addition to her legal training, she has obtained a masters in theological studies with the goal in mind of creating meaning within the professional dimensions of her life and seeking an understanding of vocation and calling. Within this capacity, she served as the president and chief executive officer for the Center for Law and Renewal. She has supported other lawyers in the process of discovering their purpose and integrating the dimensions of faith and justice. Allen's leadership journey demonstrates the importance of showing the way by encouraging others to tap into their leadership potential.

Edgar Cahn—"The Visionary"

Your vision will become clear only when you can look into your own heart.
Who looks outside, dreams; who looks inside, awakes.
—Carl Jung

Leadership starts with a vision. This is a vision of the future that enhances the well-being of others, promotes the common good, and draws people together. Dr. Edgar Cahn has a vision of a society where all people no matter their race, creed, or status have an opportunity to unveil their human capital. Cahn characterizes this as a vision of abundance, since the yield of human capital is limitless. Cahn's vision has transformed the course of history not only in the United States but across the globe. He dared to believe that he could change the world by implementing his vision of justice, which he refers to as timebanking. Timebanking is the foundation of a social economy that places premium value on the contributions each person can make in a community. Cahn and his wife, Chris, are the codirectors of TimeBanks USA. Timebanking rewards the process of reciprocity as community members share their gifts and talents and "bank" hours for their services. For example, a community timebank draws upon the assets of many members, ranging from one member with plumbing skills to another member who offers web design services. According to Cahn, timebanking is about respect, redefining work, reciprocity, and community. The mission of TimeBanks USA is to "nurture and expand a movement that promotes equality and builds caring community economies through inclusive exchange—time and talent" (TimeBanks USA, 2011). Communities from across the world have embraced these universal values and timebanking has evolved into a global social change movement.

As an extension of TimeBanks USA's mission, Cahn has codeveloped the Racial Justice Initiative. This initiative focuses on eliminating structural racism in the juvenile delinquency, special education, and child welfare systems. Cahn has organized community members, policy makers, and lawyers from across the nation to explore how to utilize alternatives to detention and create more effective tools for addressing racial disparities in juvenile justice and child welfare systems.

He began by creating a vision with his late wife, Jean Camper Cahn, to meet the legal needs of the poor and disenfranchised. He recognized that in a democratic society founded on the principles of justice and fairness courts must serve as a mechanism to protect these rights. However, without access to counsel, these rights are denied. Cahn and his late wife Jean created the blueprint for Legal Service Corporation.

Cahn is a lifelong advocate for justice who has served as a clinical law professor, a cofounder of Legal Services Corporation, a speech writer for Attorney General Robert Kennedy under President John F. Kennedy's administration, a founder of timebanking and TimeBanks USA, and a cofounder of the Antioch School of Law (which was recognized as the first law school with an explicit focus on social justice and having a clinical legal education requirement for all students).[2] Through these experiences, he has demonstrated a wealth of experience in building and sustaining social change through community engagement, organizing, and mobilizing efforts. His most recent efforts have focused on supporting an assets-based community development initiative (timebanking) and dismantling the pipeline to prison.

In essence within each of his initiatives, his primary goal is to build capacity of community members through an assets-based approach. This is evidenced in his remarks during the 2011 TimeBanks Global Conference, in which he stated: "There is tremendous wealth in this room, tremendous wealth in the nation . . . if [there] [is] ever a time to tap into it, it is right now."[3] For decades, Cahn has tapped into his intellectual wealth and has supported the growth of the social capital in the global community. The global community continues to reap the residual benefits of his efforts.

---

2. *Building a Stronger Future*, http://www.law.cuny.edu/about/location/Building AStrongerFuture.pdf.
3. Timebank USA Global Conference (Aug. 4, 2011), http://tbusaconference.org/agenda /program-at-a-glance/.

Professor Nekima Levy-Pounds—"The Motivator"

As we look ahead into the next century, leaders will be those who empower others.
—Bill Gates

Professor Nekima Levy-Pounds empowers each person that she comes in contact with to lead. She sees the leadership potential in others and aids them in unveiling this gift. This is evidenced in her teaching. As a passionate educator, she is committed to empowering the next generation of law students to serve and lead in their communities. She begins by sharing her personal experiences related to what drew her to the practice of law. Her story begins with her childhood as she recalls the challenges experienced by her community at the intersections of race and poverty.

Her passion for justice was ignited during her early childhood experiences growing up in South Central Los Angeles. She witnessed firsthand the ills of oppression, disenfranchisement, and marginalization from society experienced by communities of color. She states: "[W]hen you grow up in that type of environment . . . it plays a role in your outlook/perspective and at least for me my desire to change things when it comes to people experiencing oppression." This desire to change society led Levy-Pounds to create a clinical program, the Community Justice Project (CJP), with an explicit focus on serving in marginalized populations and working in partnership with the community to facilitate the process of social change.

Since the inception of the CJP in 2007, Levy-Pounds has become a leader in Minnesota's civil rights community. She and her students work closely with several key partners, such as the St. Paul branch of the NAACP and the Aurora/St. Anthony Neighborhood Development Corporation, to further social change. With these key partners, Levy-Pounds works diligently to dismantle systems of oppression that keep poor communities of color disenfranchised. She believes that lawyers have a moral responsibility to engage in this process of eliminating oppression and transforming these systems when she states: "I want to see the world transformed into an oasis of fairness and justice and that can only come by knowing the power and the privilege and responsibility that I have and being willing to use it."

This is a call to action. On a daily basis, Levy-Pounds works to build this oasis in partnership with community members, social justice organizations, and the future generation of lawyers—her law students. She seeks to raise the social consciousness of many as she challenges anyone who is willing to listen to become a leader who seeks justice for all. She reaches this goal by providing a critical analysis of the social conditions that disenfranchise and marginalize poor communities of color.

After empowering others to lead, she seeks to compel them to action. She often quotes Dr. King's prophetic plea to take action due to the "fierce urgency of now":

> We are now faced with the fact, my friends, that tomorrow is today. We are confronted with the fierce urgency of now. In this unfolding conundrum of life and history, there is such a thing as being too late. Procrastination is still the thief of time. Life often leaves us standing bare, naked, and dejected with a lost opportunity. The tide in the affairs of men does not remain at flood—it ebbs. We may cry out desperately for time to pause in her passage, but time is adamant to every plea and rushes on. Over the bleached bones and jumbled residues of numerous civilizations are written the pathetic words, "Too late." There is an invisible book of life that faithfully records our vigilance or our neglect.

Through this call to action, she has compelled many to take a stand by leading within their sphere of influence. She has motivated many to move from the sidelines to the forefront of a racial justice movement.

john a. powell—"The Innovator"

Leadership is the capacity to translate vision to reality.
—Warren Bennis

Professor john a. powell inspires others to strive for the realization of a vision of fairness, inclusiveness, and equity for all. He draws together professionals from all sectors to unite in this pursuit of social justice. This is a participatory leadership model that includes sociologists, economists, demographers, and lawyers. These professionals then in turn partner with key community stakeholders who are directly affected by an injustice. When working together as a collective, they can utilize law as a public language that inspires a public imagination. This imagination frees each individual from the limits of his or her professional identity to see infinite possibilities. powell admonishes lawyers and other professionals alike: "Don't define the problem by the nature of your discipline." This aids in breaking down the professional silos that limit one's ability to address deeply systemic social challenges at the macro level.

powell's vision of justice is informed by his personal values and ethics. It is deeply rooted in the interconnectedness of the human existence and a desire to foster community-building. He connects with others who share the same values, which is demonstrative of serving as a transformational leader. A transformational leader seeks to lift people to their highest place of contribution—the exercise of leadership. This provides a new vision for the future that is values-driven and strengthened through the development of collaborative relationships. powell shapes the vision through his role as educator and innovator. He is an internationally recognized authority on topics such as civil rights, civil liberties, and human rights, with an explicit focus on race, poverty and the law. He has developed theoretical frameworks, such as targeted universalism and structural racialization, and they serve as tools for engaging in systemic reform.

Further, powell is also a masterful innovator who has developed and founded key social justice institutions. powell was the director of the Kirwan Institute for the Study of Race and Ethnicity at the Ohio State University and a Williams chair in Civil Rights and Civil Liberties. He is the founder and former director of the Institute on Race and Poverty at the University of Minnesota (now known as Institute on Metropolitan Opportunity). The mission of the institute is creating greater understanding of racialized poverty and changing policies and practices that affect the well-being of low-income communities of color. He served as the director of Legal Services in Miami, Florida, and as national legal director of the American Civil Liberties Union. While at the ACLU, he was involved in developing the educational adequacy theory. Additionally, powell's leadership has extended beyond our national borders. He was an International Humans Right Fellow who worked in South Africa and consulted with the government of Mozambique. Through these leadership roles, he has promoted community participation and supported the leadership development of others.

Summary

Each of these profiled lawyers share a common passion—their commitment to serving the needs of others has inspired them to lead. Marian Wright Edelman wisely stated: "Service is the rent we pay to be living. It is the very purpose of life and not something you do in your spare time." Paying their rent in full is a daily endeavor for these lawyers as they lead national efforts to promote racial and economic justice.

Reflection Questions

As you reflect upon the profiles of these leaders, you can see that the foundation of leadership is vision. Each had a vision of justice. With this vision in focus, they were inspired to lead others in furthering the cause of justice. This vision led them to pursue a career in law, create social justice–oriented organizations/institutions, and train the next generation of new social justice lawyers.

These lawyers have made a conscious choice to serve as agents of change within their respective organizations and within the legal profession. In reflecting upon your role in creating change and realizing a vision of justice, take a few moments to ponder the following questions:

1. Why did you pursue a career in law?
2. What is your vision of justice?
3. In what ways can you further this vision?
4. What inspired you about the stories of these leaders?
5. Take a few moments and reflect upon the words of Anne Frank, "How wonderful that no one need wait a single moment to improve the world." What issues are you passionate about? Can you afford to wait any longer before taking action by cultivating your leadership skills?

Chapter 5

Building Blocks of Leadership

The exercise of leadership provides a firm foundation for initiating and sustaining social change since it draws upon each contributor's assets. Leadership skills can be utilized to guide others, motivate them, and support their leadership development during the course of social change. Through collective engagement, a multitude of assets are utilized and strategically brought to bear. The leader plays a key role in identifying and cultivating these assets that may be lying dormant or frequently overlooked. This is a process of liberating people to become actively involved in furthering the cause of justice and strengthening their leadership capacity.[1] As new social justice lawyers, these individuals in partnership with community members can employ their assets and exercise their collective power to transform systems and policies that are producing inequities.

When examining the role of the new social justice lawyer, it is important to consider the following questions: Do these lawyers promote the community's autonomy? How do they empower others to lead? How do they integrate their values and beliefs into their leadership platform? During the interviews of the profiled lawyers, I asked questions about their leadership development, leadership characteristics, and desired leadership legacy. I explored what drew them into leadership roles within social justice contexts and identified the leadership characteristics that they use to build and sustain social change. Similar to the theories of servant leadership and transformational leadership, I discovered that the new social justice lawyers'

---

1. M. DePree, Leadership Is an Art (1989).

leadership was greatly affected by their life experiences, which shaped their perspectives, values, and commitment to serve. These experiences informed their commitment to engage in social change and define their vision of justice. These lawyers then sought to connect this vision with others who share the same passion for social justice. Through these connections, these leaders realize the transformative power that lies in their hands. Tapping into this power is the exercise of leadership.

The building blocks common to the leadership of new social justice lawyers include (a) experiencing catalytic and life-changing moments, (b) framing one's vision of justice, (c) pursuing leadership as a way of life and building relationships, and (d) exercising one's transformative power (see below). Each of these building blocks will elevate you to a different level of lawyering—new social justice lawyering. You will be equipped with the tools to effectively serve and lead in the process of social change.

Diagram of Building Blocks of Leadership
1. Experiencing Catalytic and Life-Changing Events
2. Framing a Vision of Justice
3. Pursuing Leadership as a Way of Life
4. Exercising Transformative Power

First Building Block: Experiencing Catalytic and Life-Changing Moments

The Quest for Justice
Through my research, a common theme emerged among new social justice lawyers—each found their calling to lead based upon witnessing or experiencing firsthand an instance of injustice. These experiences shaped their leadership development and leadership formation based upon their active participation in the quest for justice.[2] The process of new social justice lawyering begins with a catalytic moment that can be described as an experience or encounter that fuels one's passion for the pursuit of justice. This

---

2. JEAN ANYON, RADICAL POSSIBILITIES 175 (2005).

pivotal experience helped each lawyer to discover his or her calling. Calling is manifested by being called (vocation) or sent on a task (commitment).[3] Each profiled lawyer leads based upon this passion, vocational calling, and commitment to service. This fuels his or her work and ignites the passion needed to engage in social justice lawyering. Each of the lawyers reflected upon a life experience that shaped their worldview related to justice and that still guides them today. This equates to a moment of awakening in which these lawyers view their role in the world as agents of change who have the power to create meaningful change.

The recognition of the transformative power of the law and the duty to utilize the law as a tool for furthering social justice was recognized by Dr. Edgar Cahn, Professor Nekima Levy-Pounds, Professor Bonnie Allen, and Professor john a. powell during the early stages of their lives. These experiences have had a lasting impact on both their professional and personal aspirations. Cahn reflected upon his childhood experience of being instructed by his father on the precepts of justice. Cahn recalls learning at this point in time about his role in fighting for justice.

> "Cahn grew up admonished by his father, who was a legal philosopher. Cahn's father believed that while justice was too absolute a concept for humans to grasp or attain, we are all endowed with a capacity to respond to injustice, to disparities that we feel are intolerable—and that by responding to them, we back toward an ideal of justice that we would never reach or fully realize. And so, he defined justice as the process of preventing or remedying that which would arouse our Sense of Injustice."[3]

These experiences left Cahn with an internal conviction to respond to instances of injustice in order to move closer to his vision of justice and to address issues evidenced by disparities. Further, his experiences also cultivated and developed his sense of injustice. He became aware of the many dimensions of what feels unjust and felt compelled to take action against

---

3. L.A. Parks Daloz, C.H. Keen, J.P. Keen, & S. Daloz Parks, Common Fire: Leading Lives of Commitment in a Complex World (1996).

injustice. He was reminded that justice is not a spectator sport, thus all players must be in the game. In essence, each person plays a critical leadership role in promoting justice.

Professor Levy-Pounds shares a similar experience from her childhood that served as a defining moment. This experience raised her awareness about the plight of the poor and drew her to a career in the law. She saw the law as a tool that could be used to promote justice, equity, and fairness. She describes her passion for justice being realized during her childhood. She grew up in South Central Los Angeles and saw firsthand the injustices that arise at the intersection of race and poverty. She witnessed the Los Angeles riots and their aftermath, while observing the travesties associated with the War on Drugs. Her social justice work connects with her personally based upon these experiences.

Levy-Pounds recalls these experiences as "an environment where everyone was extremely poor, and disenfranchised and marginalized from society. When you grow up in that type of environment, it plays a role in your outlook and perspective." She desires to change things when it comes to people experiencing oppression. Thus, there is a very deep connection between Levy-Pounds's work and the experiences that she had growing up.

She carries these experiences with her wherever she goes since they inform her personal identity. Therefore, she recognizes the plight of the poor and a lawyer's responsibility to address the needs of the poor. She reflects, "[I]nside of me there is still a poor person who knows what it's like to feel the weight of oppression in society or feel marginalized." She believes lawyers have a duty to keep the challenges experienced by the poor at the forefront by bridging gaps in the delivery of legal services and advocating for antipoverty reform efforts.

She expresses this sense of responsibility when she states: "I feel that I am able to help translate some of those experiences to those in mainstream society, others in academia, law makers, policy makers, law students and lawyers." Based upon their experiences, both Cahn and Levy-Pounds believe that there is a moral imperative to act in the face of injustice that moves beyond simply identifying occurrences of injustice to actively eradicating the root causes of injustice. Through observation and interviewing, I identified in both of them a deep burning desire to know that something will be done by someone in the face of injustice. This same passion was evidenced in the lives of the other featured lawyers through their words and deeds. Each lawyer recognized the interconnectedness of the human experience and the necessity of joint partnership efforts in the pursuit of justice.

Similarly, Professor Allen reflects upon a catalytic moment from early teenage years that transformed her life and informed her vision of justice. She remembers when she was in the ninth grade and participated in a church bus trip. During this trip with members of her church, she traveled to Apopka, Florida, which is an agricultural city. Allen recalls observing firsthand the challenges experienced by the migrant farmers. She characterized their work conditions as a manifestation of injustice. Therefore, this experience was a formative moment that informed her sense of unfairness and injustice. She began to reflect upon the meaning of social justice and to connect this with her core values of justice, fairness, respect for people, and human dignity. These values inform her work today and her personal commitment to touch the lives of others.

In addition to lessons learned in childhood, Cahn and Levy-Pounds also experienced a catalytic moment in their respective adulthoods that ignited their passion for justice. Cahn recalls his life-changing experience after a massive heart attack that resulted in the loss of 60 percent of his heart's functionality. While in the intensive care unit, he had an epiphany that resulted in the formulation of the theory of coproduction and the creation of timebanking as a vehicle of coproduction. Since this experience, he counts each day as an opportunity to make a difference in the world. He wakes up with a grateful heart to have another chance to make a difference in the world and to work in partnership with others. He notes that the most important part of life is "getting up with a purpose." He equates this with being "life giving." He recalls his days in the hospital and the experience of being lonely. Currently, he is no longer alone since he is surrounded by other partners who believe in the vision of coproduction and he is a part of the timebanking family. He is in fellowship with others who share the same calling and desire to live a purpose-driven life. To date, as of his most recent exam, his heart is 80 percent healed and he credits this to the impact of timebanking and coproduction on his life.

Levy-Pounds's faith also ministered to her in her adult years. Her faith was renewed and she felt called by God to engage in a different type of lawyering, one that creates transformation. She found confidence in sharing her childhood experiences and having a unique vantage point based upon these experiences. She reflects upon this confidence:

Levy-Pounds believes she was created to do what she is doing. In the past, she felt ashamed about growing up in poverty. Today, she embraces her life experiences, which have informed her moral compass. She now recognizes that society may look down on poor people but God has a different perspective. She has nothing to be ashamed of.

Her past informs her love for the work of the Community Justice Project. She recognizes that inside of her is still a poor person who knows what it is like to feel the weight of oppression in society or to feel marginalized.

Her faith coupled with the difficulty of her life experiences energizes her. It motivates her to move forward and to recognize that she has a significant contribution to make by virtue of having lived in poverty and having experienced oppression firsthand, so now she embraces who she is. Within her leadership capacity, her life experience has become an invaluable asset since it enables her to build rapport with others who were experiencing poverty or other social barriers. This has provided her with the important leadership qualities of being relational and empathetic.

Further, these lawyers heeded their calling by making a commitment to the pursuit of moral justice. They experienced or observed instances of injustice that caused them to experience a sense of conscious conflict coupled with feelings of righteous indignation. In essence, these experiences caused a conscious conflict that "violated their earlier assumptions about fairness."[4] This conflict caused an internal stirring and manifested itself in the pursuit of a calling. For some it was related to the plight of the poor (economic justice), while for others it focused on systemic inequities (racial justice). Most importantly, it was the culmination of experiences that compelled each lawyer to take action within his or her sphere of influence. Cahn's reflection on the lessons learned from his father clearly evidences this point. He described justice as a process of preventing or remedying injustices. This description

---

4. DALOZ, KEEN, KEEN & PARKS, *supra* note 3.

contains two key action words (preventing and remedying) that establish the personal responsibility to act when one encounters an injustice. One way that each of these individuals took action was by becoming a lawyer. This enabled them to use the law as a tool to engage in social engineering and as an extension of their calling. Hence, the new social justice lawyers' life experiences formed their professional identity and affected their decision to make a lifelong commitment to service.

Second Building Block: Framing a Vision of Justice

Building Connections through a Shared Vision

The catalytic moment experienced by each lawyer shaped his or her vision of justice. Building a vision of justice is also a core theme that emerged from these profiled lawyers. It provides a context for one's work, aligns with one's beliefs and values, and guides one's work related to social justice. In the process of social change, this vision is connected with others and results in building the momentum needed to facilitate social change. "Where there is no vision, the people perish."[5] Vision is crucial for the sustainability of social change. The shared vision of justice leads the people forward and establishes the agenda for the process of social change. It also serves as a reminder of the goals and objectives that the community seeks to achieve.

Dr. Cahn has a vision to change the world. This vision is based upon principles like equality (we are all created equal), justice (standing up for justice), collective engagement (establishing the feedback loop), and community-building (helping others to be all they can be). He operates at the macro level of social change by conceptualizing guiding principles and developing mechanisms for systems change. Initially, his vision was all intuitive and he referred to it as a seamless web. When communities were experiencing social justice issues and were in need of assistance, he would share with them the idea of the seamless web. He envisioned this web as a part of how systems interface with each other and affect the lives of community members while perpetuating cycles of systemic barriers. His wife and the

---

5. *Proverbs* 29:18 (King James).

director of TimeBanks USA, Chris, describes this as Cahn walking into a community meeting "like a hurricane." He would come in and share ideas for social change initiatives and social action. This was an intuitive process. However, community members were unable to implement his ideas since they did not have the opportunity to engage in the problem-solving process collectively. They were handing their problems over to Cahn to fix them instead of working together to create a plan of action for resisting systems of oppression and marginalization. When he later contacted the communities and inquired about their progress, they did not have any to report. They were still lost in ideas that left them defenseless and powerless.

After witnessing this time and time again, Chris challenged Cahn to critically reflect upon his ideas and develop a framework for community engagement and social change. Reflection upon early leadership experiences aids one in unleashing the power needed to initiate the process of social change.[6] Cahn realized this power and the end result was the development of coproduction.[7] His vision is embodied in the five principles of coproduction: (1) an asset perspective (each one has strengths); (2) honoring real work (the work the market fails to value); (3) reciprocity (empowering the recipient); (4) community (acknowledging our interdependence); and (5) respect (each voice is owed a listening).[8] These principles embody Cahn's vision of a just society that is founded upon shared values, collaborative processes, and attributes of a caring community. Within this just society, all people are equal and treated accordingly. He finds that most often the missing piece in most situations is adequate coproduction. Through his vision of justice, he shares the principles of coproduction with others and aids in building social change.

Dr. Cahn discovered that his vision is meta-frame in which the visions of others are encompassed within. Metaphorically, this can be compared to the image of an umbrella. Others who share his vision of justice seek to connect their vision with his meta-frame. As the director of TimeBanks USA,

---

6. JUDY BROWN & BONNIE ALLEN, LEADERSHIP IN THE LEGAL ACADEMY: PRINCIPLES, PRACTICES AND POSSIBILITIES (2009), http://www.law.umaryland.edu/programs/initiatives/lead/docs/LeadershipLawSchoolRpt.pdf.

7. EDGAR CAHN, NO MORE THROW-AWAY PEOPLE: THE CO-PRODUCTION IMPERATIVE (2004).

8. EDGAR CAHN, PRICELESS MONEY: BANKING TIME FOR CHANGING TIMES (2011).

his wife, Chris, compared his vision to a frame "within which visions fit." On a daily basis, people from across the world resonate with his meta-frame and add their vision to his by incorporating principles of coproduction into their daily lives. This is a process of connecting visions and fostering community empowerment. Chris explains: "It is like, 'Let me join my vision to your vision.'" As a result, Cahn's vision is "no more one man's vision," but a collective vision shared by a global family.[9]

Professor Levy-Pounds's early life experiences shaped her vision of justice. These personal convictions were related to growing up poor and witnessing the plight of poor communities. From a young age, she has committed to change circumstances for people experiencing oppression. She strives to reach this vision by helping marginalized communities to become stakeholders in the process of social change. This requires collective action against structural inequities, unjust policies, and an imbalance of power.

Levy-Pounds believes that one cannot focus on social justice in a vacuum. Some people like to disconnect social justice from a moral imperative, for example, to act. Or having some base line of what justice really is. You have to have some vision in your mind of what is just and what is unjust.

Levy-Pounds's vision of justice is action-oriented, which compels her to lead and motivates others to exercise their leadership capacity by sharing this vision. In the face of injustice, Levy-Pounds attests that you must take a stand against injustice and inspire others to stand together in solidarity.

Professor Allen shares this same conviction and has taken a stand against oppression and marginalization throughout her legal career. This has challenged her to take action in order to make her vision of justice become a reality. She was encouraged by her mentors to stay true to her passion to pursue law as a calling to serve those in need.[10] Most recently, Allen's passion for justice led her to the Mississippi Delta in order to minister to the needs of community members and protect their rights following the devastation of Hurricane Katrina.

Allen seeks opportunities to collaborate with others who share her vision of justice, which promotes fairness, human dignity, and a sense of community.

---

9. CAHN, *supra* note 7.

10. S.M. INTRATOR & M. SCRIBNER, LEADING FROM WITHIN: POETRY THAT SUSTAINS THE COURAGE TO LEAD 56 (2007).

Allen's leadership was evidenced by her ability to organize lawyers and law students in delivering legal assistance to those who survived the devastation of the storm:

Allen observed that the Katrina recovery context provided American lawyers and law students with unique opportunities to examine the critical role of law and lawyers in advancing an equitable recovery—both by mending broken lives of individual survivors and by systematically holding government accountable. Katrina gave lawyers "new eyes" to see injustice more clearly in this country, and that the rule of law, democracy, and civil society could no longer be assumed in America.

With the opening of these new eyes, Allen envisions lawyers serving as the gatekeepers of justice. Lawyers play a key role in alleviating poverty and improving social conditions for the least of these. Katrina unveiled the lack of escape routes for those living in poverty. "We saw that neither our public policies nor our economy have generated escape routes out of crushing poverty through self-help."[11] Therefore, she believes that lawyers have a social responsibility to support the adoption of equitable policies and assist the poor in deconstructing oppressive systems. Allen posits that this process of social change begins with a government that is responsive to the needs of the people. This is a vision of a government characterized by President Abraham Lincoln as being "of the people, by the people, for the people" and which focuses on serving the best interests of the community and upholding the foundational tenets of democracy.

The new social justice lawyer's vision of justice is a dream of equity and fairness that compels him or her to engage in a different kind of social justice lawyering: new social justice lawyering. These lawyers are reminded on a daily basis of what it is like to experience racism, live in poverty, and witness an injustice based upon either a personal experience, firsthand observation, or a combination of both. These profiled lawyers demonstrate (through their publications, community engagement efforts, and teaching pedagogy) that it is important to keep these visions at the forefront of their work since a vision serves as the guiding force for a social change movement. Historically,

---

11. B. Allen, B. Bezdek & J. Jopling, *Community Recovery Lawyering: Hard-Learned Lessons from Post-Katrina Mississippi*, 4 DEPAUL J. SOC. JUST. 123 (2010).

a shared vision has been the foundation of social change movements. For example, the Rev. Dr. Martin Luther King Jr.'s "dream" served as the guiding light to the path of justice during the Civil Rights Movement. On the steps of the Lincoln Memorial in 1963, King prophetically outlined the vision and goals of the Civil Rights Movement. He shared his dream for the United States to hold true to its promise of democracy by upholding one of its foundational truths that all men are created equal. This promissory note of justice has not yet been paid in full. In his vision, King refused to believe that "the bank of justice is bankrupt. We refuse to believe that there are insufficient funds in the great vaults of opportunity of this nation."[12] This is a dream that inspired a nation to seek change through the enactment of key civil rights legislation.

Similar to the late Rev. Dr. Martin Luther King Jr., a transformational leader during the Civil Rights Movement, these profiled lawyers have a dream of justice for the future and faith that the bank of justice is not bankrupt. A united group of people must continue to carry this vision until it comes to fruition and pick up the mantle of justice where King and other transformational leaders left off.[13] This vision serves as a reminder for the new social justice lawyer that the fight for justice, freedom, and equality must continue until the promissory note of justice is stamped "paid in full" for all people. The new social justice lawyer orchestrates this battle in conjunction with others who share the same passion and vision for justice.

Third Building Block: Pursuing Leadership as a Way of Life

Exhibiting Leadership Qualities through Action

After articulating a vision, the exercise of leadership compelled these lawyers to move beyond mere words to the initiation of social action. Rabbi Heschel characterized this process when he stated, "speech has power and

---

12. Martin Luther King Jr., I Have a Dream (Aug. 28, 1963), http://mlk-kpp01.stanford.edu/index.php/encyclopedia/encyclopedia/enc_i_have_a_dream_28_august_1963/.

13. Children's Defense Fund, Bounced Checks from America's Bank of Opportunity (2011), http://www.childrensdefense.org/newsroom/child-watch-columns/child-watch-documents/bounced-checks-from-americas-bank-of-opportunity.html.

few men realize that words do not fade. What starts out as a sound, ends in a deed."[14] Action is a manifestation of one's vision of justice. These lawyers shared their vision of justice with others through a tireless commitment to engage in deeds that would cause social change. Action can be manifested in many ways, such as initiating social change by building coalitions, engaging in collective involvement, empowering others to lead, and organizing policy reform efforts. It starts with simply taking a step forward and rising to take a stand.

Action is manifested through the exercise of leadership. These new social justice lawyers exhibited a range of leadership characteristics during the process of social change. The leadership characteristics discussed will include those that were self-identified (during the interviewing process), observed leadership characteristics, and leadership characteristics identified by others. These profiled lawyers operated primarily within two categories: leadership as a behavior (exhibited through their personal interactions, publications, and communication) and leadership as a relationship (evidenced by placing value on establishing key relationships and partnerships).[15]

Leadership as a Behavior
Key leadership qualities are exhibited within one's daily actions, which include your interaction with others, utilization of community-building tools, and manifestation of espoused values.

For instance, Professor Levy-Pounds's key leadership behavior is taking action in a confident manner. By organizing community action and relating to the circumstances experienced by the community, she is attempting to calm others' fears and motivate them to take action in the face of injustice. In her leadership role, she also consciously seeks to serve as a role model through acts of courage and standing for justice. This provides her with the ability to mobilize the masses, act in a strategic manner, and move forward in building social change despite the obstacles faced.

---

14. Rabbi Abraham Heschel: On Improving Catholic-Jewish Relations (2012), http://conciliaria.com/2012/05/on-improving-Catholic-Jewish-relations/
15. PETER G. NORTHOUSE, INTRODUCTION TO LEADERSHIP CONCEPTS AND PRACTICE (2009).

Further, Professor Levy-Pounds serves as a cultural guide. Daily, she is simultaneously operating effectively within the following cultures: legal profession, community-organizing, legal academe, and African American community, and she skillfully negotiates the terrain between each of these sectors. Levy-Pounds operates in multiple domains—teaching her students principles of community lawyering, serving as a board member, and exploring the history of the Rondo community. In each capacity, she is able to build rapport with others, establish coalitions, and build new partnerships. She admits, "I feel that I am able to sort of act as a bridge." Metaphorically, she is acting as a bridge by engaging in culturally responsive practices, being adaptable, and acting with compassion. Bridging is further evidenced by her ability to exhibit leadership qualities through the process of social action.

Levy-Pounds identified organizational skills, servanthood, creativity, and "getting outside the box" as key behaviors that have enabled her to lead. Organizational skills aid the leader in working with the community to develop a shared vision of justice and create a strategic plan of action. Furthermore, the curriculum that Levy-Pounds adopted in her clinic includes coursework on the topic of servant leadership. It has an explicit focus on serving the needs of others, which compels one to take action and to lead. Moreover, Levy-Pounds is often quoted challenging her students to "get out of the box and reshape it." This is a challenge not to be limited by boundaries set forth by systems or fear of the unknown. Instead, leaders should seek opportunities to utilize their creativity to address pressing social justice issues.

Cahn is able to take action by connecting theory to practice. Cahn has discovered creative ways to address a range of social justice issues from racial disparities in the juvenile court (development of the deliberate indifference legal theory) to access to economic capital (adoption of assets-based reciprocity model: timebanking). Cahn taps into his creative side by constantly exploring new theoretical perspectives, engaging in ongoing reflection, and taking strategic action. Cahn's wife, Chris, characterizes this process as serving as a scholar practitioner and she identifies Cahn as such. According to Chris, a scholar practitioner is one who moves from analysis to action then back again from analysis to action. It is a process of ongoing learning and critical reflection. The scholar practitioner develops theories, explores theories, and then provides practical application of these theories. Cahn is always learning something new and then inventing a new framework, theory, or program model.

Cahn views leadership as serving as a steward of individual assets, which requires one to work toward building social change. This is not a question of whether leaders use their assets but truly a recognition of one's moral responsibility to think ethically. A leader who embraces the role of steward leads authentically by focusing on the promotion of share value. Cahn's behavior is represented in the qualities of a wise steward who recognizes that leadership is a gift. Cahn shares this gift with others by living his values of service, community, and justice.

These lawyers demonstrate that leading as a lawyer requires creative, ongoing action. It is a behavior that can be observed by others and then later incorporated into their daily lives. Through their actions, leadership has become a way of life. Their behavior is a manifestation of their values, objectives, and skills. Based upon the findings of this study, these lawyers exhibit the following qualities: functioning as a cultural guide, serving as a bridge, utilizing creative problem-solving skills, and providing qualities of wise stewardship. The exercise of leadership is how the leader acts toward others and aids in moving a vision forward to fruition.[16] These lawyers demonstrate their commitment to stand for justice by supporting the leadership development of others and serving as a facilitator during the process of building and sustaining social change.

Leadership as a Relationship
Promoting collaboration with others and building relationships is central to the success of these lawyers. "From this perspective, leadership is centered in the communication between leaders and followers rather than on the unique qualities of the leader."[17] The profiled leaders communicate their values through interactions with community members, key partners, and other collaborators. Additionally, their ability to build relationships has aided in the development of political power and fostered community empowerment.

---

16. *Id.*
17. *Id.* at 3.

Professor Levy-Pounds builds relationships by unveiling the leadership potential of community members. She communicates the value of each person's contribution in the process of social change. She believes each person has a valuable contribution to make in order to advance the common goal of achieving justice. She said, "I think we have to begin to place a premium on people's experiences. Their contributions, gifts and talents and . . . how it takes a collective in order to push for meaningful and lasting change in society." She implements this value by encouraging community members to get involved in social change initiatives and supporting their leadership development.

Levy-Pounds has established lasting relationships with community members by empowering them to lead and by delegating responsibility to them. During a community meeting, Levy-Pounds encouraged the group to divide into subcommittees and share responsibility for implementing the strategic business plan for the nonprofit's formation.

Levy-Pounds encourages new social justice lawyers to identify the gifts, talents, and skills of community partners. She trusts these partners to carry out the different functions and duties required during social change reform efforts. This is beneficial in two ways: (1) helping to ensure that the social justice efforts are accomplished and (2) empowering the people to see themselves as leaders.

By delegating responsibility, she communicates to the community members that they are valuable contributors, and that they have what it takes to lead and the power to transform systems.

Additionally, Levy-Pounds builds relationships based upon the principles of love. She believes love is an important characteristic that lawyers serving in a leadership capacity should embrace. This love should operate within every relationship and every encounter. It also manifests itself in many different ways. According to Levy-Pounds, leadership requires "love for the people that you are serving. Love for those around you and carrying that love in the work that you do and trying to communicate that love on a regular basis." The power of love helps to create lasting relationships built upon shared values, mutual trust, and a sense of interconnectedness. Therefore, Levy-Pounds's work draws upon a relational worldview of community and mutual interdependence. In one of her law review articles, she establishes this relational worldview by advocating for the incorporation of principles of "ubuntu" in the law school curriculum.[18] Ubuntu is a communal concept that recognizes that a person is a person through others. By adopting principles of ubuntu in legal education, a connection between social justice lawyering and leadership is established. Thus, her love for others communicates her passion and commitment for the work of the Community Justice Project.

Through the founding of timebanking, Cahn places value on the power of love and the capacity to share it with others. There are countless examples on how timebanking has placed a value on the innate ability of each person to give and receive as an act of love for humanity. This may include a community member providing respite care for a senior or Homecomers (men reentering society after being incarcerated) working to renovate homes within their communities. With each of these examples, Time Dollars creates a new mechanism for exchanging transactions through human interactions. "Time Dollars are a currency designed to reward other aspect of our nature: the cooperative, caring, altruistic aspect."[19]

In addition, Cahn believes that caring is a key leadership quality. Cahn identifies one of his greatest strengths as having people know that he cares. He cares about building the leadership capacity of others and strengthening the community. His actions demonstrate his selfless, passionate commitment to the pursuit of justice. Cahn offers this sage advice: "Leadership has been avoiding . . . situations where people feel that it's about personal gain and personal ego. I think the most dangerous thing or the most destructive thing to do is for people to be saying, 'He's just in this for himself' or 'He's just showing how smart he is.' Or 'He is trying to impress them.'"

Cahn leads authentically by living his espoused values, which includes establishing strong bonds with others. Chris observes that whenever there is a call to action, Cahn invariably heeds to this call through his actions. According to Chris, despite external challenges like inconvenience, scheduling conflicts, or feeling uncomfortable, Cahn "shows his commitment in deed and the words reflect that." His actions are a reminder that action

---

18. Nekima Levy-Pounds & Artika Tyner, *The Principles of Ubuntu: Using the Legal Clinical Model to Train Agents of Social Change*, 13 INT. J. CLINICAL LEGAL ED. 8 (2008).

19. CAHN, *supra* note 7, at 80.

speaks louder than words. Further, Cahn seeks to invest in strengthening the leadership capacity of community members. The challenge is to find the untapped value in these leaders and maximize this value. The failure to use this value results in a loss for the individual of not reaching his or her full leadership potential and, more importantly, it results in a loss for the entire community. Cahn warns them that "you have to use it (value) or lose it." Cahn supports others in the process of cultivating their assets and leading in the process of social change.

Similarly, Professor john a. powell's leadership style focuses on building relationships with people and supporting collaborative efforts. He envisions moving from a transactional to a transformational paradigm, which requires redefining self in relation to others.[20] This requires a shift in thinking from viewing leadership as the influence that an individual asserts over others by virtue of skills/position to understanding leadership as a dynamic process exercised within groups.[21] He characterizes transformational leaders as upholding strong ethical values, implementing new ideas, engaging in innovative thinking, and influencing those around them.[22] Therefore, leaders are collaborators and connectors.[23]

"Leadership as a relationship" is a core value of transformational leadership that compels others to act by recognizing their self-worth and their intrinsic value. The focus is on mutual growth through the recognition that leadership is available to everyone.[24] Influence and authority are shared by the leader and followers. This approach acknowledges a sense of value in each person's contribution. Hence, relationships are fundamental to establishing partnerships and building new connections.

These lawyers have demonstrated that by combining leadership as a behavior and leadership as a relationship, leadership becomes a way of life. It is an innate part of their character to inspire and motivate others to

---

20. john a. powell, Presentation at the Des Moines African American Leadership Forum: Leadership in the African American Community (Feb. 19, 2011).

21. *Leadership and Race: How to Develop and Support Leadership That Contributes to Racial Justice*, LEADERSHIP LEARNING COMMUNITY, July 2010.

Leadership for a New Era, 2010.

22. powell, *supra* note 22.

23. *Id.*

24. NORTHOUSE, *supra* note 17.

lead by simply observing their actions, listening to their words, and seeing the fruit of their labor. Leadership is not an intentional act but evolves organically. In fact, three out of the four profiled lawyers did not use the term "leader" as a self-identified characteristic. This is further evidenced by the way Cahn shares his theoretical frameworks and simply observes as community members are motivated and begin to organize themselves. Levy-Pounds demonstrates leadership as she trains her students and challenges them to serve as agents of change. Leadership as a way of life is also illustrated in Allen's publications as she inspires others to find their call and to use the law as a tool to promote social healing, and in the way powell provides guidance for policy advocacy coalitions, like the African American Leadership Forum of Minnesota, to address the root causes of contemporary social justice issues ranging from affordable housing to economic development.

Table 5.1 provides a summary of the leadership characteristics exhibited by the new social justice lawyer. It includes the categorical designation of leadership as a behavior and leadership as a relationship.[25]

Table 5.1: Leadership Characteristics of New Social Justice Lawyers

Leadership as a Behavior	Leadership as a Relationship
Builds confidence	Promotes collaboration
• Encourages cultural competence	• Demonstrates shared values
• Acts as a bridge	• Delegates responsibility
• Demonstrates organizational skills	• Ministers love (i.e., love leadership)
• Promotes a commitment to service	• Offers care to others
• Taps creativity	• Promotes the growth and development
• Encourages lifelong learning	of others
• Requires wise stewardship	• Inspires other to lead (i.e., transformational leadership)
• Acts as a visionary	• Fosters connectedness: ubuntu
• Promotes creative problem solving	• Encourages others
• Encourages reflection and self-awareness	• Builds shared vision
• Shows respect	• Helps others serve as collaborators and connectors
• Builds trust	

---

25. *Id.*

Fourth Building Block: Exercising Transformative Power

Redefining Power and Raising Leaders

When engaging in transformational leadership, the new social justice law-yer also upholds a collective vision and supports the shared values of the community. It is a dialectic process in which the community and leader are engaging in mutual learning and empowerment.[26] During this process, com-munity members discover their leadership potential and ability to serve as change agents.[27] This is a discovery process that results in the realization of transformative power. It is based on the notion that "all people have power because all people have the ability to cause change."[28] Both, the community and the lawyer realize that they have the power to transform systems of injustice to systems of equity, justice, and hope.

The new social justice lawyer aids in discovering the innate value within people. This moves beyond a sense of value that is formulated by other external factors like social classifications and instead focuses on viewing all people as assets. According to Dr. Cahn, "the other form of value is the way in which it echoes inside you to give a sense of self-esteem, sense of purpose, sense of value." Cahn's theory of coproduction informs this value. For instance, Cahn's theory of coproduction begins where charity ends by focusing on empowering the recipient. "Reciprocity affirms the recipient as an equal and empowers the recipient as a contributor."[29] Once this value is discovered, transformative power can be derived. Collectively, the new social justice lawyers in partnership with communities can then recognize their ability to serve as leaders in their own right.

Additionally, Cahn empowers communities by offering a new vision of community in which each person is an invaluable asset. In his 2004 book, Cahn introduced the concept of "no more throw away people."[30]

---

26. BARBARA CROSBY & JOHN BRYSON, LEADERSHIP FOR THE COMMON GOOD: TACKLING PUBLIC PROBLEMS IN A SHARED-POWER WORLD (2d ed. 2005).

27. GEORGE GOETHALS, GEORGIA SORENSON & JAMES MACGREGOR BURNS, ENCYCLO-PEDIA OF LEADERSHIP (2004).

28. JERRY WINDLEY-DAOUST, LIVING JUSTICE AND PEACE: CATHOLIC SOCIAL TEACHING IN PRACTICE 93 (2008).

29. CAHN, *supra* note 7, at 15.

30. CAHN, *supra* note 7.

This concept means that each human being has value that is irreplaceable, invaluable, and unique. While in a community meeting, Cahn reminded the participants that they have the "power in our lifetime to make a difference" and encouraged them to use this power. Cahn reveres what makes people human beings, which is their ability to help other human beings. He refers to this ability as the "most special thing." Further, Cahn recognizes the power of individuals to support and uplift one another. Conceptually, Cahn frames this message by sharing a story. He recalls the great lessons that Father Fahee taught him while in the face of injustice. Father Fahee reminded Cahn that "we don't have any money but we have each other." The message is simple: Got Hope. Got Power. This was illustrative of Cahn's espoused values that power is within the hands of the community since community members have an abundance of everything that they need so long as they are working together and remain organized.

Social change movements thrive on the leader's ability to tap into the energy of the people. People exhibit a range of different energy types from anger energy to collaborative energy. Dr. Cahn through TimeBanks USA has been able to build social change by effectively reframing the notion of "value" and strategically exercising people power. Within the TimeBanks model, value has a relationship basis rather than a monetary basis. In the context of timebanking, Cahn strengthens the leadership capacity of others by unveiling their intrinsic value and their contribution to the social fabric of the global community. Social change is sustained for the long haul based upon the leader's ability to choose the best approach for utilizing this energy when appropriate. Cahn has tapped into this energy and transformative power, in order to reframe capital from being defined simply in monetary terms to focusing on the importance of human capital. According to Chris, "that is a powerful capacity for change agents" to aid others in exercising their power and directing their energy strategically.

Professor Allen assists law students in recognizing their ability to exercise power in order to transform systems and serve as agents of social change. She organized the efforts of law students who traveled to the Mississippi Delta following Hurricane Katrina. Allen described the law students who traveled to Mississippi as the "fuel of the ground game."[31] They participated in over 22 community legal clinics and performed a range of tasks from community outreach to client intake.[32] With their assistance, over 1,000 clients were served. "The students came with their hearts and minds open to serve as boots on the ground in one of the great social justice movements of our time."[33] Student engagement became a key part of the Mississippi Center for Justice's organizational structure with an explicit focus on coordinating students, organizing their efforts, and fostering their professional formation. Allen (2010) reflects upon these experiences: "[E]ngaging in this work, students experience the importance of their legal support to recovering communities to build their own leadership as agents for the positive social change envisioned by the community in each place."[34] Therefore, Allen played an integral role in training law students in the process of social change by using their legal skills to aid the community in moving closer to their vision of justice.

powell exercises leadership by providing others with the knowledge and tools to exercise their transformative power. During the observed community meeting at the Summit for a Fair Economy, powell provided the historical and legal context underlying the factors that led to the national economic crisis. powell used his legal expertise to share the history of how corporations have gained power and utilized it to maximize their own self-interest. powell proposes the need for an "economy that works for all of us." Based upon the legal precedent, he establishes that the corporations have "hijacked" the Civil War amendments to make corporations equal to citizens, which he characterizes as being too expansive. His goal is to share the history of how corporate power has evolved, its impact on American society, and methods for adopting economic policies that promote the common good.

powell offers a transformative narrative by identifying corporate misalignment as a social problem. He provides a vision of a public space and new identity. This will begin by strengthening the circle of human concern. President Barack Obama commissioned the community to expand this circle

31. Allen et al., *supra* note 11, at 111.
32. Allen et al., *supra* note 11.
33. *Id.* at 111.
34. *Id.* at 130.

when he stated, "Our task, working together, is to constantly widen the circle of concerns so that we can bequeath the American Dream to future generations."[35] The circle of human concern connects people from diverse backgrounds to build and sustain social change through the exercise of transformational thinking.

> Transformational thinking requires creativity, vision, and persistence. Transformative approaches restructure the very institutions and inter-institutional relationships that result in inequalities. Transformative solutions are those that produce sustainable, significant changes in society.
> —john powell

When these connections are fostered and transformational thinking is initiated, transformative power can be realized. According to powell, "[T]ransformational is when systems and structures and platforms that we inhabit don't work in terms of producing the outcomes we want, therefore you need to be attentive to that." powell provides key insights into how these systems work, methods for reforming these systems, and the tools for the community to exercise its collective power. He and the other speakers at the Summit for a Fair Economy challenged community members to exercise their moral imagination to engage in this transformative process. For instance, Steven Lerner (union leader, Service Employees International Union) provided the vision of creating a new world from the ashes of the old. This is a process of moving beyond the vestiges of old to build a new image of America's democracy in solidarity and partnership with others who share the same vision.

From the example of each of the profiled lawyer's collaborations with the community, it is evident that transformative power is a part of exercising human agency. Nobel Laureate Amartya Sen frames human agency as "people's ability to act on behalf of goals that matter to them."[36] Accord-

---

35. Barack Obama, Speech at McKale Memorial Center, Tucson, AZ (Jan. 2011), http://www.nytimes.com/2011/01/13/us/politics/13obama-text.html?pagewanted=all.

36. Gail Straub, The Missing Piece in the Empowerment Equation: A Strategy for Delivering Personal Agency to Women in the Developing World 2 (unpublished article) (on file

ing to Sen, within this capacity people become actively involved and are given the opportunity to shape their own destiny rather than just serving as passive recipients.

These lawyers have aided the community in tapping into their natural capabilities, and new sources of power have been revealed. Historically, power has been used as a force to engage in social change and systems reform.

During the Civil Rights Movement, King, following Gandhi's principles of satyagraha, cultivated love-force. "The whole Gandhian concept of satyagraha, satya is truth which equals love and graha is force; satyagraha thus means truth-force or love-force."[37] Similar to the exercise of love-force as a manifestation of power, the social challenges of our time call for the exercise of transformative power as a tool for empowering communities and fostering the organic growth of leadership capacities at the grassroots level. Further, this type of transformative power has been exercised by these lawyers to transform systems that lead to marginalization. New social justice lawyers understand the multidimensional nature of power since "to know power and not to fear it is essential to its constructive use and control."[38] Thus, the new social justice lawyer plays a critical role in helping the community become organized and discovering its transformative power.

Summary

The exercise of leadership provides new social justice lawyers with the capacity to work in partnership with community members to reach their shared vision of justice and exercise the transformative power that initiates the process of social change. This is a new definition of leadership that is not positional or hierarchical (endowed by title), but instead focuses on what the collective can contribute—on how people can lead together in the fight for justice. It is a definition by which "leadership is accepting responsibility

---

with author).
37. MARTIN LUTHER KING, STRENGTH TO LOVE 151 (1963).
38. SAUL D. ALINSKY, RULES FOR RADICALS: A PRAGMATIC PRIMER FOR REALISTIC RADICALS 7 (1971).

to create conditions that enable others to achieve shared purpose in the face of uncertainty."[39] The new social justice lawyer combines his/her leadership capacity and lawyering skills to create social change and transform systems in partnership with the community. The building blocks of leadership are illustrated in Figure 5.1 on page 79, which shows that leadership is initiated through life-changing experiences, framed by one's vision for justice, characterized as a way of life, and created through the exercise of transformative power.

Reflection Questions

Start to think about your leadership platform. Your leadership platform is informed by your values, beliefs, and life experiences.

1. *Experiencing catalytic and life-changing moments*: What are the life experiences that inspired you to pursue social justice?
2. *Framing a vision of justice*: What is your vision of justice?
3. *Pursuing leadership as a way of life*: Review Table 5.1 on page 79 What leadership behaviors and relationships do you currently exhibit? Are there other leadership characteristics that you would like to develop? How has leadership affected your lifestyle? A personal credo outlines your beliefs and values. Credo in Latin translates to "I believe." Take some time to reflect upon what you believe about the essence of justice and your role as a leader. Draft your leadership credo and post in a visible place as a reminder of your identity as a leader and an agent of change. Examples are available in the appendix.
4. *Exercising transformative power*: In what ways can you partner with others to harness transformative power in order to facilitate the process of social change?

---

39. Marshall Ganz, *Leading Change: Leadership, Organization, and Social Movements, in* HANDBOOK OF LEADERSHIP THEORY AND PRACTICE 509 (Nitin Nohria & Rakesh Khurana eds., 2010).

Chapter 6

Planting People, Growing Justice

When I began writing this book, I sought to explore the methods utilized by today's new social justice lawyers to effect social change. In the past, I had seen lawyers who were serving in leadership roles follow a more authoritarian model or a top-down approach. Leadership was exercised through positional and hierarchical authority. During these instances, community members were left waiting on sidelines and following commands, and lasting social change did not occur. Short-term fixes were made, but long-term systemic change remained unobtainable. Community members may have followed these leaders but only for a short period. All the while some were left waiting and longing for a fresh perspective on leadership (a more inclusive model that would utilize community members and other stakeholders as leaders). A need emerged to build an inclusive, assets-based model for community engagement in the process of social change.

This new model of social justice lawyering would focus on the premise of leadership that begins with a desire to serve (servant leadership) and continues with a desire to motivate others to lead (transformational leadership). The new social justice lawyer leads from within and views leadership as a cherished gift to share with others. He or she demonstrates a commitment to building the capacity of others to lead. The process of leadership development at the grassroots level is integral to the success of not only building but sustaining social change. People are at the center of the process of social change since "leadership is a relationship rooted in community."[1] Without the participation and active engagement of community members, the process of social change is stagnated and will never build momentum. An ancient Chinese proverb, referenced in the Introduction, provides the context for this creation of a shared vision of justice, valuing people, and working together in partnership to foster social change. The proverb provides: "If your vision is for a year, plant wheat. If your vision is for ten years, plant trees. If your vision is for a lifetime, plant people." In essence, a key frame of mind, or perspective, of these lawyers is *planting people*. Their leadership is evaluated by raising the question: Do you grow the people that you lead? Hence, new social justice lawyers can be characterized metaphorically as *planters* based upon their commitment to inspire, motivate, and encourage others to lead.

Planting People

Planting people is an organic process, which yields a great harvest over time. It starts from the ground up as a seed is planted and takes root. This seed represents resistance against marginalization and oppression in order to further the cause of social justice. The seed also represents a partnership between lawyers and community stakeholders. Together, they are able to build a shared vision of a just society and engage in community-building. As the seed begins to germinate, community members start to view themselves as leaders with the capacity to address their own challenges and realize their power to resist oppression. This is an ongoing process of collective engagement, perseverance, teamwork, and diligence. The ultimate result is creating social change, which equates to reaping a harvest of justice, fairness, and equity.

This process of social change can be envisioned through the continual growth of the banyan tree. The banyan tree as a metaphor illuminates the image of the partnership between these new social justice lawyers and

---

1. L.G. Bolman & T.E. Deal, Leading with Soul: An Uncommon Journey of Spirit (rev. ed. 2001).

Figure 6.1
The Process of Planting People (Community Empowerment Paradigm)

community partners working together in solidarity to eradicate marginalization. Unique to this tree is its ability to grow outward, since new roots are formed from the branches. Each community member represents a branch as their leadership voices begin to emerge. These branches grow upward and outward together and are intertwined as they exercise their united power and utilize their voices to advocate for social change. Collectively, the stakeholders are able to create a shared vision of community-building and establish the key steps for making this vision a reality. The branches are connecting, growing together, and supporting one another. They in turn create new roots that establish a firm foundation for the tree and extend to new growth.

The process of social change, like the growth of the banyan tree, symbolizes power and unity. Figure 6.1 outlines this four-step process of community empowerment, which is initiated by the desire to address a dire need and concludes with the implementation of a strategic plan.

Addressing a Dire Need

The seed represents the new social justice lawyer's motivation to serve and lead. It begins to grow when he or she is made aware of a dire need that is negatively impacting a marginalized community. As described by a community member, a dire need is a situation or circumstance that has a far-reaching negative impact on the quality of life experienced by community members and threatens the overall viability of a community. This dire need could include tackling a juvenile justice issue that disproportionately affects youth of color, reforming discriminatory policies, or creating community-centered, culturally specific reentry programming, to name a few challenges addressed by these profiled lawyers. During the practice of new social justice lawyering, the lawyer recalls those childhood or later life experiences that shaped his or her perspective on the quest for justice. This issue may be something that the lawyer has personally witnessed or has been made aware of by others. He or she then seeks to utilize transformational leadership skills in conjunction with legal training to address this dire need in partnership with community stakeholders who are concerned about this particular issue.

Just as transformational leaders exhibit the qualities of charisma and persuasion that challenge others to take action,[2] these new social justice lawyers' social justice convictions attract others and compel them to act in the process of reform efforts. This creates an opportunity for the seed to grow as the new social justice lawyer inspires the community to engage in social action. When a dire need occurs, the new social justice lawyer receives an invitation from community members to share in the brainstorming and problem-solving processes. It is not a scenario of the lawyer arriving on the scene with all of the answers and the solutions while the community hands over its decision-making power to the lawyer. Instead, the new social justice lawyer is asked to take part in this creative thinking process and not to control the process but to facilitate it.

---

2. PETER G. NORTHOUSE, INTRODUCTION TO LEADERSHIP CONCEPTS AND PRACTICE (5th ed. 2010).

Dr. Edgar Cahn's Story

Dr. Edgar Cahn was invited to a community meeting to address a dire need related to racial disparities in the juvenile justice and child welfare systems in Minnesota. This dire need is evidenced by the state of Minnesota having an alarmingly high rate of racial disparities in the juvenile justice system. Minnesota is among eight states with the highest disparities between youth of color and white youth in the juvenile justice system, with a ratio of 5 to 1. Further, recent research has demonstrated that alternatives to detention (ATD) are more cost-effective and can yield more successful outcomes when compared to secure detention. In Minnesota, it costs about $311 per day to incarcerate a youth versus about $65 for an ATD placement. This meeting brought together community members interested in applying Cahn's legal theory of deliberate indifference to address these disparities facing African American children and youth in Minnesota. The process of uncovering deliberate indifference is a legal remedy that seeks to eliminate racial disparities in the juvenile justice system and offer all youth equal access to effective and efficient community-based ATD.[3]

This community meeting focused on legal remedies for addressing Disproportionate Minority Contact (overrepresentation of youth of color) in juvenile justice and whether this legal framework could also be used to address the racial disparities in the child welfare system. In light of these key statistics, community members had decided to convene to learn from Cahn and create a strategic plan for reform. The meeting convener stated that there are "poor outcomes for African Americans in everything—health, mental health, education and housing. There is a need for leadership on how to improve outcomes for youth."

Cahn came to the meeting to serve as a guide on how to improve these outcomes and empower the community to lead this reform effort. He had supported other jurisdictions that were experiencing similar racial disparities with developing early prevention and intervention programs. He shared an example of the development of a youth court in Washington, D.C., where youths serve as peer jurors when nonviolent youth offenses occur. This

---

3. E. Cahn & C. Robbins, *An Offer They Can't Refuse: Racial Disparity in Juvenile Justice and Deliberate Indifference Meet Alternatives That Work*, 13 UDC/DCSL L. REV. 1–31 (2009).

court handles 70 percent of offenses in Washington, D.C., and 80 percent of youths are required to serve as jurors as part of their sentences. Based upon the empirical data, recidivism rates for the youth court participants are below 10 percent (which is much lower than the rate of comparable programs). Cahn believes that the group reached these tremendous results because in sentencing it is clear to each youth offender that "we need you in the community." The program begins with respecting the youths. Cahn tells them that they "have something I respect and need." He then challenges the youths to become change agents by raising the question: "How do we use what we know to make a difference?" This type of enlistment draws the youths into the social fabric of the community, encourages them to become actively involved in public service, and fosters their leadership potential. Those in attendance at this community meeting began to organize and explore ways to replicate some of these strategies.

Professor Nekima Levy-Pounds's Story

Professor Nekima Levy-Pounds's work focuses on the dire need of addressing the quality-of-life disparities for African American males. One such example is her leadership in the establishment of Brotherhood, Inc. Brotherhood, Inc., is a community-led initiative that began in 2007. The mission of Brotherhood, Inc., is to "enable African-American youths and young adults to envision and achieve successful futures." The focus of Brotherhood, Inc., is on the need to address both the overrepresentation of African American males in the justice system and the unemployment gap affecting these men. Levy-Pounds suggested that the group explore the Homeboy Industries model in Los Angeles as a possible model for a reintegration/ job-training program. This is a one-stop-shop model that offers employment through social enterprises, job skills development, and life skills and practical skills development.

During a community board meeting, one community leader addressed the dire need for the existence of Brotherhood, Inc. He viewed it as a matter of life or death since "brothers are dying in the streets." Levy-Pounds and the community partners are committed to the furtherance of this initiative since it is more than a project—it is an opportunity to change someone's life course. The Founder of Homeboy Industries, Father Gregory Boyle, has a mantra: "Nothing can stop a bullet like a job." Levy-Pounds and the community leaders believe that they have a chance to stop some bullets by aiding African American males in reaching success, strengthening their communities, and uplifting their families.

Creating job opportunities is imperative since unemployment is also an area of great concern. In the state of Minnesota, there is a large disparity in unemployment rates between the African American community and its white counterparts. According to a recent publication from U.S. Bureau of Labor Statistics, Minnesota's 2011 jobless rate was 18 percent for African American males.[4] That is more than 3 times the rate of unemployment for white residents, giving the state one of the largest gaps in the country. These statistics illustrate the dire need to address the structural inequities negatively affecting African American males due the barriers that restrict equal access to employment opportunities.

Professor Bonnie Allen's Story

The Mississippi Center for Justice (MCJ) and Professor Bonnie Allen have been actively involved in improving the quality of life for Mississippians and promoting economic justice and racial justice. The social conditions experienced by communities of color, in particular, demonstrate a dire need for social reform. When evaluated based upon the Human Development Index (a United Nations evaluative tool used to measure social and economic development), Mississippi ranks considerably lower in comparison with other states. In fact, Mississippi has the "lowest life expectancy, the highest rate of adults 25 and older who have not completed high school or earned a high school equivalency degree, and very low levels of personal earnings from wages and salaries."[5] This publication on the human development index in Mississippi portrays two conflicting images of the state.[6] One image is of despair characterized by dismal poverty rates and the other image is of tranquility evidenced by a rich cultural history and an abundance

---

4. www.mprnews.org/story/2012/07/03/labor-unemployment-gap.Twin cities again lead nation in black, white unemployment gap.

5. S. BURD-SHARPS, K. LEWIS, & B.E. MARTINS, A PORTRAIT OF MISSISSIPPI 3 (American Human Development Project, 2008), www.measureofamerica.org.

6. *Id.*

of lush, beautiful land. Additionally, these disparities are even greater when you take into account race and the challenges facing the African American community. For instance, the Human Development Index rate for whites in Mississippi compares with the average American in 1997, while the index rate of their African Americans counterparts compares with the average American in 1974. This is a 23-year gap in the human index rates between the two racial groups. Examples like these illustrate the dire need experienced at the intersection of race and poverty in the state of Mississippi.[7]

MCJ has framed these experiences as the current civil rights issues of our time. President and CEO of MCJ Martha Bergmark believes the mission of MCJ is to "continue the work of the civil rights movement [which is] unfinished business." A glimpse into the statistics related to the quality of life experienced by Mississippians illustrates the dire need to continue this unfinished business. MCJ has committed time, talent, and collective energy to eliminating these disparities in Mississippi by building coalitions for social change. Thus, the efforts of Cahn, Levy-Pounds, and Allen focus on addressing a dire need that involves limited access to justice for a particular group of individuals.

Asking Questions and the Process of Storytelling

When addressing a dire need, the next step in the process is tending to the plant by asking questions and sharing stories. It is a community-centered approach because the focus is on community members identifying the challenges that they are facing, prioritizing them, and building unity. Participants are asked to avoid any preconceived notions about the root causes of the challenges and the best possible solutions, and instead to begin by engaging in active listening[8] and asking exploratory questions.

Cahn uses a questioning technique as a tool for gathering information and building rapport. During the community meeting described above, Cahn began the conversation by asking each person to share about themselves and

---

7. *Id.*
8. William Quigley, *Letter to a Student Interested in Social Justice*, 1 DePaul J. Soc. Just. 7, 28 (2007).

their work. By beginning this way, Cahn created a welcoming environment. Each person appeared comfortable after their introduction, and side conversations emerged throughout as people began to network and collaborate. They started to identify common interests and organize collective efforts. This followed Myles Horton's Highlander Folk School model of bringing people together and watching the ideas emerge from them.[9] This process recognizes the leadership capacity of each individual and encourages their active involvement in the problem-solving process.

Throughout his interactions with the community members, Cahn continued to ask questions. This epitomizes his theory of the feedback loop, which focuses on enabling the community to frame its own issues and develop a plan of action. He asked some in a more rhetorical style. For example, his final question before beginning an open discussion was, "How do we enlist people we care about as coworkers?" This led community members to ponder questions such as: How can we engage in coproduction within the juvenile justice and child welfare systems? What role do children, parents, and families play in the process? He also challenged the community members to explore their leadership potential by asking the rhetorical question: "Do you understand your own power?" He offered an answer by simply stating, "We have the power to change the world."

Similar to Cahn, Professor Levy-Pounds also asks questions to foster community engagement and share collective input. She draws upon these themes in the classroom as she educates students about their roles as agents of social change. She initiates this process by asking questions on an individual basis challenging students to engage in ongoing self-reflection. She has adopted this principle in her teaching pedagogy by focusing on asking her students: "What is in your hands to make difference?" She states:

> I think of transformational lawyering as maybe a circumstance or ideal of what the true role of the lawyer who is focused on social justice would look like. For example, when we saw what was happening with the obstructing of legal process issues, transformational lawyering means not just looking at the circumstance and saying "oh,

---

9. Myles Horton, Judith Kohl & Herbert Kohl, The Long Haul: An Autobiography (1998).

that's sad. That's too bad that so many people are being arrested." But instead, saying, "you know what's in my hands? What's in my tool-box? What can I do to change the situation? Who do I have to talk to? What memos do I need to draft? Who do I need to bring on board to make sure that this injustice does not continue to happen?" And so in essence you are given an opportunity to use your legal skills and training to help transform society and to not give in to the notion that things are the way that they are and that's how they are going to be.

Levy-Pounds places a key emphasis on asking self-reflection questions that aid a new social justice lawyer in the process of professional formation. These questions focus on how each individual can make a difference in the world by furthering the cause of justice. This is a process of recognizing and cultivating the transformative power derived from the strategic utilization of one's legal training.

Like Cahn and Levy-Pounds, Professor powell uses a questioning technique to challenge community members to think critically about how social inequities have evolved. During the Summit for a Fair Economy, he discussed the original intent of the 14th Amendment, which was to protect the rights of citizens but later evolved into the protection of corporations. He raised questions such as, "How did this happen? How did corporations gain these protections after the Civil War?" When asked to examine the future policies to consider, powell suggests looking at policies through a certain lens and raising the question: "Are they generating the outcomes that we want?"[10] This is to ensure that system and democratic practices are responsive to the needs of the community.

Asking questions serves as an evaluative tool and fact investigation mechanism for the new social justice lawyer. As an evaluative tool, it is important for the new social justice lawyer to assess progress in achieving a goal, which is evident through Cahn's feedback loop (community engagement technique) and powell's process of inquiry (exploration and education process). Both focus on evaluating progress from the community's perspective and

---

10. African American Leadership Forum, *Q & A with John Powell*, 1 REVIVE! TWIN CITIES 36 (2011).

encouraging community engagement. Similar to the community organizer, the new social justice lawyer's most frequent word is "why?"[11] By raising questions, such as "Why do racial disparities exist in the juvenile justice system?" or "Why are the current policies not working and how are they influenced by social systems/structures?," these new social justice lawyers are constantly examining the life challenges facing marginalized communities. Thus, when engaging in the process of social change, ongoing inquiry and deliberation are key practices.

Enlisting Partners in Social Action

Another technique used by these new social justice lawyers is establishing key partnerships, which lay the foundation for building and sustaining social change. This is the recognition that social change emerges through collaborative processes. Building partnerships focuses on the value that each person brings to the table and enables community members to take ownership over addressing their own challenges. Additionally, it recognizes the power derived from building alliances with a range of community partners who can establish a united front in the fight for justice.[12] This parallels with fertilizing the ground by preparing for the growth process.

New social justice lawyers play an integral role in enlisting partners to engage in social change efforts. Cahn recognized the importance of partnerships during a presentation with his wife, Chris, at a plenary session sponsored by the Schumacher Society. Chris's words reflected the vision of the future of timebanking. She stated it is "no more one man's vision."[13] Cahn writes, "When Chris finished sharing the key message, it became very clear the extent to which I am no longer alone. I have a genuine partner. And I have a vast, global extended family. And that family is growing."[14]

---

11. SAUL D. ALINSKY, RULES FOR RADICALS: A PRAGMATIC PRIMER FOR REALISTIC RADICALS 7 (1971).

12. Joseph Stewart, *Policy Models and Equal Educational Opportunity*, 24 POL. SCI. & POL. 167 (1991).

13. EDGAR CAHN, NO MORE THROW-AWAY PEOPLE: THE CO-PRODUCTION IMPERATIVE (2004).

14. *Id.* at xii.

These partnerships establish a unified vision for changing the perception of the commodity of time and the value of money by focusing on the future growth of the social capital derived from collective engagement.

While working with community members, Cahn places an explicit emphasis on enlisting partners. During the observed community meeting, he encouraged the group to "enlist partners, respect their contribution, and value their contribution." He warned the group that "nothing works unless you enlist persons you are working with as partners." He posited that this is the reason why human services have failed since these organizations focus primarily on service delivery and operate from a deficit model. He then offered a solution through implementation of coproduction. He characterized coproduction as "helping others to be all they can be." Coproduction places value on the contributions of each individual and each person is drawn into the social fabric of the community.[15] This is a process of reciprocity. It goes beyond the notion of "let me help you solve your problems" to recognizing the inextricable nature of the human existence. It focuses on how we can help each other to thrive. This is the recognition that human beings need each other to survive, thus partners are needed for social systems to thrive.

Levy-Pounds believes all partners have equal value based upon each individual's unique composition of gifts and talents, life experiences, and overall ability to lead in a meaningful way. The new social justice lawyer is able to recognize these hidden talents in others and aid partners in unveiling them. She envisions the ability of each partner to serve and work toward the common good. She emphasizes that this ability needs to be respected and recognized:

> So I think each person needs to recognize the contribution that he or she can make. I think other stakeholders also have to be willing to see the value that other people are bringing to the table. Whether they have a bachelor's degree or not, whether they have a high school diploma or not. Whether they have an advanced degree or not. So often we place so much stock in those who are the most highly educated when

---

15. *Id.*

often times you know it's the person who has street knowledge or experience from having lived a long life that is valuable [...] I think we have to begin to place a premium on people's experiences, their contributions, gifts and talents and how it takes a collective in order to push for meaningful and lasting change in society.

Levy-Pounds's philosophy/approach of engaging stakeholders as a collective represents leadership at the center of social change. The stakeholders are leading and directing the course of social change. This collective can range in size but the most important part is enabling each partner to assume his or her unique, individualized role.
"Now, that collective may be five people or 5,000 people. I think the most important thing is figuring out who's with you, what sacrifices they are willing to make, and then striking at the right time in order to change things."
—Professor Levy-Pounds

Levy-Pounds establishes that each person is a valuable contributor in the process of social change. The leader aids the people in maximizing their full potential and taking strategic action to usher in social change. Further, Levy-Pounds exhibits the qualities of policy entrepreneurship by recognizing the need to strike at the right time as a "window of opportunity" opens wide.

Professor Bonnie Allen and MCJ's community lawyers actively engage in building new partnerships and strengthening existing relationships. Their work focuses on creating equitable policies that improve the quality of life for all Mississippians by building healthy communities. This advocacy work is furthered through collective and collaborative efforts of community partners. These partners include faith leaders, teachers, elected officials, community advocates, and health care professionals. Together, they work to promote justice, fairness, and equity in a wide range of areas (like health care reform, affordable housing, foreclosure prevention, and consumer lending). For instance, the campaign to reform payday lending in Mississippi is led by a number of partners who have established a policy coalition. According to Allen (speaking in 2011), "Mississippi has the highest interest rate in the country. . . . [I]f you roll over a few times with a payday loan it's up to like 574% [interest rate]—it's terrible." This coalition educates community members on the impact of these lending practices and aids in organizing the community to challenge these policies. These reform efforts are coalition-driven initiatives that rely on the collective engagement of community partners to reach their desired objectives.

Through this process of enlisting partners, new social justice lawyers exemplify servant leadership qualities and community-organizing skills. The servant leader's key goal is to "grow people" in their leadership capacity.[16] Servant leadership is a facilitative approach that supports growth and development of partners, and the role of follower and leader are intertwined.[17] When enlisting partners, the new social justice lawyer is growing the people around him or her. The central focus then becomes lawyering with the people, and not simply lawyering for the people.

Re-Imagining Justice and Creating Equal Access

These new social justice lawyers have added yet another dimension to social justice lawyering: the power of moral imagination. During the process of social change, the new social justice lawyer and community partners need to allow for opportunities to unleash their moral imagination. Based upon John Dewey's philosophy of moral imagination, this occurs through imaginative processes and allows for examining a range of possible outcomes despite the parameters of societal rules, myths, customs, and rituals.[18] Dewey characterizes this as empathetic projection as one imagines another person's goals, desires, and aspirations as one's own.[19] The new social justice lawyer exercises moral imagination by exhibiting compassion for the poor, marginalized, and those in need.[20] This compassion informs one's vision

---

16. ANN MCGEE-COOPER & GARY LOOPER, THE ESSENTIALS OF SERVANT LEADERSHIP: PRINCIPLES IN PRACTICE (2001).

17. STEPHEN BROOKFIELD & STEPHEN PRESKILL, LEARNING AS A WAY OF LEADING: LESSONS FROM THE STRUGGLE FOR SOCIAL JUSTICE ix (2009).

18. S. FESMIRE, JOHN DEWEY AND MORAL IMAGINATION: PRAGMATISM IN ETHICS (2003).

19. *Id.*

20. L.A. PARKS DALOZ, C.H. KEEN, J.P. KEEN, & S. DALOZ PARKS, COMMON FIRE: LEADING LIVES OF COMMITMENT IN A COMPLEX WORLD (1996).

of justice and desire to address the social justice issues affecting marginalized populations. In addition, the new social justice lawyer facilitates the rehearsal process of creating a shared vision of justice and re-imagining the essence of community. This equates to the flower emerging before the plant bears fruit.

The flower reflects the long-anticipated gift of bearing fruit. In the case of new social justice lawyering, this is the possibility of transforming justice and fostering social equity. These lawyers have a vision for justice and they use their moral imagination to achieve this goal. Levy-Pounds believes lawyers can exercise their moral imagination by engaging in social engineering. A lawyer as a social engineer is "the mouthpiece" for those living at the margins of society and is a protector of their legal rights.[21] The law can be used as a tool to dismantle structural systems that are inequitable. Coupled with this is the moral responsibility of lawyers to facilitate the process of social change. Levy-Pounds characterized the utilization of this tool as being given an opportunity to use your legal skills and training to help transform society and to not give in to the notion that the status quo must prevail. Her early life experience of growing up poor and facing oppression has served as a motivation for leading social change. She seeks to leave a better future for her children and generations to come.

Levy-Pounds's vision of justice is inclusive. It includes protecting the interest of children and other vulnerable populations who face oppression by envisioning a more just society and equal justice under the law. This vision is a manifestation of Levy-Pounds actively exercising her moral imagination. She is continually creating new ways to address marginalization and eradicate systems of oppression. Further, she also exhibits strong moral character by imagining and identifying with the quest for justice sought by marginalized communities. The future of justice imagined by Levy-Pounds leads and guides her work in the Community Justice Project.

Professor Allen also demonstrates the power of moral imagination in social change efforts. According to Allen, "leadership for change starts with imagining a new reality—for ourselves, our institutions, and our

---

21. R.A. Fairfax, *Wielding the Double-Edged Sword: Charles Hamilton Houston and Judicial Activism in the Age of Legal Realism*, 14 HARV. BLACKLETTER L.J. 17–44 (1998).

communities."[22] She has led a paradigm shift in how the role of lawyers is viewed. She envisions the law being used as a vehicle of social healing with the goal of healing conflict versus perpetuating it. This is a new vision of using lawyering as a tool for effecting social change.

Allen believes leadership begins with moral imagination as the starting point for building relationships with key partners. The vision of MCJ is "re-imagining" Mississippi as the Social Justice State.[23] Through the cultivation of key partnerships, MCJ is working toward this goal through the exercise of moral imagination. "[Demonstrating moral imagination] involves working the process toward uncertain ends, negotiating the space between different and often clashing groups, and demonstrating bold action and moral courage."[24] A shared vision provides a firm foundation for nurturing collaborative relationships between the new social justice lawyer, community members, and other stakeholders. Allen characterizes this vision as "a vision for change, a vision for making the world a better place in some sort of specific way." This vision aids the "leader" in leading in an authentic manner and inspiring others to do the same. According to Allen, a lawyer engaging in leadership and promoting social change initiatives also has the ability to bring people together from diverse backgrounds, identify their gifts, and encourage their leadership to emerge. This manifests the individual's ability to lead in a collaborative and team-oriented manner.

Through the exercise of moral imagination, the community can envision its future and develop a strategic plan for reaching its goals. "Imagination in Dewey's central sense is the capacity to concretely perceive what is before us in light of what could be," therefore providing the community with the freedom to imagine justice in action.[25] Cahn offered the example of community members envisioning a new set of rules that are fair, equitable, and just. According to Cahn, the community desires to have the ability to

---

22. S.M. INTRATOR & M. SCRIBNER, LEADING FROM WITHIN: POETRY THAT SUSTAINS THE COURAGE TO LEAD 56 (2007).

23. B. Allen, B. Bezdek & J. Jopling, *Community Recovery Lawyering: Hard-Learned Lessons from Post-Katrina Mississippi*, 4 DEPAUL J. SOC. JUST. 123 (2010).

24. E. ENOMOTO & B.H. KRAMER, LEADING THROUGH THE QUAGMIRE: ETHICAL FOUNDATIONS, CRITICAL METHODS, AND PRACTICAL APPLICATIONS FOR SCHOOL LEADERSHIP 86 (2007).

25. FESMIRE, *supra* note 18, at 65.

shape its own destiny and move toward a shared vision of the future.[26] As understanding increases about how these rules operate and can be altered, people can change the rules of social systems.[27] Community members can then realize the power to transform the rules that govern social systems. This is evidenced by the way in which community members have re-envisioned market value through timebanking. Timebanking participants now recognize that the monetary system alone cannot determine who is valuable and what it means to give.[28] Alternatively, timebanking recognizes that all people are valuable contributors, thus everyone has something to give.[29] These community members have a new vision of what it means to build strong, caring communities of support.

The new social justice lawyer exercises moral imagination by envisioning the future of social change and working collaboratively with others to make this vision a reality. "We must believe that it is the darkness before the dawn of a beautiful new world; we will see it when we believe it."[30] First, unleashing one's moral imagination is an art and not a science. It focuses on the artistic values (doing) and the aesthetic values (intellectual thinking) underlying a social justice dilemma. The new social justice lawyer engages in "improvisational thinking" by assessing how to change law and policy to usher in this "new world." This requires creativity, expressiveness, and foresight.[31] This is analogous to the experience of the artist. Metaphorically like the artist, the new social justice lawyer has the courage to discover new possibilities and guide others on this path. "Moral deliberation can be artfully developed only through a socially responsive imagination that skillfully perceives paths of mutual growth."[32] Secondly, socially responsive imagination begins by connecting with others to promote the common good. It acknowledges that a sense of community is manifested through interdependence, expressing care, and commitment to others. These social connections serve as a catalyst for change.

---

26. Cahn, *supra* note 13.
27. *Id.*
28. Cahn, Priceless Money: Banking Time for Changing Times (2011).
29. Cahn, *supra* note 13.
30. Alinsky, *supra* note 11, at 196.
31. Fesmire, *supra* note 18.
32. *Id.* at 126.

Moral imagination also informs the strategy of the new social justice lawyer. He or she engages in dramatic rehearsal of possible outcomes of strategies, which provides key insights about system responses, possible outcomes, and alternative courses of action.[33] "The action in the rehearsal phase moves beyond imagining possibilities to proposing actual courses of action."[34] During this process, one is also challenged to anticipate the unintended consequences of one's actions, evaluate potential blind spots, and assess how others might respond to the course of action. Dr. Cahn and Chris train their students in this dramatic rehearsal process. In their systems changes class, they teach their students about the dynamics of how systems operate, possible system responses, and the utilization of power. This process provides the new social justice lawyer with valuable insights and the foresight needed to chart the course of social change. It also recognizes the limitations of traditional litigation since the primary focus of litigation is to challenge or uphold legal precedent. However, social change may require changes in the policy arena and altering the way systems currently operate. By considering alternatives to litigation (e.g., policy advocacy, community-organizing, and social engineering), the new social justice lawyer is challenged to engage in a multifaceted approach to problem solving. This is evidence of the exercise of dramatic rehearsal. Hence, by unleashing their moral imagination, communities in partnership with new social justice lawyers can discover the path to justice and take the steps necessary to achieve their shared goals.

Setting a New Social Justice Agenda and Building Coalitions

When a long-term strategic plan is created, additional opportunities for planting more seeds emerge. The community takes ownership of its own problems and collaborates to create durable solutions. This is an organic process in which the leader is a part of a collective that takes action to

---

33. *Id.*
34. Enomoto & Kramer, *supra* note 24, at 101.

challenge instances of injustice.[35] Together, they realize their power to overcome marginalization and break down systems of oppression. This phase is a preparation for the harvest since each person emerges as a leader within his or her own right.

The new social justice lawyer naturally exits the process when the community realizes its collective power, yet he or she continues to serve as a resource. For example, during the community meeting, when Cahn's remarks drew to a natural close, the group members began to organize themselves. Cahn simply sat back as the two community leaders led the group in developing a strategic plan. I came in with a misconception about how this meeting would be conducted. I thought that Cahn had come to share the knowledge, but I soon found that the knowledge base was already well-established there in the room. The people gathered had the answers within themselves since they were talking about things that they cared about and had firsthand knowledge of. Cahn came only to facilitate a dialogue and share a few helpful tools for community-organizing and public policy advocacy. They took the initiative and began organizing themselves. This process was not about Cahn at all. They started to discuss how they could be of support to one another and build their own timebank. This was illustrative of Cahn's guiding principle that power is within the hands of the community since it has an "abundance" of everything that it needs. The outcome of this community meeting also exemplifies his leadership style. The Chinese philosopher Lao-tzu once stated: "A leader is best when people barely know he exits. When his work is done, his aim is fulfilled, they will say: we did it ourselves."[36] Cahn was able to exit from the community meeting in a manner that empowered the community members to lead. Community members were left with the confidence that they could chart the course for the future themselves.

Levy-Pounds also recognizes the need for the community to set its own agenda and lead its own efforts. She is often found quoting: "We must remember that one determined person can make a significant difference and that a small group of determined people can change the course of history."

---

35. BROOKFIELD & PRESKILL, *supra* note 17.
36. NICHOLAS VON HOFFMAN, A PORTRAIT OF SAUL ALINSKY: RADICAL 177 (2010).

Levy-Pounds uses this quote to inspire community members, and encourage them to lead their own change and set their own agenda.

At the Summit for a Fair Economy, Professor powell was leading a group of determined people in the process of social reform with the goal in mind to create a more equitable, sustainable economy. The essence of this new economy evolved through the unleashing of powell's moral imagination and his engagement in dramatic rehearsal with the community participants. Together, they were able to imagine their collective identity, shared humanity, and power to effect social change. They also could envision their power to challenge an economic system that was not meeting their needs. One community organizer shared her strategy for reaching this vision. She stated the need to "start empowering the people. Look you can't fight by yourself, you can't fight these big corporations by yourself. You gotta have the tools and that's by uniting." This sense of unity combined the voices of community members by organizing them as a collective force and building coalitions of support.

This collective force is harnessed within coalitions that provide the organizational base needed to train, organize, and inspire community members to lead. During this summit, former Secretary of Labor Robert Reich challenged the participants to get involved in the process of public policy reform. He warned: "Nothing good happens in Washington unless people are mobilized, energized, and make sure things happen." Reich's words serve as a reminder of the importance of community members engaging in agenda setting by preparing for social change when the "window of opportunity" opens and serving as policy entrepreneurs through active involvement in policy reform.

"When ideas are used as seeds, they take root, grow and become reality in the life in which they are planted. The only risk in the seed approach: once it grows and becomes a part of those in whom it's planted, you probably will get no credit for originating the idea. But if you're willing to do it without credit . . . you'll reap a rich harvest."
—Dr. Richard C. Halverson

These new social justice lawyers have supported small groups as they start with an idea and as those groups are now building social change in communities locally and globally. They could be metaphorically characterized as planters of seeds of ideas, which are evidenced through their leadership styles.

The profiled lawyers have demonstrated that through planting people, community voices are taking root and ideas are growing into justice.

New social justice lawyers are constantly planting people with encouragement, support, and motivation. When these lawyers enter a room, you can feel anticipation in the atmosphere. I witnessed this experience firsthand as I observed each of these lawyers in the field and recorded their interactions with community stakeholders. For instance, when Dr. Cahn was participating in a community meeting, the people all seemed to be suddenly uplifted. Some appeared to be waiting for practical solutions to the issues that they were facing in furthering social justice initiatives. Others appeared to be waiting for encouragement and motivation to get involved in the change process. It is as if a gust of wind has swept through the room—a wind of renewed hope—when the new social justice lawyer appears. This renewed hope is an integral part of building and sustaining social change since community empowerment is the foundation.

Summary

The new social justice lawyer utilizes a wide range of methods to engage community members in the process of social change and motivate them to lead. This is not a linear process but instead it naturally evolves as trust and rapport is built over time. The new social justice lawyer is invited into the community to provide his or her legal knowledge and leadership skills to engage in problem solving around a social justice issue. The new justice lawyer listens to the stories of the people, helps to establish a strategic plan of action, and aids in facilitating the process of social change. Collectively, the community members and the new social justice lawyer begin to unleash their moral imagination by looking beyond the limitations of the current circumstances to realizing their shared vision of justice. Other connections are also established in order to build strong partnerships and form coalitions. Overall, these four profiled lawyers are planting people in the hopes of yielding a great harvest—growing justice.

Reflection Questions

1. According to John Maxwell, "empowering is giving your influence to others for the purpose of personal and organizational growth." How have the profiled lawyers given their influence to others?
2. What steps can you take to foster community empowerment?
3. How can you apply the principles of servant leadership (leading by serving first) and transformational leadership (motivating others to lead) to your work in the community?
4. In what ways can you engage in "planting people" and demonstrate the qualities of a "planter" based upon your commitment to inspire, motivate, and encourage others to lead?
5. The banyan tree serves as a metaphor for an image of community partnerships. What other images come to mind when you think of the lawyer's role of building partnerships with the community?
6. *Addressing a Dire Need.* Read a local community newspaper and/or interview a local community leader. What are the dire needs affecting the viability of your neighborhood?
7. *Asking Questions and the Process of Storytelling.* Attend a community meeting or town hall forum. What are some of the common themes shared by community participants as it relates to challenges experienced by the community?
8. *Enlisting Partners in Social Action.* Select a social justice issue to focus on. Who is working on this issue and how can you support their efforts?
9. *Re-imagining Justice and Creating Equal Access.* How can you unleash your moral imagination in order to aid you in reaching your vision for justice?
10. *Setting a New Social Justice Agenda and Building Coalitions.* How can you support community members in setting their own agenda and embracing a sense of agency?

Chapter 7

The New Social Justice Lawyer's Toolbox: Redefining Money, Power, and Lawyering

The tools needed to facilitate the process of social change have evolved. In the arena of civil rights, mass litigation and civil suits had become indispensable tools. The success of these tools is exemplified in the renowned case of *Brown v. Board of Education*, which ended de facto segregation in schools. However, today the landscape of civil rights law has changed, which is evidenced by limited access to the courts and a limited ability to eradicate the underlying root causes of systemic inequity. Out of necessity a new breed of lawyers has emerged who focus not only on employing their legal training as a tool for social change but who also recognize the importance of utilizing a multifunctional toolbox. These lawyers assess and determine which tools are best suited for a given situation, whether it be engaging in public policy advocacy or utilizing community-organizing with the goal in mind of facilitating the process of social change.

These particular lawyers employ a variety of tools in order to further the cause of social justice, starting with the fundamental lawyering tools that include legal research/analysis, oral advocacy, and writing as advocacy, to name a few. These tools are the base and built upon this firm foundation are additional advocacy skills that were gained out of necessity in response to the complexity of today's social challenges. As new social justice lawyers, these lawyers combine these tools with their leadership skills and public policy advocacy experience to build and sustain social change. Leadership is exemplified as the lawyer works to motivate, educate, empower, and inspire community members to initiate leadership in the process of social change. Public policy advocacy tools are exhibited as these lawyers engage in community-organizing and coalition-building. The culmination of these tools provides a framework for engaging in collaborative processes that can influence the future of social change. The new social justice lawyer is a steward of these tools and utilizes them to advance the cause of justice by being adaptable and creative and recognizing when and how to use the tools effectively.

The new social justice lawyer is not a single actor, nor are lawyering skills the default tool of choice. Instead, he or she recognizes the importance of combining lawyering skills with a range of other multidisciplinary approaches that include systems mapping, ethnographic approaches, policy entrepreneurship, and qualitative research. These tools are all valuable instruments for building and sustaining social change. Each tool is equal in value and serves an indispensable function. Further, the new social justice lawyer recognizes the importance of combining one's tools with other tools by working collaboratively with professionals from diverse backgrounds to address the root causes of social and structural inequities and the interrelated nature of social justice issues.

Keys to the Kingdom: The New Social Justice Lawyer's Tools

The new social justice lawyer possesses the tools that are needed to build and sustain social change. The profiled lawyers recognize the importance of lawyers utilizing their tools to effect social change. This process begins with identifying these tools and recognizing the moral responsibility to use them for the greater good. Professor Bonnie Allen believes lawyers are in a prime position to facilitate the process of social change through the use of their lawyering skills as a tool. Allen acknowledges that lawyers have "more tools than most good advocates." These tools include oral advocacy, legal research and writing, and understanding how the law, systems, and government function. According to Allen, the legal profession endows lawyers with great leadership responsibility and an esteemed position. She notes when referring to the role of a lawyer that "we have the keys to the kingdom." The keys to the kingdom are evidenced by the lawyer's ability to have access to the courts, exercise technical training, and demonstrate understanding of how systems operate. These keys (when leveraged as tools) aid in furthering the cause of social justice and opening the doors to the realization of justice.

Since lawyers possess the keys to the kingdom, they are challenged to put them to good use. This goes beyond having keys in one's hands to taking the action of opening the door for others. Dr. Edgar Cahn believes lawyers have a responsibility to use the law as a tool to build a shared vision of justice and equity. Cahn provides that a lawyer has a job to do similar to the professional role of an architect. An architect has the power to create and innovate. Similar to an architect, the lawyer has the power to create a redesign by transforming structural injustices into new inroads for justice.

Cahn describes lawyers as social architects whose "job in part is to structure the institutional vehicles into which and through which people can channel their energy and contribute in ways that are collectively more powerful."

These institutional vehicles provide opportunities for the community to become engaged in the process of social change. This framework moves beyond lawyering in a case-by-case format to lawyering in partnership with the community. The emphasis on lawyering in partnership with the community demonstrates the multifaceted nature of the new social justice lawyering approach, which includes coalition-building, policy entrepreneurship, and community-organizing.

Drawing upon the teaching pedagogy of Charles Hamilton Houston, lawyers have a moral duty to use the law as a tool to fight for those who cannot fight back for themselves.[1] Cahn's work is demonstrative of the characteristics of a social architect. The role of social architect places an emphasis on social and ethical responsibility endowed upon lawyers to

---

1. GENNA RAE MCNEIL, GROUNDWORK: CHARLES HAMILTON HOUSTON AND THE STRUGGLE FOR CIVIL RIGHTS (1983).

engage in new social justice lawyering. Based in the philosophy of social engineering, the lawyer has a responsibility to create the vehicles for social change by utilizing the law and one's legal training to guide this process.

Levy-Pounds also advocates for using the tools that lawyers have been given to advance the cause of justice in society. It begins with process of inquiry about how a lawyer's tools can be used. She asks, "What's in my hands? What's in my toolbox? What can I do to change the situation? Who do I have to talk to? What memos do I need to draft? Who do I need to bring on board to make sure that this injustice does not continue to happen?" By reflecting on these questions, the lawyer can begin to recognize the responsibility and privilege of carrying these tools. During her own reflection experience, Levy-Pounds discovered that she had an important role to play in engaging in the process of social change. She stated, "I want to see the world transformed into an oasis of fairness and justice and that can only come by knowing the power and the privilege and responsibility that I have and being willing to use it."

Once the lawyer is able to understand the responsibility of possessing this toolbox, he or she is compelled to act and effectively utilize these tools. There are examples of lawyers who maximized the use of their tools and as a result transformed the legal system and the world. According to Professor Levy-Pounds, "There are many lawyers that we have to look up to as an example. I think back to Charles Hamilton Houston and the phrase that I love and he says that either a lawyer is an engineer of social justice or he is a parasite. I think that was pretty strong language that he used. But it was necessary to awaken people from apathy and lethargy and indifference and to say, you have the tools to change things—*use them.* Don't just focus on self."

Professor Levy-Pounds advocates for using these tools in the furtherance of justice by proactively seeking to address social inequities. Therefore, new social justice lawyers play an integral role in social change movements when they use their legal training as a tool coupled with other advocacy tools to set in motion the process of social change.

Developing a Multi-forum and Multi-strategy Toolbox

This new type of lawyering calls for the use of a multifunctional toolbox that draws upon diverse perspectives and a range of strategic courses of action. During her interview, Levy-Pounds distinguished the role of traditional lawyering from the role of the new social justice lawyer. First and foremost, the new social justice lawyer (according to Levy-Pounds) is not "inside of a box based upon a title," such as the title of lawyer. Instead, the new social justice lawyer seeks to build key partnerships and establish new coalitions. Traditional lawyering focuses on trial advocacy and stating your case before a judge or jury. Conversely, lawyers engaging in social justice lawyering can envision the complexity of effectuating social change, which includes recognition of the many layers of influence needed to create change. Levy-Pounds believes lawyers are "really pushing for change in the court of public opinion." This draws upon the essence of Charles Hamilton Houston's 1936 public advocacy framework. In his article titled "Don't Shout Too Soon,"[2] he educated community members about the importance of civil rights and creating access to justice. He then challenged community members to become actively involved in the fight for justice by challenging systemic inequities. This is a two-step process of (1) education and (2) mobilization of the masses to formulate the people power required to facilitate the process of social change. The end result is a shift in the court of public opinion since it moves people from inaction to active participation and from observers to leaders. This unleashes the collective power of joint action.

A Shift in the Court of Public Opinion

Levy-Pounds also offered key guidance on how to utilize a multi-strategy approach for building social change. In one such example, community members had expressed concerns about the overrepresentation of people of color in gang databases, inaccurate information about who is a gang member within the databases, and overly broad selection criteria for entry into the databases. In particular, although African Americans make up about 5 percent of the population in Minnesota, they represented 54 percent of those listed in the Gang Pointer File and 42 percent of those listed in GangNet,

---

2. Charles H. Houston, *Don't Shout Too Soon*, CRISIS, Mar. 1936.

which is an alarming representation of 7,108 individuals.[3] Levy-Pounds and her students used traditional lawyering skills, which included legal research, writing, logical reasoning, and oral advocacy, to engage in gang database reform efforts. However, Levy-Pounds's transformative approach begins where traditional lawyering ends by utilizing key lawyering skills in preparing for windows of opportunity for social justice policy reform and engaging community members in the process of setting new policy agendas that focus on eradicating injustices.

Professor Levy-Pounds provided a detailed account of the role that she and her law students played in dismantling a gang database system in Minnesota that negatively and disproportionately affected communities of color, African Americans in particular. Levy-Pounds provided this as an example of her work with educating and mobilizing the community around reforming gang databases to ensure fairness and equity. This process is illustrative of all three pillars of new social justice lawyering (social justice lawyering, leadership, public policy advocacy) being used as tools to build and sustain social change.

Model for Community Engagement

Similarly, the Mississippi Center for Justice (MCJ) engages in a multi-strategy and multi-forum approach that begins with community engagement. In furtherance of MCJ's mission, the focus of its work is policy advocacy, systemic change, community education, and community-organizing. Each dimension of MCJ's work is community-centered since community members help to identify the key goals, build a strategic plan, and guide the process of social change. Allen distinguishes this from traditional legal services of direct service delivery and individual client representation. According to Allen, MCJ focuses on "helping communities identify their own social justice goals and then working in collaboration with grassroots groups as well as regional partners and also national partners" to bring this vision to

---

3. N. Levy-Pounds, F. Aba-Onu, J. Salmen, & A. Tyner, *Evaluations of Gang Databases in Minnesota and Recommendations for Change*, 19 INFO. & COMM. TECH. L. 223–254 (2010).

fruition.[4] Allen refers to this as the community lawyer having a multi-form and multi-strategy toolbox. Picking the appropriate tool to use is determined by the individual issue presenting itself.

Members of MCJ's staff described the profound impact and sense of gratification experienced when utilizing their advocacy tools and combining their tools with the community's immense assets. Development Director Norman Chronister described his work as being a "powerful motivator: [you] can do something to make a difference." One of the lawyers, Beth Orlansky, describes the proactive nature of MCJ's work when she expressed pride in being "a part of the solution, not identifier of the problem." Marni von Wilpert, a lawyer leading the HIV/AIDS law clinic, discussed the impact of MCJ's work, which is helping people to "live better." The work of each member of the MCJ team in partnership with the community contributes to the collective efficacy by utilizing their individual tools to further the cause of justice.

The gang database reform work of the Community Justice Project and the Mississippi Center for Justice's coalition-building work serve as exemplary models of lawyers utilizing a wide range of tools to create a multifaceted, multi-strategy approach. The process of building and creating social change is incremental, coordinated, and strategic. With each step, the new social justice lawyer must be ready and prepared to coordinate collective action.

The New Social Justice Lawyer's Toolbox

The new social justice lawyer moves beyond characterizing lawyering as a single tool that can be compared metaphorically to a hammer. According to Abraham Maslow, "If the only tool you have is a hammer, you tend to see every problem as a nail."[5] The vision of only a certain tool in mind limits the power of discovery of narrowly tailored solutions to social justice issues as they arise. The new social justice lawyer recognizes the possibilities of maximizing the full range of the toolbox's contents and seeing beyond the

---

4. Interview with Bonnie Allen (Oct. 28, 2011).
5. Abraham Maslow Quotes, www.brainyquote.com/quotes/authors/a/abraham_maslow .htm

hammer. The profiled lawyers demonstrated how to strategically employ tools to promote social justice. Thus, the new social justice lawyer has an eye toward the future by seeking to realize a vision for justice that extends beyond its current state.

Analyzing Laws and Policies

The first tool employed by the new social justice lawyer is conducting legal research and analysis related to the injustices experienced by the community. In order to make an impact, the new social justice lawyer must gain an understanding of the aspects of the law that are producing oppression or leading to discrimination. According to Levy-Pounds, this tool requires a close examination of the underlying policies and laws that are leading to inequities.

The above-referenced gang database reform efforts illustrate this point. During this process, the Community Justice Project (CJP) also examined the best practices from around the country in order to conduct a comparative analysis. Within the CJP, law students conducted research related to the methodology and practices utilized by service providers, governmental agencies, and other social justice–oriented institutions to explore cutting-edge, innovative models for policy reform. In the context of gang database reform, this included researching data collection procedures (storage, purging, and auditing), performing legislative history research, and hosting community listening sessions.

Another example of how the CJP has used this tool is evident in the project focused on addressing the racial disparities in charging of obstructing of legal process (OLP). Poor African Americans were being arrested for making an inquiry about arrest procedures or in some way interfering with an officer executing an arrest. The CJP drafted a memo analyzing the law and its application (as it applied to the circumstances in St. Paul) and offered key recommendations for change. This report was submitted to the St. Paul city lawyer during a community stakeholders meeting. The CJP found that the police department was applying OLP charging in an overly broad manner, which was inconsistent with relevant case law on OLP. The city lawyer agreed with the analysis and retrained his team according to the findings of the report. He also communicated these changes with law enforcement leadership about the practices that may have produced this injustice. This collaborative effort demonstrates how CJP's legal research and analysis had a lasting impact on policy reform. Its efforts went beyond representing an individual client on an OLP charge to protecting the rights of an entire community. To date, there has been a precipitous decline in the rate of charging of obstructing legal process. Thus, this particular situation provided Professor Levy-Pounds and her students with a vital analytical and evaluative tool. Through the utilization of this tool, teacher and students could closely examine some of the root causes of social inequity and develop methods for addressing these issues. More importantly, this example demonstrates the wide reach of public policy reform efforts in creating systemic change.

Another example of the successful utilization of the tool of policy analysis is the work of MCJ lawyers who conducted research related to consumer lending practices and regulations in order to address the impact of payday lending. Cahn's research and analysis of juvenile justice laws aided in the development of the deliberate indifference theory.[6] Professor john a. powell thoroughly analyzed laws and policies that affect the allocation of wealth, economic structure, and corporate power in the United States.

The tool of analyzing laws and policies can provide you with a deeper understanding of the underlying policies and practices that are resulting in social inequities for your client or within the greater community.

Developing New Theories and Frameworks

New social justice lawyers develop new social justice frameworks to aid in the process of problem solving around social justice issues and seizing opportunities to bring forth social change. One such example is Professor powell's introduction of "targeted universalism." Targeted universalism provides an analytical framework for critically examining the context of social justice challenges and also provides a method for addressing them. For instance, in the context of racial justice, target universalism "recognizes racial disparities and the importance of eradicating them, while acknowledging their presence within a large inequitable, institutional framework."[7]

---

6. Cahn & C. Robbins, *supra* note 6.

7. john a. powell, Presentation at the Des Moines African American Leadership Forum: Leadership in the African American Community (Feb. 19, 2011).

powell's framework provides that as human beings have a linked fate, we can grow together, and we should embrace collective solutions.[8] Targeted universalism establishes that "goals are universal and strategies are targeted based on your situation. You have an overall umbrella goal and targeted strategies."[9] Further, powell recognizes that strategies cannot be a one-size-fits-all approach since, although everyone has the same value, their situations are not all the same.[10]

powell warns that sometimes leaders focus on the particularity of people's experiences, hence overlooking the universal goals. Other times, the focus is only on strategies and people are not all in the same situation. Targeted universalism balances both of these interests—universal goals and narrowly tailored approaches.[11] powell has shared this framework with national organizations, such as the African American Leadership Forum, to offer guidance in taking a holistic approach to addressing the needs of communities. Thus, frameworks serve as a tool for aiding community members in organizing and mobilizing to engage in the social change process.

Cahn also uses this same tool, the framework of targeted universalism, to introduce alternative legal theories for addressing social inequities. For instance, Cahn proposed to apply the legal theory of "deliberate indifference" to eliminate the racial disparities in the juvenile justice system. The theory, codeveloped by Cahn and Professor Cynthia Robbins, was first introduced in a 2009 article titled "An Offer They Can't Refuse: Racial Disparity in Juvenile Justice and Deliberate Indifference Meet Alternatives That Work."[12] This theory focuses on addressing racial disparities in the child welfare and juvenile justice systems under a 14th Amendment Equal Protection cause of action. Cahn explained that once you prove the existence of a disparity and establish that existing programming and initiatives have not worked, this can equate to evidence of intent to engage in discriminatory practices.

---

8. *Id.*

9. African American Leadership Forum, *Q & A with John Powell*, 1 REVIVE! TWIN CITIES 36 (2011).

10. *Id.*

11. *Id.*

12. E. Cahn & C. Robbins, *An Offer They Can't Refuse: Racial Disparity in Juvenile Justice and Deliberate Indifference Meet Alternatives That Work*, 13 UDC/DCSL L. REV. 1–31 (2009).

According to Cahn, this provides policy makers with a choice between utilizing alternatives that work and are cheaper (e.g., youth court and community-based alternatives to detention) and conducting business as usual. Once policy makers are put on notice, then there is a right to bring suit for the failure to utilize the knowledge that policy makers were given of the availability of effective and efficient alternatives to detention. The failure to act in effect is an intentional disregard of the consequences of one's act of omission, which equates to deliberate indifference.

Cahn, Robbins, and the staff of the Racial Justice Initiative have worked to establish notice of viable alternatives to detention by holding public hearings. These hearings draw together service providers, scholars, and community leaders to share proven practices that yield positive results and successful outcomes for youths. During the 2011 Timebank USA Global Conference held in Rhode Island, a public hearing was convened in order to address racial disparities in the child welfare system. Clinical law professors, service providers, and grassroots community leaders shared information about effective, efficient, and equitable alternatives being used in child welfare systems. These practices are being used to strengthen and support families and youth in need. "Deliberate indifference" is only one example of how Cahn's development of legal theory and vision for strategic legal action can be employed as a tool to further social change. The impact of these theories is analogous to a ripple effect since change in policies and practices have a far-reaching impact. Thus, the development of legal theories lays a firm foundation for the work of the new social justice lawyer.

Cahn's development of coproduction as a theoretical framework is another example of how he has created new thought paradigms and developed innovative community-based social change initiatives.[13] This tool aids in redefining money, power, and lawyering. Cahn's vision of coproduction informs how he views the role of lawyers in the process of social change. He acknowledges the shortcomings of case-by-case representation and mere service delivery. In these situations, the lawyer seeks to help individuals and the individuals become reliant on the lawyer's assistance. This creates

---

13. EDGAR CAHN, NO MORE THROW-AWAY PEOPLE: THE CO-PRODUCTION IMPERATIVE (2004).

a relationship of dependency that diminishes the capacity of the individual or community to become involved in the process of change and emerge with their own leadership capacity. The client or community is viewed as a problem, and hence their job is to merely consume services. As perceived by professionals, their duty as recipients of services is to enable a specialist to do his or her job.

Within their professional capacity, lawyers are trained to resolve problems and serve as leading problem solvers. However, according to Cahn, people are not problems. People are told to present a new problem—bigger each time they seek professional services in order to get a professional's attention. Professionals believe that they are fulfilling a need and they establish one-way transactions with their clients. According to Cahn:

> Government entitlements are based on need. Charity is based on need. Volunteering is based on need. We mean well and all of those efforts are to be honored. Too often, helping is a transaction that starts between two strangers who remain strangers. And with the best of intentions, one-way transactions often send messages unintentionally. They say "We have something you need—but you have nothing we need or want or value." And they also say: "The way to get more help is by coming back with more problems."

Cahn critiques this unilateral process and its failure to unleash the potential of the client. He often says that being a part of the honored helping professions, like the law, is not merely about service delivery. He reminds professionals that "we are not delivering pizzas, you can't deliver justice. But you can build community." Instead, lawyers and other helping professionals (e.g., those in human services and social services) have an important role to play in eliminating dependency as the price paid for providing help. Cahn warns these professionals to stop devaluing those whom they help while they profit from their troubles.[14] Cahn offers an alternative by encouraging

14. EDGAR CAHN, PRICELESS MONEY: BANKING TIME FOR CHANGING TIMES (2011).

reciprocity and promoting coproduction. "Reciprocity affirms the recipient as an equal and empowers the recipient as a contributor."[15]

Cahn's legal training has provided him with the analytical tools needed to analyze rules and laws, deconstruct systemic inequities, and develop new models for social change. His colleague Professor Cynthia Robbins describes Cahn as a social change agent first who then uses being a lawyer as a tool. As a social change agent, Cahn develops new frameworks to create new solutions, inspire others to take action, and lead authentically. Hence, through the creation of new theories and frameworks, the new social justice lawyer is able to develop new conceptual paradigms for addressing social justice challenges.

Writing as Advocacy

The new social justice lawyer uses writing as a tactical tool for advocacy by advancing the cause of social justice reform efforts. These participants have published their work in a wide range of outlets in order to inform, engage, and mobilize others. Professor Allen uses writing as a form of advocacy in a wide variety of ways and reaches others through her written publications. Her publications include law review articles, reflective writing/devotionals, and policy papers. For instance, one of her most recent law review articles explored the formation and development of the first legal services clinic following Hurricane Katrina. This community recovery lawyering clinic was founded by the University of Maryland School of Law in partnership with MCJ. Community recovery lawyering refers to "a long-term, comprehensive, community-driven process by which community organizations and enterprises seek to reduce poverty and recover from disinvestment."[16] Over 1,500 law students and youth volunteers were drawn to the Mississippi Delta and New Orleans to minister to the needs of the people.[17] This was the largest representation of student involvement in social change efforts

---

15. *Id.* at 15.

16. LEADING EDGE, UNIVERSITY OF MARYLAND SCHOOL OF LAW LEADERSHIP, ETHICS, AND DEMOCRACY INITIATIVE 10 (2009), http://www.law.umaryland.edu/programs/initiatives/lead/docs/LEAD_F09_newsletter.pdf.

17. B. Allen, B. Bezdek & J. Jopling, *Community Recovery Lawyering: Hard-Learned Lessons from Post-Katrina Mississippi*, 4 DEPAUL J. SOC. JUST. 123 (2010).

in Mississippi since Freedom Summer in 1964 (Civil Rights Movement).[18] These students were the "fuel of the ground game" since they participated in over 22 community legal clinics and assisted over 1,000 clients.[19] Thus, Allen's article serves as a guide for clinical professors when developing a community lawyering clinic that focuses on building a collaborative strategy for social change.

Allen also exercised writing as advocacy when she wrote a policy paper that was commissioned by the Mississippi Access to Justice Commission. Allen organized the public hearings and drafted the subsequent report. Allen begins the report with the statement, "To be poor in America is to face myriad challenges in everyday life."[20] The report is organized like a legal argument because it explores the barriers experienced by the poor when seeking to obtain legal services (issue), contrasts their experiences with current practices (rule), provides firsthand accounts of everyday people (analysis), and offers practical solutions for change (conclusion).

The law review article and report demonstrate how writing can serve as a multifaceted tool and reach a diverse audience. It can be used to educate, mobilize, organize, and inform, more generally. These written publications may reach law professors, law students, community advocates, lawyers, and policy stakeholders. Overall, the goal is to inform these audiences and challenge them to take action in eradicating the root causes of social injustices.

Utilizing Media Advocacy and Communication Tools

Further, Allen and the MCJ team recognize that writing as advocacy also takes additional forms that move beyond traditional written materials. As technology continues to advance, new social justice lawyers must adapt to change by finding new ways to reach their audience and must build new connections with community partners. Moreover, media advocacy and interactive communication tools are an additional attribute of writing as advocacy. Allen believes that the new social justice lawyer must be "highly knowledgeable and skilled in the field of communications, media, framing

---

18. *Id.*
19. *Id.*
20. MISSISSIPPI ACCESS TO JUSTICE COMMISSION, REPORT OF PUBLIC HEARING ON THE UNMET CIVIL LEGAL NEEDS OF LOW-INCOME MISSISSIPPIANS 1 (2007).

message development." MCJ strategically utilizes social media tools such as Facebook and Twitter to facilitate its policy campaigns. In addition, MCJ has a communication specialist on staff who manages its interactive website, frames the policy campaign issues and messaging, and develops newsletter communications. The communication specialist uses her expertise to reach audiences both near and far. According to Allen:

> After Katrina, we had a lot of opportunities to be in national press, sort of the major newspapers and TBS and other outlets—radio, television and then local papers as well. And now more and more we're using social media to reach people, particularly constituents on the ground. . . .

This tool can be used to communicate with individuals from a range of different backgrounds and to build new partnerships.

As evidenced above, the tool of communication can be used as a part of policy entrepreneurship by advocating for policy changes[21] and coalition-building by leveraging the political power of collective engagement.[22] Therefore, this tool aids in engaging in agenda setting, enlisting the community in reform efforts, and developing community-centered advocacy coalitions.

Like Allen, Cahn effectively utilizes writing as a form of advocacy through a range of venues from book publications to law review articles. Cahn's 2004 book, *No More Throw Away People: The Co-Production Imperative*, provided a framework for coproduction and timebanking. The goal of this book was to provide an exploratory analysis of the principles of coproduction and offer hands-on techniques for applying the principles through timebanking. Cahn opens the book with the story of Moses and the tablets. In this section, he discusses how Moses broke the tablets after watching the children of Israel worshiping the golden calf. Moses is then given a second set of tablets. Cahn applies this story to the current state of humanity by writing: "one set of broken tablets is enough. Time Dollars say:

---

21. J.W. KINGDON, AGENDAS, ALTERNATIVES, AND PUBLIC POLICIES (2d ed. 2003).
22. Joseph Stewart, *Policy Models and Equal Educational Opportunity*, 24 POL. SCI. & POL. 167 (1991).

Reject the Golden Calf. We have each other. Co-Production says: Amen."[23] This statement recognizes that having each other is the greatest gift to the world. As we recognize the interconnectedness of our existence, all things become possible.

Through his writing, he introduces a transformative framework, the theory of coproduction, for building a transformative community that aligns with timebanking as a vehicle for social change. Coproduction redefines the value of work and reestablishes key partnerships within the community. According to Cahn, work has to be redefined to value whatever it takes to raise healthy children, build strong families, revitalize neighborhoods, make democracy work, advance social justice, and make the planet sustainable. This is the kind of work that needs to be honored, recorded, and rewarded. It is the foundation of caring and vibrant communities.

Coproduction is based on five core principles: (1) assets, (2) redefined work, (3) reciprocity, (4) social networks, and (5) respect (TimeBanks USA, 2011). First, people are valuable assets and have something to give. Second, the contributions of each person are valued—and rewarded—as real work. Third, Cahn posits that the question: "How can I help you?" needs to change so we begin to ask: "How can we help each other build the world we both will live in?"[24] Fourth, coproduction acknowledges that we need each other since networks are stronger than individuals. Finally, coproduction acknowledges that every human being matters.

Through his writings on timebanking and coproduction, Cahn is positing that each member of the community has a crucial role to play in reaching the full vision of community. This could be characterized as a "labor of love" between individuals. It is using your labor (time, energy, and talents) to better the world. The focus is laboring together to bring forth social change. Cahn's publications have helped to extend his vision to thousands of others as they read about how coproduction has transformed his life and the lives of others. It is an engagement tool that introduces others to the vision of collective engagement and collaboration. Readers can use the book to

---

23. CAHN, *supra* note 12, at x.
24. TimeBanks USA, Mission and Values of TimeBanks USA (2011), http://timebanks.org/.

develop timebanking in their communities and educate others about the timebanking approach.

This is only one example of the multitude of scholarly contributions that Cahn has made to the discipline and exploration of social justice. His other works include law review articles, policy papers, and short essays. One such notable example is an article that he coauthored with his late wife, Jean Camper Cahn. The 1964 article, titled *The War on Poverty: A Civilian Perspective*, was credited by Sargent Shriver, director of President Kennedy's Office of Economic Opportunity, as the genesis of legal services since it provided the blueprint for the National Legal Services.

With each publication, Cahn is exercising the tool of writing as a form of advocacy. This tool can be used to reach a wide audience beyond geographic borders and professional disciplines. Writing as advocacy provides the opportunity to reach others who are exploring ways to address the social challenges in their communities. Cahn has also used the tool of writing to serve the important function of education for policy leaders, lawyers, community members, and other professionals. It provides them with relevant research, analysis, and practical solutions for addressing the social justice issues at hand. Additionally, writing can aid in shaping a collective message and establishing a shared public narrative; these manifestations can provide the momentum for a social change movement when implemented. Thus, writing as advocacy is an indispensable tool for initiating policy reform efforts and providing educational resources.

Another example of the power of writing as advocacy is Professor powell's efforts in helping frame social justice issues, developing practical solutions to these issues, and generating new partnerships. He has an extensive bibliography that includes scholarly articles, books and book chapters, and newspaper articles. The topics explored range from the history of the Fair Housing Act to the introduction of the theory of targeted universalism. Each publication is used as a tool to inform and engage his readers about social justice, history, policies, and laws.

Overall, powell views communication as a powerful tool. In the Kirwan Institute, in addition to written publications, a wide range of communication tools is used in order to reach a wide audience. powell describes the range of communication tools utilized by the Kirwan Institute, which includes writing, speaking, developing system maps, and hosting film festivals and plays. powell describes not being wedded to any particular type of advocacy. He suggests the importance of a multimedia approach through writing, blogging, and publishing newsletters. The approaches vary similarly by organizational style.

By using a range of communication tools, powell and members of the Kirwan Institute stand ready to advance the Institute's mission by reaching a diverse constituency and developing a comprehensive plan of action. The Institute may reach one person who attends a play, another who watches a webinar, and yet another who reads an online blog post. No matter the venue, the Kirwan Institute advances its mission in a comprehensive manner that reaches audiences both near and far. Therefore, writing as advocacy is a tool that connects people and builds a sense of community beyond physical borders to foster dialogue and create public spaces.

Additionally, writing as a form of advocacy has been an indispensable tool utilized by Professor Levy-Pounds within her work at the Community Justice Project. According to Levy-Pounds, she uses this tool more and more frequently. During this process, legal research and writing is compiled into various reports. In 2007, a report titled "Recommendations for Improving Quality of Life for African Americans in Saint Paul," served as an illustration of the power of this tool.[25] This report laid a firm foundation for addressing quality-of-life issues affecting the African American community in Saint Paul, Minnesota. It focused on two key issues: (1) lack of available programs for youths in the juvenile justice system or who are at risk of becoming involved with gangs and (2) the need to improve community and police relations.

The report was submitted to the mayor of Saint Paul and the chief of the Saint Paul Police Department. This report was used as a tool for advocacy. For example, the section related to community and police relations focused on strategically improving these relationship. One of the outcomes following the report was that the mayor conducted an audit of the St. Paul Police

---

25. Recommendations for Improving Quality of Life for African Americans in Saint Paul (on file with author).

Department. The audit findings were used to improve and strengthen the police department.

Another example of the power of this indispensable communication tool is a report written about the gang database practices in Minnesota. Titled "Evaluation for Gang Databases in Minnesota and Recommendations for Change,"[26] this report was a culmination of the legal analysis, policy evaluation, and exploration of best practices in data collection. An advanced version of the report was released to the public for additional input. The final version of the report was used as an advocacy tool to reform the gang database policies since it included guidance for systemic changes.

These reports were written with the intent to include the voices of the community and encourage their involvement in the process of social change. According to Levy-Pounds, the goal is to communicate in a clear and concise manner in order to make the process of social change inclusive. Within her work, she seeks to "incorporate the voices of those who have been disenfranchised or oppressed throughout the process and ensure that they become key stakeholders in whatever change we are pushing to effect."

Writing as advocacy provides a key tool that can be used to educate and mobilize the community. This tool provides the information needed to educate the community and key stakeholders about a particular social justice issue. Levy-Pounds's scholarly writings fulfill this role. She reaches a wide audience as she explores topics like the impact of the War on Drugs on communities of color, collateral consequences of a criminal record, and the impact of parental incarceration on children of color. Writing also can serve as an advocacy tool for organizing and engaging the community. The gang database report was used by the community as a guidebook and a legislative advocacy tool since it provided an overview of relevant statutes, laws, and policies, and outlined key talking points for legislative advocacy.

Writing as advocacy is a tactical tool that can be employed to build and sustain social change. It can be used as a tool to educate diverse audiences, organize social change initiatives, and advocate for social reform.

---

26. Levy-Pounds et al., *supra* note 3.

Establishing Social Justice–Oriented Organizations

Social justice–oriented organizations are the foundational base for mobilizing the masses and preparing for social action. According to Stewart (1991), changes in policy are the product of individuals acting rationally and strategically within an organization.[27] Therefore, organizations serve as a firm foundation for the execution of the new social justice lawyer's work. They provide the public space needed to gather together key partners (e.g., community members, students, other professionals) to engage in collaborative problem solving.

The culmination of Cahn's tools and work is evidenced through his creation of social justice–oriented institutions and working in partnership with diverse professionals to further the mission of the institution. As referenced above, Cahn is able to effectively maximize institution-building as a tool, which is evidenced by the development of Antioch Law School and the model for Legal Services Corporation. Subsequently, he has developed TimeBanks USA and its subsidiary, the Racial Justice Initiative. Founded in 1995, the mission of TimeBanks is to nurture and expand a movement that promotes equality and builds caring community economies through an inclusive exchange of time and talent. TimeBanks leaders across the United States and internationally work to strengthen and rebuild community, and they use TimeBanks to achieve a wide range of goals, such as achieving social justice, building bridges between diverse communities, and promoting local ecological sustainability. There are currently 300 timebanks in the United States and timebanks are operating in 36 countries.[28]

In addition to the founding of social justice–oriented institutions, Cahn has also served in a leadership role in developing innovative, groundbreaking initiatives. One such example is the Racial Justice Initiative, which was founded in response to the racial disparities in the juvenile justice, child welfare, and special education systems. The purpose of this Racial Justice Initiative is to provide judges and officials with resources about evidence-based practices that promote the best interests of children. Homecomers Academy offers another example of a social justice initiative that Cahn has played an

---

27. Stewart, *supra* note 22.
28. TimeBanks USA, *supra* note 24.

instrumental role in developing. This initiative focuses on creating opportunities for successful reentry for men who are returning home to their communities after serving time in prison. These men are drawn back into the social fabric of the community to form new roots and evolve as key leaders in the community.

These institutions and initiatives serve many purposes, including building a community base, enlisting new partners, training the next generation of new social justice lawyers, conducting key research, offering solutions for policy reform, and introducing new frameworks. Institutions by definition serve as organizations devoted to the promotion of a particular cause that is public or charitable in nature.[29] The institutions created by Cahn and other participants, like Professor powell, serve as tools for not only initiating social change efforts but also to sustaining the momentum needed to establish lasting change. These institutions bring together key stakeholders to problem solve around some of the most challenging social justice issues and develop ways to bring about change.

One of powell's key tools is the ability to build new social justice–oriented institutions and lead within institutions focused on social change. "The secret of institution building is to be able to weld a team of such people by lifting them up to grow taller than they would otherwise be."[30] These institutions weld together a team by drawing together professionals who represent a range of disciplines for developing comprehensive, multidisciplinary approaches for social change. The Kirwan Institute is one such example. powell describes it as a multidisciplinary research and policy-focused organization "with a keen focus on marginalized groups and democratic practices, norms that support everyone." The mission of the Kirwan Institute is to "partner with people, communities, and institutions worldwide to think about, talk about, and engage in issues of race and ethnicity in ways to create and expand opportunity for all." There are at any time 30 to 50 professionals on staff. These professionals use a range of methodologies based upon their professional training as demographers, mappers, sociologists,

---

29. AMERICAN HERITAGE DICTIONARY 666 (1985).
30. Interview with john a. powell, August 29, 2011.

economists, and lawyers. According to powell, the Institute also builds key partnerships with "partners from various walks of life."

At the helm of the leadership within the Kirwan Institute, powell focused on collaborative problem solving and systems change.[31]

powell instills a key principle into the work of his staff and the Institute's operations: "Don't define the problem by the nature of your discipline. Let the problem define itself and bring the necessary tools to actually solve [it] and if you don't have them find someone who does." This message acknowledges the immense benefits of the staff working together as a team to build and sustain social change. One professional's expertise does not trump the value of another's expertise; instead, each is encouraged to find new ways to work together. All are equal in value and are needed to address the multifaceted nature of social justice issues.

The collaborative nature of the Kirwan Institute's approach demonstrates the importance of the new social justice lawyers as leaders who work in partnership with other professionals. Traditionally, professionals work together in a model of technocracy by which each respective professional group uses the expertise of others. Their work is framed by the silos of their professional backgrounds and crossing these borders is not permissible. The example powell provides is of lawyers using only psychologists and social workers for assessments or expert testimony. Alternatively, powell offers a new paradigm by emphasizing the importance of collaborative processes that are not driven by lawyers and do not frame an issue through the lens of one's respective discipline. This is a framework in which everyone is equal and adds equal value. Each professional plays an important role in working together and problem solving together.[32]

Allen also has played an active role in establishing and supporting a new social justice–oriented organization. Allen served as the president of the Center for Law & Renewal, based at the Fetzer Institute in Kalamazoo, Michigan. She also has served as the executive director of Just Neighbors Immigrant Ministry, Inc., and codirected the Project for the Future of Equal Justice. Shortly after MCJ's inception in 2003, Allen served as a volunteer

---

31. powell, *supra* note 7.
32. GEORGE P. LOPEZ, REBELLIOUS LAWYERING: ONE CHICANO'S VISION OF PROGRESSIVE LAW PRACTICE (1992).

and later joined the staff as the director of access to justice partnerships in 2005. In 2007, Levy-Pounds established the CJP, which serves as the organizational base for the promotion of racial justice and civil rights. Hence, building new institutions with a focus on partnerships and collaboration is an essential tool for the new social justice lawyer to utilize.

Fostering Key Partnerships and Engaging in Coalition-Building

Key partnerships aid in establishing coalitions and organizing community members. The new social justice lawyer recognizes the importance of building partnerships in order to establish a community empowerment model (as referenced in chapter 3). The utilization of this tool aids in bringing together those who share common values and interests to facilitate the process of social change. Together, they seek to realize a shared vision of justice.

The Kirwan Institute's foundational base is built upon key partnerships with organizations and groups who share common values. According to powell, the work of the Kirwan Institute is values-driven and not issue-based; therefore partnerships represent alignment of key values and ongoing relationships with people. Issue-based advocacy, on the other hand, focuses on a hierarchical structure of leadership and is limited to resolving the issue at hand. powell shares his vision of values-driven work when he describes the Kirwan Institute's partnerships: "We have deep relationships with some community-based groups, we look at partnerships and a partnership is just that—it's not them just directing us or us just directing them, it's a relationship."[33] powell identified 24 key partnerships of his own (past and present) that have fostered collaboration within a range of social justice initiatives, from improving diversity in schools to addressing disparities in the foreclosure crisis. This is demonstrative of Kirwan's tagline "many differences, one destiny." These partnerships provide the support needed to bring the vision of equal opportunity and justice to fruition.

Levy-Pounds encourages community involvement in the process of change; therefore she is continuously creating new opportunities for enlisting partners. For instance, during the gang database reform efforts, Levy-Pounds testified before the American Indian tribal chiefs, since the American Indian

---

33. powell, *supra* note 30.

community was also disproportionately affected by the gang database practices. The CJP also connected with Hmong and Latino community leaders. The goal of these exchanges was to gain insights about the diverse experiences of community members. Subsequently, the CJP under her direction met with government stakeholders at the city, county, and state levels to share the community's concerns and offer the community's recommendations for change. As referenced in chapter 3, the community is at the center of social change and at the wheel in navigating the process. Professor Levy-Pounds and members of CJP recognize the valuable contributions of a wide variety of stakeholders. As I observed her in action, I saw her repeatedly encourage community members to use their voice as a tool to facilitate social change. Their insights inform the focus of social justice issues by identifying their desired goals, developing a strategic plan, establishing partnerships, unleashing their moral imagination, and setting the agenda.

Coalition-building is a vital component of MCJ's community lawyering toolbox since MCJ arranges its social justice advocacy into policy campaigns. Policy campaigns inform, engage, and mobilize community members related to social justice policy issues. They serve as a framework for organizing collective political power and strategically employing this power when the window of opportunity opens.[34] Metaphorically, initiating these policy campaigns can be compared with ripening the time. In the early stages of the Civil Rights Movement, Dr. Benjamin Elijah Mays, former president of Morehouse College, stated, "I'm sure some of you say the time is not right, but if you have a Christian purpose, then it's your job to ripen the time."[35] MCJ has recognized its responsibility to ripen the time for social change and has drawn the community into this process. The driving force behind MCJ's policy campaigns is community-based coalitions. MCJ has 20 national advocacy partnerships and a multitude of local partnerships.[36] These partnerships connect people together as they advocate as a collective

---

34. KINGDON, *supra* note 21.

35. J. BRYANT, LOVE LEADERSHIP: THE NEW WAY TO LEAD IN A FEAR-BASED WORLD 177 (2009).

36. Previous partners were named on its website, www.mscenterforjustice.org/about-center. Mississippi Center for Justice, 2012.

to bring forth social change. This provides a political base, shared vision, and a mechanism to develop a strategic plan.

Presently, MCJ and its coalition partners have organized policy campaigns in the spheres of health, education, affordable housing, child care, food security, and economic security. The health campaign focuses on increasing access to Medicaid and removing barriers to enrollment. Recently, an HIV/AIDS law clinic has been launched to address employment law issues, health care disparities, and housing discrimination faced by those infected with the virus. MCJ's education campaign focuses on dismantling the school-to-prison pipeline. Further, MCJ has co-convened strategic action meetings with the Mississippi Coalition to Prevent Schoolhouse to Jailhouse. In addition, MCJ and its partners were at the forefront in advocacy related to persuading policy officials to target recovery funds to address the needs of low-income homeowners following Hurricane Katrina.

Furthermore, MCJ has organized child-care campaigns to increase access to child-care certificates funded through Temporary Assistance to Needy Families (TANF) dollars. Moreover, MCJ has organized a food security campaign to address the growing number of food deserts in Mississippi. This campaign was informed by a related report titled: "Savor the Coast: A Recipe for a Sustainable Coast," which recommended improving consumer access to healthy food options and improving food production as possible remedies to the problem. Finally, as referenced in chapter 6, MCJ has supported economic security campaigns to address the predatory nature of payday lending.

Each campaign is built upon enlisting key partners and engaging in coalition-building. Allen notes, "In each of these campaigns there are coalitions associated with it so that is very much of a coalition driven initiative." MCJ assists with helping to set up these coalitions and supporting the partnerships. Over time, Allen has witnessed new partnerships blossom and grow. Some coalitions have started as a community-based group and then evolved to become a strong coalition with a robust political voice and mighty force. According to Allen, "coalition-building is really important, understanding how the legislature works, how to move a bill, how to defeat a bill, having people that know how to hang out at the legislature when it's in session, the policy advocacy is very important." Coalition-building provides community members with the power to effectuate long-term systemic changes. Thus, people are the nucleus of coalitions and the new social justice lawyer is able to build strong partnerships and engage in coalition-building to harness the collective power of these individuals. Through the implementation of this tool, people power is realized and the process of social change begins.

Providing Community Education

A key tool for promoting community mobilization and community engagement is education. Community education provides new insights about the law and policies. powell uses a historical study of law and policies as a tool to transform systems and address present-day challenges. At the Summit for a Fair Economy, he provided those in attendance with an in-depth analysis on the emergence of corporate power and its impact on the economy. powell stated:

> We are in the midst of the most extreme corporate realignment in 100 years. We are not only experiencing corporate welfare . . . low taxes but also undue influence of our political systems and our lives. This movement threatens our democracy, our environment, our civil and human rights. This may be one of the greatness challenges facing our country in the 21st century. But I believe we can rise to the challenge.

powell shared his perspectives on the history of how corporations have gained their power and utilized it to maximize their own self-interest. According to powell, a source of this problem is the courts, since the courts have used the Civil War amendments to make corporations equivalent to citizens. This expansive approach has limited regulations of corporations and diminished protection of the citizenry's interests within the market economy.

Through this education process, powell provided the audience with an analysis of the precedent related to the emergence of the corporate voice. He began with the U.S. Supreme Court's ruling in *Lochner vs. New York* (1905). The period following this case was referred to as the "Lochner Era," since this case set the precedent that the courts limited regulation of corporations. Subsequently, in 2010, the U.S. Supreme Court in *Citizens*

United v. Federal Election Commission[37] failed to distinguish between an individual's voice and a corporation's voice.

This community education tool provided community members with the knowledge and understanding of the root causes of the current economic challenges and corporate misalignment. It also served as an organizational tool to educate and inform those in attendance about the need for their collective action to remedy this misalignment in order to promote a fairer economy. Therefore, this example demonstrates how education can be used to both organize and mobilize community members. As a result of the utilization of this tool, the community becomes equipped with a new tool, which is the knowledge needed to deconstruct inequitable systems. Hence, the utilization of community education as a tool plays a fundamental role in raising the community's consciousness and aiding it in the process of moving from abstract ideas to collective action. It is a manifestation of the adage "educate to liberate."

Allen advocates for a lawyering model that places people in the center of advocacy efforts. More specifically, the ability to work with people to advocate for social change is what drew her to Mississippi and MCJ. Upon her visit to Mississippi (following Hurricane Katrina), she described herself as being "hooked on the work and hooked on people." Allen envisions working with people as a key attribute of the new social justice lawyer, which begins with using public education as a tool. She believes that those who are working in the arena of social change need to become more knowledgeable and skilled in utilizing public education as a tool. However, she also acknowledges that lawyers are not traditionally trained to do that.

MCJ lawyers and other professionals have learned how to effectively use public education as a tool. MCJ's work is built upon public education and outreach, in order to mobilize and organize the community around key social issues. This is an effort to demonstrate that experiences of social injustice are not merely isolated instances but also include systemic challenges. Therefore, these issues are not merely individual travesties but widespread social problems. For example, MCJ has focused on educating the community about the impact of predatory consumer lending. Due to difficult economic

---

37. 558 U.S. 310 (2010).

times, many people may seek financial assistance to make it until their next paycheck; therefore they may use payday lending and title lending services. These loans however can further exacerbate the cycle of poverty with the challenge of refinancing, severe default penalties, and usury interest rates (up to 572 percent). MCJ has worked to educate community members about these circumstances and develop a coalition for reform of payday lending practices. This resulted in statewide attention to predatory lending during the 2011 session of the Mississippi Legislature. The coalition was granted a hearing before the Banking and Financing Committee in the Mississippi House of Representatives. These examples demonstrate the power of public awareness and knowledge in shedding light on key social justice issues and compelling others to engage in reform efforts.

New Eyes: Training Law Students to Become New Social Justice Lawyers

An additional tool maximized by the new social justice lawyer is the ability to prepare law students to engage in social justice lawyering and develop their leadership skills. This is a process of guiding law students in their professional formation by placing an explicit focus on training students in the principles of social justice lawyering, public policy advocacy, leadership, and community empowerment. These participants have provided law students with experiential learning (in the context of initiating social change initiatives) with the goal in mind of training the next generation of social justice lawyers.

Allen and the lawyers of MCJ are committed to bringing up the next generation of lawyer-leaders. In the wake of the devastation of Hurricane Katrina, law students traveled from across the nation to offer legal services and lend a hand at MCJ (*Leading Edge*, 2009).[38] MCJ served as the volunteer hub by organizing these students, coordinating the legal services, and partnering with legal clinics (like University of Maryland School of Law). These law students participated in a number of community legal clinics and

---

38. LEADING EDGE, *supra* note 16.

performed a range of tasks from community outreach to intake. With their assistance, over 1,000 clients were served.[39]

While the law students were in Mississippi, Allen collaborated with other members of MCJ and law professors to develop a clinic model that focused on training students in community recovery efforts.[40] The conceptual framework focused on law, community recovery, and democracy-building. The teaching tools utilized by Allen focused on critical reflection (learning through reflection) and experiential learning (learning by doing).[41] The process of critical reflection begins by stepping back and answering the question "What are we learning from what we are doing?" Through this reflection, the students are able to explore the meaning of justice and democracy and to move from an abstract vision of social change to conceptualizing their role in building a stronger community. Additionally, this experience raised their social consciousness and provided an opportunity to learn about the crucial role of lawyers in community recovery efforts.[42]

The community recovery clinic was founded upon the principles of experiential learning. Allen characterized this clinic experience as a learning laboratory.[43] Students received hands-on training in community lawyering and policy advocacy. Subsequently, in the field (community settings), they applied these skills. For example, law students played an integral role in the affordable housing campaign in order to protect the rights of those displaced after the devastation of the storm.[44] They collected data related to eviction rates, analyzed this data, and identified trends in court actions that had a disproportionately negative effect on those who appeared in housing court pro se. Through this process, law students gained valuable tools of qualitative research, fact investigation, client counseling, and interviewing. These law students also offered direct legal services under the supervision of licensed lawyers. They wrote appellate letters on behalf of those who were denied Federal Emergency Management Agency benefits.[45] Between 2009

---

39. Allen et al., *supra* note 17.
40. *Id.*
41. LEADING EDGE, *supra* note 16.
42. *Id.*
43. Allen et al., *supra* note 17.
44. *Id.*
45. *Id.*

and 2010, law students labored for the cause of justice by "using a mix of representation, legal clinics, document review, and teach-ins, to stave off imminent homelessness."[46] Through this experience, students learned the importance of using a multifaceted approach to systems change by combining traditional lawyering skills (legal research, writing, and analysis) with community education, policy advocacy, and community-organizing tools.

Metaphorically, Allen characterizes this learning experience as law students gaining "new eyes."[47] The law students involved were able to "see" through a new lens as they learned to recognize the critical role of lawyers in advancing equity and protecting the rights of individual survivors. They can also now see the importance of holding the government accountable for remedying systemic failures. According to Allen, "Katrina gave lawyers 'new eyes' to see injustice more clearly in this country, and that the rule of law, democracy and civil society could no longer be assumed in America."[48] These new eyes informed their professional formation as they began to see themselves as engineers of social change with the ability to stand up for justice. The law students recognized the power that lies within, using their legal training as a tool to effectuate social change.

Dr. Cahn is a pioneer in legal education with the cofounding of Antioch Law School in partnership with his late wife, Jean Camper Cahn. Their ingenuity led to the development of a comprehensive clinical legal education model and laid the foundation for the future of social justice lawyering. In 1971, the Antioch School of Law was founded by the Cahns with the goal of training public interest lawyers. This training began with the introduction of their comprehensive law clinic, which served as an inaugural model for clinical education adopted by law schools across the world. Based upon their commitment to serve the needs of the poor and disenfranchised, the Cahns also developed the framework for the creation of the National Legal Services program during the War on Poverty.

This initial clinical model incorporated principles of ethnography by focusing on gaining an understanding of the client's lived experiences. All students were required to live with clients in order to establish rapport with

---

46. *Id.* at 118.
47. *Id.*
48. *Id.* at 119.

their clients and build community connections. This requirement introduced a model of clinical legal education that concentrated on lawyering in partnership with the community. Within this model, the lawyer recognizes the abundance of assets within the community and the importance of releasing these assets in the process of social change. This is done in recognition that the process of social change requires the active engagement of many stakeholders and especially those who are directly affected by a given injustice.

Antioch Law School later became one of the predecessors to the University of the District of Columbia David A. Clarke School of Law (UDC-DCSL). Since founding Antioch, Cahn has continued to develop innovative clinical models. At UDC-DCSL, Cahn has incorporated principles of coproduction into the framework of clinical legal education. For example, in the Child Advocacy Clinic at his law school, clients "pay" for legal services by serving as parent advocates, which is an extension of principles of coproduction. This type of partnership is outlined in the clinic's retainer agreement and explained during client intake. It is a "pay-it-forward" imperative that recognizes that each client can make a valuable contribution and provide a support network for others who share similar experiences.

The new social justice lawyer utilizes education as a tool to model social justice lawyering and leadership. The classroom is a knowledge laboratory where students grapple more broadly with issues like structural inequities, discrimination, and injustices. Students are encouraged to reflect upon their role as agents of change and how to use law as a tool to promote social justice. This teaching technique is characterized as critically reflective learning, which is a learning process that focuses on developing critical thinking skills and forming one's professional identity. Each participant played a key role in helping law students to contextualize these social justice–related experiences and engage in reflective learning. As mentioned earlier, Professor Allen teaches law students in the community recovery clinic (University of Maryland School of Law) and Dr. Cahn teaches a law and justice course and leads the Community Service Program (University of District Columbia David A. Clarke Law School). Professor powell taught civil rights at the Ohio State University Moritz College of Law and Professor Levy-Pounds teaches in a civil rights clinic at the University of St. Thomas School of Law in Minnesota. From these educational experiences, students are exposed to surrounding injustices, examine their root causes, and develop strategies for fostering social change. Students gain new eyes related to their future roles in building and sustaining social change.

Other Essential Tools

The profiled lawyers also demonstrated additional tools that were unique to their respective work. These tools serve as mechanisms for problem solving related to social justice issues.

Dr. Cahn's Toolbox: Conducting Systems Mapping and Analysis

Cahn utilizes his analytical skills to examine how systems operate and affect community members. This analysis enables him to aid community members in developing a strategic action plan for transforming systems. Cahn and his wife, Chris, also share this knowledge with their students in their systems change class. According to Cahn, the process of systems mapping and analysis begins with lawyers exploring these questions:

- What is the largest system that you are operating?
- Who are all the players?
- What are the dynamics between the players?
- For the people whom you are seeking to advocate on behalf of, what might be their voice, their incentives, and their roles?

After exploring these questions, the Cahns then teach their students to create maps of the relationship between various players and explore how these players would respond to legal action.

This process of systems mapping draws upon foresight, strategy, and creativity. In most circumstances, lawyers are taught to respond to an injustice; however this course of action does not anticipate the long-term impact of one's chosen action or the policy implications on a larger scale. This can be compared to the metaphor of playing the game of "Battleship"; sinking one battleship is only one play in a series of others to reach the desired outcome of sinking all of the battleships and declaring your victory. Similar to that game, each move or action during the process of social change affects the overall outcome. Chris characterizes this strategic methodology when she described the victory of one injustice without taking into account system considerations. "[It is like:] boom, injustice dealt with. . . .but you know there are all these intersecting people and players and things." The lawyer is challenged to also rethink and reexamine the map and possible outcomes since systems change is multifaceted. Chris challenges lawyers to examine the multi-layered nature of systems mapping. She encourages you to "zoom in [. . .] and zoom out in order to clearly see the range of courses of action available. This will inform which steps one should take and when to take strategic action.[49]

This is a process of continual assessment, collaborative thinking, and problem solving. Each dimension of evaluation offers a new layer of analysis and informs the best course of action in initiating the process of social change.

The new social justice lawyer must be aware of the dynamics of how systems operate and how they create injustices. Failure to understand systems reform at the macro level can leave the new social justice lawyer unprepared to sustain social change. Systems mapping as described by Cahn and Chris provides key insights on how to transform social systems by anticipating system responses and being prepared with appropriate solutions. This process provides the new social justice lawyer with the intellectual tools to critically examine a situation in an in-depth, multileveled manner. It also enables the new social justice lawyer and community partners to be strategic in their approaches and create narrowly tailored solutions to long-standing social justice challenges.

Dr. Cahn's Toolbox: Changing the Rules and Offering Alternatives

With a smile, Cahn jokingly characterizes himself as the only man who is able to produce money legally without facing criminal charges. Through the implementation of principles of coproduction and timebanking, Cahn is deconstructing and redefining the very essence of money and the nature of a capitalist economy. Cahn has been able to change the rules related to

---

49. Interview with Dr. Edgar Cahn and Chris Cahn, August 2, 2011.

time, community-building, and collective engagement through the adoption of the timebanking framework. Cahn has developed an alternative economy that focuses on the abundance of human talent and gifts as capital. Cahn has introduced an assets-based approach that places value on each person's contribution to society. "An asset perspective says: maybe we already have enough to get where we are going."[50] These assets are invaluable and provide the support needed to facilitate the process of social change. Dr. Cahn demystifies the characteristics of assets, when he expresses an understanding that whatever money is, it's not what it looks like. According to Cahn, "[Money] has a dynamic of its own and ultimately its dynamic is determined by how it measures value and how it affects the creation of value. I came to understand that there are two forms of value. One form of value is what you can use it to exchange for. What you can buy extra. The other form of value is the way in which it echoes inside you to give you a sense of self-esteem, sense of purpose, sense of value."

Dr. Cahn has aided communities in tapping into this internal value as a source of strength and power. Case in point: Cahn found untapped value in the lives of young people in the juvenile justice system. He offered an alternative to the juvenile justice system through the creation of a juvenile peer court, Timedollar Youth Court. Within this model, youths serve as jurors of their peers when other youths commit nonviolent offenses. According to Cahn, this court handles 70 percent of offenses in Washington, D.C., and 80 percent of youths are assigned to serve as jurors as a part of their sentencing. Based upon empirical data, recidivism rates for the youth court participants are below 10 percent, which is significantly below rates of recidivism in comparison with juvenile corrections and similar alternative programming. This tremendous success is due to Cahn challenging the youths to become change agents by raising the question: "How do we use what we know to make a difference?" This type of enlistment draws the youths into the social fabric of the community, cultivates their assets, and encourages them to become actively involved in public service and civic engagement.

Cahn has shown that the new social justice lawyers are not bound by existing systemic structures that lead to inequities or by the present solutions

---

50. CAHN, *supra* note 12, at 87.

available to these challenges. Instead, they alter the rules by offering alternatives for change, such as Cahn's development of the peer court model or his creation of a human capital framework (coproduction), to transform systems. These alternatives are community-centered and draw upon the community's engagement. They also promote leadership development within the community and unveil the multitude of assets that may be lying dormant in the lives of community members. This is analogous to the community lawyering model of lawyering together toward change.[51] For Cahn, this includes promoting economic justice and racial justice. Hence, the community and new social justice lawyers are working together to achieve a shared vision of justice by shifting the rules of engagement.

Professor powell's Toolbox: Applying a Multidisciplinary Approach

Professor powell acknowledges that a good lawyer has certain tools to further social change. However, when he thinks of issues of social justice, he believes that "you really need a composite group of people with the hearts and minds and resources to engage." This may include bringing together professionals with a range of backgrounds from economists to demographers. These professionals provide valuable tools for implementing a multidisciplinary approach in addressing social justice issues. He does not accord privilege to the tools of one profession over those of another, since they are all of equal value and each individual serves as an indispensable part of the mosaic of social engineers and transformational contributors. powell sees the advantages of a diverse group of committed people working together to bring forth social change, since collaborating together brings a great deal of value. This value is the benefit of a composite of intellectual capital.

Professor Levy-Pounds's Toolbox: Creating New Public Spaces and Utilizing a Varied Approach

The CJP hosts community town hall meetings in order to provide community education, garner community support, and seek community input. Within each of their publications, CJP makes recommendations based

---

51. L. White, *To Learn and Teach: Lessons from Driefontein on Lawyering and Power*, Wis. L. Rev. 699–770 (1988).

upon community input by exploring questions about how the community perceives the current social justice issue. What are its desired goals and objectives? The community's responses help to formulate the recommendations for change and develop a strategic reform plan. In the case of gang database reform efforts, the CJP incorporated the community's feedback into its published report. Community members offered new insights on revising the gang criteria and developing youth gang prevention and intervention programs. Additionally, the CJP mobilized the community to attend legislative hearings and participate by testifying. Thus, lawyers can host town hall forums in order to create a new public space for community engagement, collaborative processes, and strategic planning.

When utilizing the tools in her toolbox, Levy-Pounds recommends using an approach that combines education, lobbying, and community-organizing. When reflecting on the gang database reform initiative, she recalls employing a varied approach that included direct advocacy, legal research, community education, and the convening of key stakeholders. Moreover, the CJP encouraged community members to contact the database administrators and inquire whether their names were in the database. Community members from all walks of life participated, from community elders to concerned high school students. This was a process of getting people involved and tapping into their collective power. Through a collective effort, they were able to work strategically to "dismantle a system that served as a source of oppression for the people in the community," according to Levy-Pounds. She recalls how this experience empowered community members as they took a stand for justice. Another part of the multifaceted approach was the community members sharing their message by wearing advocacy T-shirts that indicated support of their reform campaign. The NAACP Youth Committee purchased and distributed shirts that read: "Am I in Gangnet? Are you?" These shirts were a provocative advocacy tool.

According to Levy-Pounds, lawyers have a wide range of tools at their disposal when furthering the cause of justice. The challenge is often in knowing when and how to use each tool. The complexity and multifaceted nature of social justice issues creates the need for a varied approach. The CJP's approaches have combined community-organizing techniques, legislative advocacy, and framing a new public narrative.

Summary

This chapter provides key insights into how the new social justice lawyer applies key tools to build and sustain social change (see Table 7.1). Beginning with the process of redefining money, these participants have demonstrated the ability to use social capital and intellectual capital as tools for engaging in social change. Next, these participants have demonstrated how to redefine power as they build community partnerships, establish social justice–oriented organizations, and organize policy campaigns. Finally, they are redefining lawyering, since they have identified and employed new tools that combine social justice lawyering, leadership, and public policy advocacy. They are teaching these tools to their students in order to prepare them to serve as new social justice lawyers.

Table 7.1 The New Social Justice Lawyer's Toolbox

Tools Utilized by the New Social Justice Lawyer
Analyzing laws and policies
• Developing new theories and frameworks
• Writing as advocacy
• Establishing social justice–oriented organizations
• Fostering key partnerships and engaging in coalition-building
• Providing community education

Reflection Questions

"Each time a man stands up for an ideal or acts to improve the lot of others or strikes out against injustice, he sends forth a tiny ripple of hope."
—Robert Kennedy[52]

---

52. *Collected Quotes Pertaining to Equal* Justice, NATIONAL LEGAL AID & DEFENDER ASSOCIATION, http://www.nlada.org/News/Equal_Justice_Quotes (last visited Apr. 18, 2014).

1. Each of the profiled lawyers has described the social and moral responsibility for lawyers to pursue justice. How do you characterize the role of lawyers?

2. Lawyers have "the keys to the kingdom," according to Bonnie Allen. This means that lawyers are equipped with the tools needed to lead social change. Take a few moments to identify the tools in your toolbox. Create a two-column chart. In the first column, start by listing your core lawyering skills and competencies. This may include legal research and writing, analytical skills, and oral advocacy). In the second column, identify the new social justice lawyering tools that you utilize. See Table 7.1. Are there additional new social justice lawyering skills that you would like to develop? What steps will you take to develop these skills?

Conclusion

The magnitude of the challenges facing marginalized communities today is great and far-reaching. Communities are experiencing a widening justice gap, limited access to resources, and poverty rates increasing at an astronomical rate. To address these challenges, leaders near and far must take a stand. Lawyers are in a prime position to take this stand and to lead social change. Our legal training provides us with the tools needed to advance the cause of social justice. Whether it be our analytical skills or zealous advocacy, lawyers have indispensable leadership tools. As a civil rights lawyer, I began to ponder my role in creating social change and what methods I could use to reach this goal. I was left with more questions than answers. This sense of questioning compelled me to write this book. What are the leadership characteristic of lawyers currently engaged in social justice efforts and what tools do they use to build and sustain social change?

To answer this question, I studied the leadership style of four lawyers who have demonstrated leadership in social change movements: Bonnie Allen (Mississippi Center for Justice), Edgar Cahn (TimeBanks USA, University of District of Columbia David A. Clarke School of Law), Nekima Levy-Pounds (Community Justice Project), and john a. powell (formerly of the Kirwan Institute).

Each of these lawyers has played an active role in the process of social change with the goal in mind of eliminating racial disparities and addressing injustices in the areas of criminal justice, juvenile justice, education, and affordable housing. They work in partnership with community members to reach these desired goals and make their shared vision of justice a reality.

During this process of exploration, I developed a new model for leadership within the context of social justice advocacy: new social justice lawyering. This type of lawyering offers innovative and creative ways for engaging in social change efforts. It is built upon the following three pillars: (1) social justice lawyering, (2) leadership, and (3) public policy advocacy.

Key Themes of New Social Justice Lawyering

The foundation of new social justice lawyering is leadership development. In chapter 3, I explored the building blocks of leadership for new social justice lawyers, which included identifying their key leadership characteristics. These lawyers view leadership in social justice contexts as a way of life that abides within the very essence of their being. Leadership is a manifestation of their values of community-building and justice. They exhibit leadership as a behavior by modeling such characteristics as foresight, critical thinking, vision, and self-awareness. They also demonstrate that leadership is about relationships since a leader is purposeful in preparing others to reach their full leadership potential and modeling the way. These relationships are the foundation of community-organizing since the focus is on empowering others to lead and mobilizing the community.

Leadership is a participatory process that focuses on influencing others to reach a shared, collective vision. This model of leadership focuses on collaboration and collective engagement. This is a new definition of leadership that is not positional or hierarchical, but instead focuses on what the collective can build together—how people can lead together in the fight for justice. It aids the community in realizing its transformative power, which must be harnessed to transform systems of injustice to systems of equity, justice, and hope.

In chapter 6, I introduced the concept of "planting people, growing justice." This chapter examines the relationship between the lawyers and community partners. While engaging in new social justice lawyering, I discovered that the process of leadership development at the grassroots level is integral to the success of not only building but also sustaining social change. This is referred to as the process of "planting people." New social justice lawyers believe that people are at the center of the process of facilitating social change and that partnerships are firmly rooted in shared values. Therefore, their work in partnership with the community is values-based and not simply issues-based. The result of their efforts has a lasting impact of "growing justice." This is evidenced by continual momentum for seeking social change. The theoretical frameworks of social engineering, policy entrepreneurship, coalition-building, and community-organizing guide this process.

In chapter 7, I examined the tools utilized by the profiled lawyers to build and sustain social change. These tools move beyond using traditional lawyering skills to combining multidisciplinary approaches that include systems mapping, ethnographic approaches, policy advocacy, and institution building. The new social justice lawyer works in partnership with community members and other professionals—social workers, community organizers, educators, and faith leaders to take a multifaceted approach to address the root causes of injustice. Therefore, effective leaders recognize that individuals are stronger together than they are apart.

Leadership Lessons Learned

Leadership is a process of influence that motivates the collective to move toward a shared vision and purpose. Effective leaders lead from the heart. At the forefront of their agenda is a desire to show humility and love for others. The exercise of leadership is the materialization of their personal values. They lead by example (leadership as a behavior) and build a natural connection with others (leadership as a relationship). Thus, a title is not relevant; leadership for them has become an essence of their being and way of life.

Leadership as a Behavior

Leadership is a behavior that is evidenced through the leader's actions, which includes interacting with others (leaders encourage storytelling and an exchange of ideas), modeling of leadership (leaders serve as guides and facilitators), and living authentically according to one's espoused values (leaders aid in aligning personal values with the vision of the collective). These behaviors inform the process of leadership as the leader seeks to collaborate with members in the community who share similar interests. This serves as the cornerstone of collective efficacy as the group realizes that its goals are within reach.

Leadership Is about Exercising the Stewardship of Influence

Leadership is characterized as a process of influence that inspires others to become leaders and to facilitate the process of social change. The exercise of leadership occurs in a group context. The focus is how to reach shared goals and fulfill a mutual purpose.[1] New social justice lawyers are stewards of both their legal training and leadership skills. As stewards, they play a critical role in upholding the precepts of justice. This is what Levy-Pounds referred to as a "duty and responsibility" to serve and lead in the community. Most importantly, Levy-Pounds acknowledged the duty to use the law as a tool to facilitate the process of social change. The acknowledgement of this duty causes one to reflect upon personal duty, responsibility to others, and the need for collective action. This process of reflection was explored in the three questions raised by the legendary sage Rabbi Hillel: "If I am not for myself, who will be for me? When I am for myself alone, what am I? If not now, when?"[2] By reflecting upon these questions, new social justice lawyers (while serving within their leadership capacities) recognize their ability to influence the process of social change and their responsibility to answer the call to social action.

Leadership Requires Re-imagining the Very Essence of Principles of Community and Justice

Moral imagination provides the leader with the capacity to see a vision of justice, rehearse the steps needed to reach this vision, and develop ways to work collaboratively with others to make this vision a reality. It moves beyond the limitations of today to see the range of possibilities in the future.[3]

Cahn provides an example of the power of moral imagination with the development of TimeBanks USA. In the face of widespread economic uncertainty, the elderly population being neglected, and communities becoming fragmented, Cahn envisioned a way to reconnect the network of caring communities. The basic premise is that all people are valuable assets and have something meaningful to contribute. Cahn has helped others to unleash their moral imagination in creating timebanks around the world that address a range of social justice issues from respite care models to prison-based timebanks. Thus, these examples illustrate that the possibilities are endless; if

---

1. Peter G. Northouse, Leadership Theory and Practice (5th ed. 2010).
2. M. Ganz, *Hillel's Questions: A Call for Leadership*, Being Jewish 1 (2007), http://www.beingjewish.org/magazine/spring2007/article6.html.
3. S. Fesmire, John Dewey and Moral Imagination: Pragmatism in Ethics (2003).

you can envision it and work together, a vision for change can soon become a reality.

A Leader Recognizes the Limitations of the Present Societal Paradigm and Creates New Rules for Engagement

We are living during a time of monumental flux and change in the United States and throughout the global community. Flux and change illustrate the inevitably of constant change and one's ability to influence this process.[4] Notable changes happening currently in the global community are evidenced by economic crises, the foreclosure epidemic, and political and social unrest. Despite the challenges that lie ahead, lawyers can lead change by engaging in collaborative problem solving, mobilizing community members, developing solutions to a range of long-standing social justice challenges, and supporting the leadership development of others.

For instance, john powell stood at the forefront of policy changes by offering guidance in addressing the root causes of poverty and providing solutions to promote affordable housing. Edgar Cahn fellowshipped and shared principles of timebanking with those participating in Occupy D.C. (a coalition of solidarity formed to challenge economic inequities) located at McPherson Square. He reminded the participants that the monetary system alone cannot determine who is valuable and what it means to give. Alternatively, timebanking recognizes that all people are valuable contributors.

Another example is the development of policy campaigns related to education, juvenile justice, and food security, which were created to advance racial and economic justice by Bonnie Allen and the Mississippi Center for Justice. Nekima Levy-Pounds has focused her efforts on addressing the impact of the incarceration crisis on the African American community. This includes the development of Brotherhood, Inc., a one-stop-shop approach for comprehensive social services and employment services for African American males who have come in contact with the criminal justice system or are at risk. These are representative examples of the many ways that these lawyers have been actively involved in building and sustaining social change.

---

4. G. MORGAN, IMAGES OF ORGANIZATION (2006).

Flux and change are also apparent in the legal profession as a whole. Some have predicted the end of lawyering as we know it. In the foreseeable future, there will be a shift in the traditional role of lawyer as expert and deliverer of legal services.[5] The changes in social conditions have called forth a new breed of lawyers in the 21st century who serve in a leadership capacity and are committed to being gatekeepers of justice. They are the new social justice lawyers. They possess a new set of leadership qualities that are deeply rooted in community empowerment and inspiring others to lead. These qualities include the ability to utilize a multidisciplinary approach, engineer social change, and influence change processes. Further, their leadership has laid the foundation for covertly building a revolution in the realm of social change. With this revolution, they have redefined the role of lawyers, community engagement, and systems change.

Leadership as a Relationship

Leadership as a relationship is manifested through a leader communicating his or her values to others.[6] Leaders communicate their values through their words and deeds. In turn, others can observe the leader's ability to lead authentically and can be inspired to also tap into their leadership potential. The leader also provides followers with the guidance needed to develop their own leadership capacity. The profiled lawyers inspire others to lead and become actively involved in facilitating the process of social change.

A Leader Promotes the Growth and Development of Others, Which Is Essential to the Success of This Alternative System

The role of leader is to aid others in cultivating their leadership development and reaching their full leadership potential. This is a process of mutual growth and development. The leader assumes the role of guide by championing others in their leadership development. He or she invests time and resources in supporting the growth of others. The focus is on the mutual growth of each person since leadership is available to everyone and full participation is needed to advance social change. The manifestation of

---

5. R. SUSSKIND, THE END OF LAWYERS? RETHINKING THE NATURE OF LEGAL SERVICES (2008).

6. PETER G. NORTHOUSE, INTRODUCTION TO LEADERSHIP CONCEPTS AND PRACTICE (2009).

"power over people" is no longer the focus of leadership; instead the focus is on advancing the "power of the people" (i.e., people power).[7] Therefore, the measure of a leader's effectiveness is the assessment of whether he or she helped to grow the people being led.[8] Growth is apparent as community connections become stronger and a sense of unity is embraced. New social justice lawyers are growing the community partners, students, and other stakeholders that they work with. For instance, Edgar Cahn has the natural ability to grow other leaders. He trained community members to use a new set of advocacy tools and empowered them to begin advocating for reform in child welfare and juvenile justice systems.

In particular, each of the featured lawyers has focused on building the leadership capacity of their students. Within their role as educators, they seek to prepare their students to assume the responsibility of leadership and serve as agents of change. Case in point: Nekima Levy-Pounds has incorporated principles of servant leadership and community lawyering into the Community Justice Project's curriculum. Notably, her students also engage in hands-on training and skills development since this is a mobile clinic that is deeply embedded in the community. The fruit of their labor is evidenced by changes in policies ranging from addressing the racial disparities in the juvenile justice system to eliminating barriers to employment experienced by those with a criminal record. The students are immersed in the social fabric of the community through organizing and hosting community meetings, listening sessions, and town hall forums. Overall, the new social justice lawyer intentionally focuses on developing the leadership potential of the next generation of lawyers. This is a process of planting seeds with the goal in mind of reaping a future harvest as law students develop the tools needed to become effective leaders and strategic change agents.

The New Social Justice Lawyer Leads from the Heart

Leadership begins with exercising the power of love. This is a love for the work and love for the community. Levy-Pounds notes that leadership is

---

7. SAUL D. ALINSKY, RULES FOR RADICALS: A PRAGMATIC PRIMER FOR REALISTIC RADICALS (1971).

8. ANN MCGEE-COOPER & GARY LOOPER, THE ESSENTIALS OF SERVANT LEADERSHIP: PRINCIPLES IN PRACTICE (2001).

informed by love: "love for the people that you are serving." This desire to give to others, foster interconnectedness, and empower others to lead is the foundation of love leadership.[9] Love leadership is exercised when lawyers work in partnership with others to further the cause of justice. This love keeps them motivated and inspired to continue their work. Professor Allen captured the essence of this notion when she described why she unexpectedly relocated to Mississippi shortly after the devastation of Hurricane Katrina. She describes being "hooked" on the people and the work. Cahn also ministers to others through demonstrating love. He identifies one of his greatest strengths as having people know that he cares about them and their well-being. Hence, new social justice lawyers have a love for the people, which drew them into leadership roles in order to exercise the influence needed to create social change.

The New Social Justice Lawyer's Toolbox: Building and Sustaining Social Change

Lawyers are the gatekeepers of justice who are endowed with certain technical skills (practical, analytical, and critical thinking skills) to aid in this function. However, these traditional lawyering skills are only one component of the new social justice lawyer's toolbox. This toolbox is multifunctional and versatile; therefore, it contains other advocacy tools like leadership and policy advocacy skills. These additional tools are required to facilitate the process of social change in partnership with other key allies. The new social justice lawyer is able to combine their legal aptitude and leadership competence in order to build and sustain social change. This process begins with understanding how and when to use new social justice lawyering tools. The question of how to use these tools is informed by practical experience but it is still versatile since each approach is situational (explored within the appropriate context). At the same time, the question of when to use each tool encourages creativity and innovation since the new social justice lawyer is committed to thinking outside the box.

---

9. J. BRYANT, LOVE LEADERSHIP: THE NEW WAY TO LEAD IN A FEAR-BASED WORLD 177 (2009).

The New Social Justice Lawyer Utilizes a Distinctively Different Approach to Address Contemporary Social Justice Challenges

Historically, public interest–related advocacy and social change reform efforts have focused primarily on litigation strategies. This is characterized by class actions suits and mass litigation. Despite these customary practices, the new social justice lawyers have chosen a different path and employed a range of varied strategic approaches. The new social justice lawyer recognizes that the social justice issues of the 21st century are multifaceted and interrelated. Therefore, new approaches are needed to uproot these social injustices.

Additionally, one who engages in social change efforts may become deeply entrenched in the complexity of these issues to the point of becoming weighed down and feeling powerless. The tide of social justice issues may seem to be insurmountable, leaving those passionate about social justice with sentiments that "the sea is so wide and my boat is so small."[10] Despite these challenges, new social justice lawyers are charting a new course that moves beyond traditional litigation strategies to transforming systems, policies, and paradigms of thinking. They are no longer bound by the parameters of the historical lawyering strategies; instead they have found ways to develop innovative approaches for promoting social justice. This includes strategies like grassroots community-organizing and community engagement strategies.

New social justice lawyers are seasoned strategists who examine each layer of an issue since these layers impact other aspects of another issue. For example, john powell warns that you cannot address housing without addressing unemployment, and you cannot solve unemployment without addressing education.[11] Additionally, Cahn has recognized the limits of current social services delivery and its impact on those who receive services. He warns that these practices create a sense of dependency and disempower those receiving services. Therefore, these interrelated and multifaceted challenges call for a comprehensive response that draws upon a range of strategies and multidisciplinary approaches. Their work demonstrates that

---

10. P. EDELMAN, SO RICH, SO POOR 8 (2012).
11. African American Leadership Forum, *Q & A with John Powell*, 1 REVIVE! TWIN CITIES 36 (2011).

there is no one-size-fits-all approach but that each strategy must be narrowly tailored to address a particular issue in a specific community. This is a community-centered approach that is for the people (community develops the agenda) and by the people (community leads the agenda).

Further, new social justice lawyers recognize that each person is an invaluable asset; therefore they seek opportunities to collaborate with other professionals and community members. Allen works with a range of professionals at MCJ from community organizers to communication specialists. Each plays an indispensable role in community outreach efforts, public policy campaigns, and systems change. The Kirwan Institute has at any given time between 30 to 50 members of the team who represent professional disciplines like sociology, law, and economics. They share their professional tools and each brings a unique vantage point in the process of problem solving around social justice issues and developing a strategic action plan.

In addition, Cahn works with community members to produce their desired outcomes through an exercise of the principles of coproduction. Coproduction recognizes that each individual has unique and valuable assets and tapping into these assets is essential for societal growth and sustainability. Finally, Levy-Pounds in her work with the Community Justice Project utilizes an integrative approach to community engagement that focuses on building a strong base of community leadership. This empowers community members to lead their own change processes and set their own agenda.

The New Social Justice Lawyer Must Recognize Limitations of the Law and the Need for a Collective Approach

The new social justice lawyer recognizes the need to move beyond the restraints of traditional lawyering of case-by-case litigation. White (1988) describes this uncharted territory as *lawyering together toward change*, which focuses on channeling the power of the community to foster social change and organize as a collective force. The profiled lawyers build this type of partnership with the community in their work by raising "awareness that their real strength lay not in 'the law' but in their own capacity to talk and act and imagine together."[12]

---

12. L. White, *To Learn and Teach: Lessons from Driefontein on Lawyering and Power*, WIS. L. REV. 743 (1988).

This type of partnership recognizes that there are additional tools needed to build a new vision for justice. These tools include policy entrepreneurship, coalition-building, writing as advocacy, and social engineering.

The Pursuit of Justice Is an Eternal Struggle

Justice is dynamic and the pursuit of justice is a lifelong quest. Judge William Hastie once stated, "Democracy is a process and not a static condition. It is not being but becoming. It can be easily lost and never fully won. Its essence is eternal struggle."[13] This description of the democratic process is analogous to the process of social change in furtherance of justice. Similarly, justice is a process and not a static condition; it is an eternal struggle. Lawyers have a key role in transforming the legal system into this state of "becoming." This process of "becoming" ensures that the laws and policies become more just and equitable.

Cahn and powell share the sentiments of justice being an active pursuit and ongoing process. Both advocate that there is more work to be done. powell notes, "justice is not a resting place." Cahn also advocates for active involvement in the pursuit of justice. He stated, "I do not regard the future as a spectator sport so I am unwilling to simply wait to take action until there is a shift in values or an acceptance of the limitations of government." These lawyers focus on the pursuit of social justice as a call to action. This action is manifested through the utilization of the tools within their reach that can be used to create transformation.

The Maximization of Power Must Be Understood as an Indispensable Tool for Engaging in New Social Justice Lawyering

The new social justice lawyer recognizes the importance of maximizing power. He or she strategically seeks to cultivate the power of the collective and create transformation. I am reminded of a conversation with Dr. Mahmoud El-Kati, distinguished scholar and historian. He reminded me that power only respects power and without power there are no changes. Dr. El-Kati directed me to Mary McLeod Bethune's "Last Will and Testament"

---

13. Freedom Riders, Freedom Rides Quotes (2011), http://www.uen.org/freedomrides /downloads/Freedom_Rides_Quotes.pdf.

for additional exploration on the impact of the calculated, strategic exercise of power. In 1955, Bethune wrote:

> We live in a world which respects power above all things. Power, intelligently directed, can lead to more freedom. Unwisely directed, it can be a dreadful, destructive force. During my lifetime I have seen the power of the Negro grow enormously. It has always been my first concern that this power should be placed on the side of human justice.[14]

The new social justice lawyer maximizes the law as a tool of power to effect social change and empower others in tapping into the power that lies in their hands. They challenge others to use the power that may be lying dormant in their lives by becoming actively engaged in the process of social change. This is evidenced by the work of Allen and the MCJ in organizing policy campaigns, and by the work of powell and the Kirwan Institute in partnering with community organizations to address a range of disparities, from creating access to quality health care to eradicating food deserts. All of the profiled lawyers have used the variety of tools in their possession to transform legal, social, and political systems to move closer to the side of human justice.

New social justice lawyers have also challenged the traditional dynamics of lawyers exercising power over individuals by instead positing a new paradigm. This is a focus on lawyering in partnership with the community. Power then becomes a shared tool for manifesting change and resisting oppressive systems. New social justice lawyers are constantly reflecting upon the questions: What power do I have to facilitate social change? How can I use my power endowed by technical legal training to create change? Also, they critically examine their own action and inaction by asking: How do I perpetuate oppression through acquiescence that things are just how they are and will remain so? This reflection process is a reminder of Justice Burger's premise that "concepts of justice must have hands and feet";

---

14. Mary McLeod Bethune, Last Will and Testament 2 (1955), http://www.cookman.edu /about_BCU/history/lastwill_testament.html.

consequently lawyers aid in materialization of justice.[15] Therefore, they must exercise power as a tool to ensure the fair administration of the law and create equal access to justice.

Community-Organizing Is an Essential Tool for Building People Power

In order to sustain social change, the community must be organized. According to Saul Alinsky, legendary community organizer, "community itself means an organized, communal life; people living in an organized fashion."[16] The new social justice lawyer plays an integral role in supporting this organizational structure of community advocacy and enlisting community organizers as partners in the social change process. Former President of South Africa Nelson Mandela serves as an ideal model of a new social justice lawyer since he "was able to teach people how to organize themselves for the purpose of achieving their freedom."[17] Like Mandela did, new social justice lawyers organize communities by hosting community town hall forums, offering public education workshops, and, most importantly, empowering the community to lead. They also work in partnership with community-organizers in order to employ multidisciplinary approaches to problem solving. The new social justice lawyer recognizes that "change comes from power, and power comes from organization. In order to act, people must get together."[18] They employ the tool of community-organizing as a vehicle to build a solid foundation for a coalition based upon shared, collective interests fueled by people power.

Additionally, community-organizing positively affects the community by creating the atmosphere for empowerment. Empowerment affects multiple levels of one's identity and view of self. It is a process of establishing self-actualization, self-awareness, and self-identity, and fostering community connections. The community is at the center of this change as its members seek to guide the reform process. "It is absolutely essential that the

---

15. *Collected Quotes Pertaining to Equal* Justice, NATIONAL LEGAL AID & DEFENDER ASSOCIATION, http://www.nlada.org/News/Equal_Justice_Quotes (last visited Apr. 18, 2014).

16. ALINSKY, *supra* note 7.

17. Bangalee Trawally, Nelson Mandela the Transformational Leader: The Struggle for Justice, Equality and Democratic Change in South Africa 49 (unpublished Master of Arts in Leadership thesis, Augsburg College, 2009).

18. ALINSKY, *supra* note 7, at 113.

oppressed participate in the revolutionary process with an increasing critical awareness of their role as subjects of the transformation."[19] The new social justice lawyers aid in the transformation of the community by offering public education and sharing their knowledge, building community-based institutions and coalitions, and supporting the leadership development of others. Through these encounters, community members are transformed into agents of social change and leaders within their own right.

Writing as Advocacy Is a Tool That Can Be Used for Educational and Organizing Purposes

Writing as advocacy is an indispensable tool for promoting social justice. It provides a venue for shedding light on the challenges facing those who live at the margins of society and gives voice to their concerns. It also serves the outreach function of mobilizing community members around collective interests. For these profiled lawyers, writing is a powerful tool for reaching a wide audience from judges to grassroots community groups. Within the Community Justice Project (CJP), Professor Levy-Pounds and law students publish policy reports on key social justice issues, which provides a detailed analysis of the particular issue and key recommendations for change. CJP then utilizes these reports as advocacy tools to engage in policy reform efforts. The genesis of this work is embodied in a report that was submitted to a local mayor. The report identified and analyzed quality of life challenges (in the arenas of education, criminal justice, policing) experienced by members of the African American community. This report laid the foundation for comprehensive policy reform. Similarly, powell's extensive body of research aids in framing social justice issues, deconstructing systemic inequities, and offering a vision for future reform.

New social justice lawyers have maximized the benefits of technological advancement by publishing and sharing resources in the virtual arena. With over one billion users of social media worldwide, technology has become an essential tool for utilizing writing as advocacy. The Kirwan Institute hosts a blog and publishes updates through e-newsletters. TimeBanks USA utilizes

---

19. P. Freire, BrainyQuote.com, http://www.brainyquote.com/quotes/quotes/p/paulofreir166475.html.

social media sources to connect with timebanking members throughout the world. The Mississippi Center for Justice provides video clips online related to its policy campaigns, which serves as educational outreach. The Community Justice Project shares its policy reports through online venues. Each profiled lawyer demonstrated the importance of using a range of strategies to share his or her work and the far-reaching impact of utilizing writing as advocacy as a tool. For instance, a simple click of the send button can distribute an e-mail action alert to millions of people who could serve as key allies and ambassadors for social change. Hence, writing as advocacy serves as a tool to bring the social justice challenges of our time to the forefront of public discourse.

The Development of New Conceptual Frameworks Serves as a Tool for Redefining Money, Power, and Community

With a paradigm shift and change in modus operandi, there is also a need for a change in public discourse and the reframing of issues. This requires developing a new public narrative,[20] setting a new policy agenda,[21] and employing power strategically.[22] Social change is evidenced by the ways in which new social justice lawyers have redefined money and its characteristics. Money is not defined by them as only financial capital but is built upon human capital. Levy-Pounds defines wealth and capital as a process of placing a premium on people's lived experiences and innate leadership qualities. This equates to the community having an abundance of capital and the ability to use this capital as leverage for facilitating social change. For Cahn, money is not what it looks like, therefore its characteristics are fluid and not static. Therefore, Cahn changed the interpretation of the terms of time and banking by introducing a new framework, timebanking, which focuses on people being indispensable assets. It places value on their time being used as a mechanism to build caring communities and networks of

---

20. M. Ganz, *The Power of Story in Social Movements* (2001), http://www.hks.harvard.edu/organizing/tools/Files/MG%20POWER%20OF%20STORY.pdf; M. Ganz, *Leading Change: Leadership, Organization, and Social Movements*, in HANDBOOK OF LEADERSHIP THEORY AND PRACTICE 509–550 (N. Nohria & R. Khurana eds. 2010).

21. J.W. KINGDON, AGENDAS, ALTERNATIVES, AND PUBLIC POLICIES (2d ed. 2003).

22. M. FOUCAULT & C. GORDON, POWER KNOWLEDGE: SELECTED INTERVIEWS AND OTHER WRITINGS (1980).

support. Thus, these examples demonstrate how new social justice lawyers have created an alternative economy that is fueled by people power.

These profiled lawyers have also offered new conceptual frameworks for redefining power and community. This paradigm shift has aided in analyzing social justice issues and developing practical solutions for policy reform. For example, Dr. Cahn has codeveloped a theory of deliberate indifference, which can be used to address the overreliance on secure detention and racial disparities in the juvenile justice system. This legal theory focuses on addressing racial disparities in the child welfare and juvenile justice systems under a 14th Amendment Equal Protection cause of action.

In addition, powell has introduced the principle of targeted universalism as a framework for accomplishing a range of social justice goals from creating access to affordable housing to developing livable-wage jobs. This conceptual framework acknowledges that goals are universal but strategies are targeted based upon one's situation and context. Both frameworks demonstrate how new social justice lawyers aid in developing innovative and comprehensive problem-solving techniques. Their formulation of new theories and frameworks provides community members with the tools to reconceptualize social justice challenges as opportunities to create social change. The community is then empowered to assume its own leadership in shaping its future.

The Establishment of Coalitions, Institutions, and Initiatives Serves as a Tool

An organizational structure is necessary for developing the capacity to lead social change initiatives. These structures provide a firm foundation for training, education, collective problem solving, and strategic planning. Further, these structures support the development of coalitions that support a common goal.[23] Each new social justice lawyer should play an active role in developing and leading within social justice–oriented coalitions, institutions, and initiatives. For example, Professor Allen served as the president of the Center for Law and Renewal and presently is the director of access to

---

23. Joseph Stewart, *Policy Models and Equal Educational Opportunity*, 24 POL. SCI. & POL'Y. 167 (1991).

justice partnerships at the Mississippi Center for Justice. Professor powell is the founder of the Institute on Race and Poverty at the University of Minnesota and was previously the executive director of the Kirwan Institute for the Study of Race and Ethnicity. Dr. Cahn cofounded Antioch Law School and laid the foundation for the development Legal Services Corporation. Today, he leads TimeBanks USA and the Racial Justice Initiative. Professor Levy-Pounds developed the Community Justice Project, a civil rights legal clinic. The development of these organizational structures has provided an infrastructure for a social justice learning community and policy advocacy incubator. This is a place where people are encouraged to gather together to share ideas and formulate reform strategies.

New Social Justice Lawyers Have a Living Legacy Since They Are Training the Next Generation of Lawyer-Leaders

New social justice lawyers are instrumental in training the next generation of leaders. This is an exercise of their leadership since they are influencing their students to achieve a common goal,[24] which is building and sustaining social change. Leadership is further evidenced by their ability to work with their students to create a shared vision for the common good[25] and compelling others to serve while modeling a commitment to service to others.[26] This can be characterized as a living legacy. The Honorable Justice Alan C. Page of the Minnesota Supreme Court has characterized the essence of a living legacy as (a) future experience—living beyond you (everlasting contribution to society) and (b) present experience—looking ahead to the future while reaching back to lead the course.

These new social justice lawyers train law students in learning laboratories located within their respective law schools and organizations. This setting can be compared to a "garden of leadership" where seeds are planted into the lives of law students.[27]

---

24. PETER G. NORTHOUSE, INTRODUCTION TO LEADERSHIP CONCEPTS AND PRACTICE (5th ed. 2010).

25. DEBRA REN-ETTA SULLIVAN, LEARNING TO LEAD: EFFECTIVE LEADERSHIP SKILLS FOR TEACHERS OF YOUNG CHILDREN (2003); NORTHOUSE, *supra* note 24.

26. ROBERT K. GREENLEAF, THE SERVANT AS LEADER (1970).

27. JOHN ADAIR, HOW TO GROW LEADERS: THE SEVEN KEY PRINCIPLES OF EFFECTIVE DEVELOPMENT (2005).

Schools are gardens for leadership—the places where seeds are planted and first green shoots spotted, tended, and encouraged.[28]

These seeds take root and bear fruit as their students also pursue the quest of new social justice lawyering. Allen characterizes this process as the law students gaining and opening "new eyes." In describing her work of founding a post-Katrina legal services clinic, she explains that Katrina gave law students new eyes to see injustices clearly and the challenges related to preserving the precepts of democracy and justice.[29] In the context of the devastation of Katrina, the existing paradigm of oppression became apparent and clearly visible. As law students witnessed firsthand the devastation of the storm, they were able to see firsthand the importance of the law in protecting the rights of the most vulnerable members of our society. This was not a textbook case study but instead represented the lived reality of the community members. Through this experience, law students learned that the law is a powerful tool for protecting the rights of others and addressing injustices.

Allen is committed to teaching the next generation of lawyers to "use [their] intellect, education, leadership abilities, and will [as well as] the law and our systems of justice to advance equality and prosperity for all people." The other profiled lawyers share the same passion for inspiring law students to lead. Cahn has trained generations of new social justice lawyers. Levy-Pounds focuses on influencing the leadership development of her students by fully integrating them into the social fabric of the community. Hence, new social justice lawyers plant seeds in the lives of their students and young lawyer they are mentoring, which bear fruit as they become empowered to challenge injustices. This is the manifestation of a living legacy.

---

28. John Adair, How to Grow Leaders: The Seven Key Principles of Effective Leadership Development (2005).

29. B. Allen, B. Bezdek & J. Jopling, *Community Recovery Lawyering: Hard-Learned Lessons from Post-Katrina Mississippi*, 4 DePaul J. Soc. Just. 123 (2010).

Conclusion

This exploration was a journey of growth and development within my own leadership capacity. One of the pivotal moments was when I was asked whether new social justice lawyering is truly demonstrative of lawyering or whether it is something else (e.g., community-organizing or social work). For instance, did Mohandas Gandhi and Nelson Mandela really use their lawyering skills? Do we need lawyers operating in this arena of social change? Initially, I shuddered during this fiery line of questioning that felt like a cross-examination, since I had mistakenly thought that I had left the Socratic method behind in law school. However, these questions compelled me to continue this journey of exploration, recognize the significance of lawyers serving in leadership roles, and begin to conceptualize the framework of new social justice lawyering.

I discovered that new social justice lawyering begins where traditional lawyering ends. In certain circumstances, the law alone cannot change the underlying inequitable policies, procedures, or systems that are causing the injustices. In reflecting upon the question of why Gandhi and Mandela would be considered new social justice lawyers, I offer the following hypothesis: (1) they understood the limitations of the law, (2) they recognized that policies can have an impact on law and social change, (3) they knew the importance of community-organizing, since the community is the lifeline of any movement, and (4) they could see from a systems perspective (an understanding of how systems perpetuate inequities). Further, they used their analytical skills to change the rules of how systems operate and to introduce new rules that were equitable and just. Hence, legal training provided them with a unique vantage point of assessing the possible strategies for building social change and their leadership skills provided them with the tools to execute this strategy.

We can learn key leadership lessons from the four trailblazers of justice featured in this book. These lawyers engage in new social justice lawyering, which is an integral component to a collective effort for building and sustaining social change. They also demonstrated the importance of legal training being used a tool to facilitate social change and the exercise of leadership as a moral endeavor. Further, they established the importance of building strong coalitions with other professionals, students, and most importantly, community members. These new social justice lawyers and community partners have worked together to facilitate the process of change.

Throughout the research process, the themes of community empowerment and transformative power continually emerged. These themes served as a source of inspiration hence the book title *The Lawyer as Leader: How to Plant People and Grow Justice*. An ancient Chinese proverb, shared earlier in the book, provides the context for this creation of shared vision of justice, valuing people, and working together in partnership to foster social change. The proverb provides: "If your vision is for a year, plant wheat. If your vision is for ten years, plant trees. If your vision is for a lifetime, plant people."

People and communities are at the center of the process of social change. They help to identify the legal problem/experience of injustice, shape the course of action, and work in partnership with the new social justice lawyer to facilitate the process of social change. This means that the lawyer cannot simply assert, "I am super lawyer—hand over all of your problems to me." Instead, he or she ought to state: "I am here in the struggle with you for social change. I have tools to contribute to building this change." The new social justice lawyer recognizes that each individual has a unique set of tools. Together, the tools can be strategically utilized to address social injustices and eradicate their root causes. Thus, the new social justice lawyer raises the question, "How can we grow justice together?"

New social justice lawyers are compelled to take action through the utilization of their tools based upon their personal convictions. An early life experience has informed their commitment to realizing their vision of justice and serving as leaders. More importantly, as leaders they connect with others who share a similar vision, a similar purpose, and similar values. Together they learn and grow. This is the manifestation of planting people and growing justice. In the end, "the true meaning of life is to plant trees, under whose shade you do not expect to sit."[30] New social justice

---

30. N. Henderson, Dictionary quotes, http://www.dictionary-quotes.com/the-true-mean ing-of-life-is-to-plant-trees-under-whose-shade-you-do-not-expect-to-sit-nelson-henderson/.

lawyers across the globe are planting seeds of change that will continue to bear fruit as the manifestation of their leadership legacy. The challenge is now left to you. How will you lead change? This is the quest of planting people, growing justice.

Afterword

My passion for social justice lawyering was ignited during my college years and has continued to be fueled by the hopes of a better tomorrow. I started my vocational journey with a dream of becoming a high school English teacher. However, when I began student teaching, I witnessed firsthand the disparities in the school system influenced by factors such as race and poverty. This was a formative moment in my personal and professional development. Something had to be done to change these circumstances so that every child was granted equal access to a quality education. I became committed to shaping public policy and standing up for children. At this point, I also recognized that the law is a language of power and I wanted to learn this language to empower others in my community. Gandhi wisely stated that "you must be the change you wish to see in the world." I became this change by enrolling in law school.

While in law school, I studied the work of great lawyers, like the late Dean Charles Hamilton Houston, Justice Thurgood Marshall, and Marian Wright Edelman, who used their legal training to effect social change. I was inspired by their work and was committed to also create meaningful change with my law degree. Following in their footsteps, I was able to exercise this leadership role as an agent of change within my role as a member of the Clinical Law Faculty by codeveloping the curriculum and program model for the Community Justice Project (CJP) civil rights clinic. CJP's curriculum is the first of its kind since it focuses on holistic problem-solving approaches for creating equal justice under the law for underserved communities. CJP students are trained to engage in community-building and utilize innovative problem-solving techniques. I also instruct the students in theoretical perspectives of social justice lawyering and leadership development with a goal in mind of training them to become not just lawyers but engineers of social change.

In partnership with affected communities of color, the CJP has been instrumental in deconstructing systems of oppression, creating a social justice narrative, and empowering community members to pursue civic engagement. I envision CJP continuing its work and building social justice movements locally, nationally, and internationally. With this ideal in mind, I sought to understand the following: how do lawyers who engage in social justice efforts stay motivated, build coalitions, empower others to lead, and sustain social movements?

My leadership journey provided me with opportunities to explore this question by interviewing lawyers who lead in social change movements and applying the leadership lessons learned from these seasoned practitioners into my work. This experience informed my understanding of how I can create access to justice, transform systems and policies, and leave a legacy of change for future generations. It also led to the development of the theoretical framework of new social justice lawyering and informed the principles of planting people, growing justice.

New social justice lawyering in action is evidenced by my leadership in policy campaigns focused on creating access to affordable phone calls between prisoners and their loved ones, bridging the racial jobs gap, and strengthening the economic development of marginalized communities.

Prison Phone Justice

The Campaign for Prison Phone Justice seeks to ensure that prisoners and their loved ones can exercise a fundamental human right—communication. For far too many families, this right is restricted due to the high costs of prison phone calls. The harsh reality is that a 15-minute collect phone call received from a loved one who is incarcerated can cost as much as $17. The high cost of prison phone calls is due to the associated commissions and kickbacks paid to prisons from phone companies. Prisons and phone companies enter into contracts for phone services. As a result, these phone companies pay commissions to the prisons, which yields about $143 million in revenues to state prisons or the private corporations who operate them. In Minnesota, state prisons receive 49-percent commissions on phone calls made from prisons, which generates $1.5 million in revenue each year. In turn, families must bear the burden of choosing between accepting a loved one's call from prison and meeting their basic budgetary needs.

Prison phone calls are the most accessible means of communication since prisoners are incarcerated an average of 100 miles away from home and their families. Therefore, phone calls are truly a vital source of communication in order for families to remain connected. The Campaign for Prison Phone Justice seeks to ensure that children and families can remain in contact with their incarcerated loved ones by advocating for the costs of prison phone calls to be capped at a reasonable amount. A recent Federal Communications Commission ruling offers a glimpse of hope, but change has been long overdue. On August 9, 2013, following a hearing on the policies associated with interstate phone calls, the commission voted 2–1 to cap the costs of interstate prison phone calls, determining that $.12 per minute was a reasonable "safe harbor" rate and imposing an absolute cap of $.25 per minute for collect calls. However, intrastate calls remain subject to egregiously high call rates.

The Community Justice Project has been actively involved in promoting community education and engagement. CJP students hosted a listening session to gain knowledge of the firsthand experiences of those who encounter this injustice. They also employed writing as a tool for advocacy by publishing op-ed pieces, blogs, and news articles, which shed light on the imminent need for prison phone justice reform and challenged community members to take a stand for prison phone justice.

Racial Jobs Gap

Nearly 65 million people in America have a criminal record (which includes an arrest or a conviction). These records have a haunting impact on the lives of many individuals who have turned their lives around after a brush with the law, since community members with a criminal record are routinely denied employment opportunities. This is because more than 92 percent of employers use background checks, and as many as two-thirds refuse to hire applicants with criminal or arrest records, regardless of the length of time since conviction or relevancy to the job. A criminal history serves as a bar to employment. Communities of color experience this barrier at a disproportionate rate, especially since people of color make up about 30 percent of the United States's population but account for 60 percent of those imprisoned.

As those who have been incarcerated embark on the journey to reintegration, their criminal background is a looming reminder of the past with present-day ramifications. Promoting changes to employers' use of background information will give those with a criminal background the chance to compete in the job market. The U.S. Equal Employment Opportunity Commission (EEOC) added new guidelines to address the employment challenges that people with criminal records are facing. The EEOC limited the scope in which past criminal records could be evaluated and set forth guidelines limiting an employer's ability to examine past criminal records. The EEOC offers a comprehensive model for fair-hiring practices. An employer must first look at the nature and gravity of the offense or conduct. Second, the employer must look at the amount of time that has passed since the offense or conduct in question. Third, the nature of the job the applicant is applying for must be evaluated. These guidelines provide parameters for employers to evaluate an applicant's criminal history while looking to the future by creating access to employment opportunities.

The work of the Community Justice Project has focused on addressing this issue at a local level through policy reform initiatives. Our team has conducted a comparative analysis of states that have undergone reform in order to explore possible models for future reform.

Timebanking

Difficult economic times are widespread both nationally and locally. In Minnesota, African Americans are facing tough economic times, which are evidenced by 37.2 percent of families living in poverty and the largest unemployment gap disparity in the nation (between blacks and whites). The Community Justice Project and the St. Paul Chapter of the NAACP are working together to develop practical solutions for addressing the economic challenges affecting the African American community and other diverse populations. One such solution is supporting the growth and development of TimeBanks locally.

Timebanking follows the traditional community values of respect, love, and service that are embodied in the notion of "It takes a village." Deeply rooted in African American tradition and culture, we recognize that it takes a village to build strong and vibrant communities. Timebanking establishes an opportunity for each community member to serve as a valuable contributor and play a key role in maximizing our human capital. Similar to traditional notions of banking, members of TimeBanks earn and redeem Time Dollars with each hour of a service exchange. The recipient of services redeems hours while the service provider earns hours when performing the given task.

Timebanking is being used to promote economic development around the globe. Nationally, there are over 250 TimeBanks in the United States and TimeBanks are operating in 26 countries. Timebanking can also be a vehicle to address other social issues like juvenile justice reform, reentry/reintegration initiatives, and elder-care programming. Communities have narrowly tailored the timebanking model to meet their needs. One notable example is Homecomers Academy, which incorporates the principles of timebanking into a reentry/reintegration initiative that provides job development and builds community support networks for those who are returning home from prison. Homecomers Academy participants help to rehabilitate houses in their local communities. Another example is a timebanking initiative in Rhode Island that provides respite care for seniors ranging from meal preparation to transportation services, in order to ensure that they can maintain their homes and live independently. Both of these examples demonstrate how timebanking helps to build a support network in communities and ensure that communities can remain viable.

The founder of timebanking, Dr. Edgar S. Cahn, opened the TimeBanks Global Conference with the following remarks: "There is tremendous wealth in this room, tremendous wealth in the nation . . . if [there] [is] ever a time to tap into it, it is right now." Tapping into village currency has empowered communities to build networks of support and exercise servant leadership.

Each of these policy reform campaigns represent the transformative power of planting people, growing justice. Through the exercise of leadership and lifting of their voices, community members in partnership with lawyers have leveraged their collective power to lead change.

Appendix

Leadership Toolbox

Leadership Resources
What are the leadership tools in your toolbox? Every effective leader has a toolbox of indispensable tools. These tools may include your ability to:

- Build a vision for your organization
- Collaborate with others
- Innovate and create new ideas
- Apply technical competence based upon your professional training

No matter which tool you employ, you need to learn when and how to use it. Leadership is a learning process. This section provides key leadership resources to guide you on your vocational journey.

Leadership Assessment Tools
An essential part of learning and growing as a leader is assessing your leadership skills. These assessments will aid you in discovering your leadership strengths, gaining new insights, and developing new leadership tools.

- Emotional Intelligence Assessment: http://danielgoleman.info/ei-assessments/
- 360° Assessment: http://www.ccl.org/leadership/assessments/assessment360.aspx
- Servant Leadership Inventory: http://www.leadersource.org/resources/instruments/personal-competencies/servant-leader-inventory.html
- Strengthsfinder: http://www.strengthsfinder.com/home.aspx

Personal Credo Exercise

Your personal credo serves as a vision statement for your leadership platform. It informs who you are and what you believe.

Think of a creed as a way of living with your whole being.

- Your head knows *who you are*
- Your heart beats with *purpose*
- Your two arms embrace your relationships:
  - your *family* on one hand
  - the rest of the *world* on the other
- Your two legs ground you:
  - *acceptance* of your reality
  - *action* to change it

Joyful Days-Live Well. Be Happy.

http://www.joyfuldays.com/how-to-write-a-personal-creed/ (2013).

Sample Credos serve as guiding principles for your leadership journey.

- "Stay Hungry, Stay Foolish." —Steve Jobs
- "Only those who dare to fail greatly can ever achieve greatly." —Robert F. Kennedy
- "Don't settle for a spark . . . light a fire instead." —Dove Chocolates

Leadership Activity

My Vision of Leadership

The purpose of this exercise is to begin the process of developing one's vision of leadership. Begin to envision a goal that you would like to achieve; this process will aid you in identifying the skills needed to achieve this goal, engaging in the development of an action plan, and building a network of support.

Please fill in the blanks.

This is my vision of leadership. As a leader, I hope to (list goal). I will reach this goal by exercising (list core leadership competencies) and cultivating (identify key strength areas). I am confident that I can achieve my goal with the support of (name your personal Leadership Board of Directors) and through perseverance, commitment, and dedication. This vision will be a reality—I claim my success!

Goal-Setting Exercise

Goal setting is an essential part of leadership development. This process provides you with an opportunity to set the course of your leadership journey. You can identify what you would like to achieve and develop a strategic plan of action.

Harvard Business School Case Study:

> Ten year study conducted by Harvard Business School establishes the importance of goal setting. In 1979, graduates of Harvard Business School were asked to set clear goals for their future. **Only 3% of these graduates actually wrote their goals,** 13% had written goals but had not created an implementation plan and 84% failed to set goals or outline their objectives. Guess what- the 13% earned twice as much as the 84% (who failed to set goals). **The 3% who set clear goals earned 10 times more than their classmates.**
> (Mark McCormick, *What They Don't Teach You at Harvard Business School*)

Goal setting lays a firm foundation for your future success. Imagine if you were like the 3 percent and set your leadership goals today. Could goal setting yield ten times more on your investment of time in strengthening your leadership platform, expanding your client base, growing your firm, or expanding into new practice areas and markets?

Desired Goal (What goals would you like to achieve?)	Steps you will take to reach your goal (What steps will you take to reach these goals?)	Network of Support (Who can aid you in reaching your goals?)	Timeline (When will you achieve your goal?)
Example: Pillar #3- Develop public policy advocacy skills	Study policy entrepreneurship Join ABA Washington Summary (for updates on current legal related policy issues) Join an advocacy group	Schedule a meeting with an elected official to learn more about his/her policy agenda Attend a legislative committee hearing	Register for ABA Washington Summary (today)

Reflection Journal

Reflection is a critical part of leadership development. This practice will provide you with the sacred space and time to explore your leadership potential. The focus of reflection is to develop an acute awareness of your leadership strengths, values, and ethics. Socrates characterizes this as the process of "knowing thyself." By endeavoring to know yourself, you will enhance your leadership skills and discover your signature leadership brand.

"Do not wait for leaders; do it alone, person to person."
—Mother Teresa

Dr. Tyner's Reflection on Leadership as a Ministry
Leadership is a part of a ministry, a ministry of love and service. The word ministry has been defined as one that serves as a means; an instrumentality. Ministry is an action-oriented noun since it is a tool and can be used as an instrument to further the cause of social justice. It requires the strength, dedication, and perseverance of the actor. The actor makes a conscious effort to engage in a daily ministry of service to others.

On the streets of Calcutta, one leader began her ministry of love. The challenges surrounding her were great and some would call them insurmountable. Despite the mountain of challenges and perceived impossibilities, she decided to take a stand. She made a lifetime commitment to a ministry of service starting person to person. She opened her heart to the least of these and showed love, mercy, and grace.

Her charisma and passion motivated others to join this service ministry. Not only did she reach other nuns but she inspired people from all walks of life, from business leaders to community members. They were inspired by her acts of kindness and compassion. She liberated others to not simply wait for someone else to further the cause of justice but to discover their own individual ministry and leadership potential. She acknowledged that the task ahead may seem daunting or look impossible, but her message of inspiration was to simply do it anyway, person to person.

I salute Mother Teresa for serving as a beacon of hope and servant leader. Her ministry of service transformed the world and inspired others to become servant leaders. She once stated:

People are often unreasonable, irrational, and self-centered. Forgive them anyway. If you are kind, people may accuse you of selfish, ulterior motives. Be kind anyway. If you are successful, you will win some unfaithful friends and some genuine enemies. Succeed anyway. If you are honest and sincere people may deceive you. Be honest and sincere anyway. What you spend years creating, others could destroy overnight. Create anyway. If you find serenity and happiness, some may be jealous. Be happy anyway. The good you do today, will often be forgotten. Do good anyway. Give the best you have, and it will never be enough. Give your best anyway. In the final analysis, it is between you and God. It was never between you and them anyway.

"It begins with the natural feeling that one wants to serve, to serve first. Then conscious choice brings one to aspire to lead."
—Robert Greenleaf

Dr. Tyner's Reflection on Servant Leadership

This quote causes me to reflect upon the qualities of a servant leader. A servant leader is one who is a visionary, motivator, relational, and strategic problem solver. This is a leadership role that everyone can assume since each person has the capacity to serve. Through serving, everyone can contribute to the growth and development of a strong community. Dr. King (1968) described the significance of service in his speech titled "The Drum Major Instinct." In this speech, he deconstructed the notion of individualism and self-centeredness within communities, while offering an alternative paradigm of service and interrelatedness. This new paradigm empowers each individual to become servant leaders. He stated: "If you want to be important—wonderful. If you want to be recognized—wonderful. If you want to be great—wonderful. But recognize that he who is greatest among you shall be your servant. That's the new definition of greatness."

Robert Greenleaf, who coined the term servant leadership, explores this definition of greatness through the fictional characterization of Leo. The character of Leo is drawn from Herman Hesse's *Journey to the East*. Leo accompanies a group of men on a mythical journey as the servant who performs routine menial tasks. Leo remains on the journey as a servant while uplifting the men and guiding the journey. One day, Leo disappears and is found by one of the men many years later. It is then discovered that Leo is also a great leader, a noble guiding spirit, in addition to being an indispensable resource to the group of traveling men. Leo's inner strengths as a motivator and giver empowered him to serve in a merged role as both a servant and a leader. This serves as an example of a servant leader's ability to uplift and motivate others through random acts of kindness.

The most powerful dimension of Leo's work was his ability to lead through his actions. For many on the journey he went unnoticed until he had left. The group of traveling men on the journey then knew that Leo was the source of strength for their group. He was the glue that held them together. This image of Leo demonstrates leadership as a capacity to influence more with your actions than through words. Leo's actions showed his commitment to serving others with dignity and grace. We each can learn from Leo how to become a leader by serving others. This has a far-reaching impact as those watching you are reminded that your leadership capacity is measured by both words and deeds. Your deeds are a manifestation of your words and values in action.

Words of Inspiration

"Your vision will become clear only when you look into your own heart. Who looks outside, dreams; who looks inside, awakes." —Carl Jung
"We must realize that our future lies chiefly in our own hands." —Paul Robeson
"Where there is no vision, there is no hope." —George Washington Carver

Quotes on Leadership and Social Justice

Effective leadership requires self-awareness. This is the process as characterized by Socrates of knowing thyself. The quotes below serve as a tool for continuing the process of reflective learning. After reading each quote, take a few moments and explore how the quote informs your definition of leadership.

"The progress of the world will call for the best that all of us have to give." —Mary McLeod Bethune
"My life is my message." —Mahatma Gandhi
"To command is to serve, nothing more and nothing less." —Andre Malraux
"Instead of counting your days, make your days count." —Author Unknown
"Do not wait for leaders; do it alone, person to person." —Mother Teresa
"I am only one; but still I am one. I cannot do everything; but still I can do something; and because I cannot do everything, I will not refuse to do something that I can do." —Edward Everett Hale
"Leadership is influence." —John C. Maxwell
"A man who wants to lead the orchestra must turn his back to the crowd." —Max Lucado
"Leaders are not born, they are made. And they are made just like anything

*else, through hard work. And that's the price we'll have to pay to achieve
that goal, or any goal."* —*Vince Lombardi*

This I Believe
I believe the day will come
    when rich and poor will stand equal before the law
  And I believe the day will come when Black and White
    Hispanic, Asian and Native American,
  Young and old, man and woman
    will stand equal before the law *This I believe*
  And I believe the day will come when the monopoly
    over law and legal knowledge—the lawyers' monopoly
    the law schools' monopoly—will be broken
When men and women and yes, even children will know that which
    is expected of them and that which they can expect of others:
    to refrain from harm
    to honor their word
    to respect the dreams of others and the right of others
    to dream in their own way *This I believe*
And I believe that the day will come when courts of law
    will be courts of justice, courts for people, not courts for lawyers—
    above all, courts to render simple justice, to see
    that promises are honored
    that the injured are made whole
    that the weak are protected from the powerful and the greedy
    This I believe
For in the fullness of time, I must believe that the voices of love
    shall prevail over the voices of hate and the forces of justice
    shall triumph over the forces of injustice and inhumanity
    This I believe
But in the here and now, there can be no safety, no guarantees and no
easy way.
    At each point, our faith will be tested and when weighed in the balance,
    if we are honest, our best efforts will be found wanting
    This is true, this I believe

And so, all that we have, in the here and now is
  our love for each other,
  our willingness to forgive each other,
  our willingness to come to each other's rescue,
  and our unwillingness to stand by silent or passive
  in the face of injustice.
This is my belief, this is our joint belief and this we shall try to honor
  so long as life and breath permit.

Edgar S. and Jean Camper Cahn

Time Dollar Credo
We take halting steps one by one by one
  Our math is simple: one equals one equals one
  One is tiny, the smallest absolute
  But absolute is absolute

  To be human is what we do and what we are
  To care, to love, to reach out, to come to each other's rescue
  To grieve, to celebrate, to reach consensus,
  To stand up for what's right, to stand against what we know is wrong

  These are not acquired though may be honed
  They are in our DNA—They are being and our doing
  Our shaping and creating and weaving
  That's what one hour of our being means

  We stand for what it means to be human
  And human beings are not chattel;
  There are domains which are above market, beyond price
  Family, loved ones, justice, democracy, our planet
  all that is holy
  Not for sale at market price, at any price

One hour, one piece of eternity.
Fleeting but nonetheless, precious, sacred, eternal
That is what Time Banking means, declares, affirms and reaffirms
We are—and We will not be diminished. Let it be.

Glossary

Empowerment: Empowerment focuses on enhancing the capacity of poor people to influence the state institutions that affect their lives by strengthening their participation in political processes and local decision making. And it means removing the barriers—political, legal and social—that work against particular groups and building the assets of poor people to enable them to engage effectively in markets. (World Development Report, 2000)

Justice: "The principle of moral rightness, equity; conformity to moral rightness in action or attitude" (*American Heritage Dictionary*, 1985, p. 694).

New social justice lawyering: I developed the theory of new social justice lawyering, which draws upon leadership principles, public policy advocacy strategies, and notions of social justice lawyering in order to work in partnership with marginalized communities to foster and support social change.

Servant leadership: Servant leadership provides a theoretical framework of service that inspires each individual to serve and lead. "It begins with the natural feeling that one wants to serve, to serve first. Then conscious choice brings one to aspire to lead" (Greenleaf, 1991, p.7).

Social change: The process of changing systems, policies, and administration of justice in order to create access to justice, equity, and fairness.

Social justice: This concept involves "the goals of equality, of access, opportunity and outcome" (Bok, 1992, p. 15).

Transformational leader: An individual who seeks to influence and motivate followers to reach their own leadership potential. According to Northouse (2010) "transformational leadership is the process whereby a person engages with others and creates a connection that raises the level of motivation and morality in both the leader and the follower" (p. 172).

Bibliography

Abraham Lincoln Online. (2012). *The Gettysburg address*. Retrieved from http://showcase.netins.net/web/creative/lincoln/speeches /gettysburg.htm

Adair, J. E. (2005). *How to grow leaders: The seven key principles of effective leadership development*. London, England: Kogan Page.

Adams, M., Bell, L. A., & Griffin, P. (2007). *Teaching for diversity and social justice* (2nd ed.). New York, NY: Routledge.

African American Leadership Forum. (2011). Q & A with John Powell. *REVIVE! Twin Cities, 1* (1), 36.

Alinsky, S. (1971). *Rules for radicals: A pragmatic primer for realistic radicals*. New York, NY: Vintage Books.

Allen, B., Bezdek, B., & Jopling, J. (2010). Community recovery lawyering: Hard-learned lessons from post-Katrina Mississippi. *DePaul Journal for Social Justice, 4,* 97–130.

American Bar Association. (2002, April). Public perceptions of lawyers consumer research findings. Retrieved from http://www.cliffordlaw .com/abaillinoisstatedelegate/publicperceptions1.pdfAmerican Bar Association. (2010). Model rules of professional conduct. Retrieved from http://www.americanbar.org/groups/professional _responsibility/publications/model_rules_of_professional_conduct /model_rules_of_professional_conduct_preamble_scope.html

American Bar Association, Section of Legal Education and Admissions to the Bar. (1992). Legal education and professional development: An educational continuum. Minneapolis, MN: West Publishing Company.

American Heritage Dictionary. (1985). (2nd ed.). Boston, MA: Houghton Mifflin Company.

Answers.com (2011). Abraham Joshua Heschel. Retrieved from http://www.answers.com/topic/abraham-joshua-heschel

Anyon, J. (2005). *Radical possibilities: Public policy, urban education, and a new social movement.* New York, NY: Routledge.

Atkinson, R. (1998). *The life story interview.* Thousand Oaks, CA: Sage Publications.

Autry, J. A. (2004). *The servant leader: How to build a creative team, develop great morale, and improve bottom-line performance.* New York, NY: Three Rivers Press.

Barbuto, J.E. Jr., & Wheeler, D.W. (2006). Scale development and construct clarification of servant leadership. *Group and Organizational Management, 31,* 300–326.

Bass, B. M. (1985). *Leadership and performance beyond expectation.* New York, NY: Free Press.

Bethune-Cookman University. (2008). History. Retrieved from http://www .cookman.edu/about_bcu/history/index.html

Bethune, M. M. (1955). Last will and testament. Retrieved from http://www.cookman.edu/about_BCU/history/lastwill_testament .html.

Bezdek, B. L. (2004). To forge new hammers of justice: Deep-six the doing-teaching dichotomy and embrace the dialectic of "doing theory." *University of Maryland Law Journal of Race, Religion, Gender and Class, 4,* 301.

Black, H. (2009). Black's law dictionary (9th ed.). B.A. Garner (Ed.). St. Paul, MN: West.

Blanchard, K. H., & Hodges, P. (2003). *The servant leader: Transforming your heart, head, hands, & habits.* Nashville, TN: J. Countryman.

Bogdan, R.C., & Bilken, S.K. (2007). *Qualitative research for education: An introduction to theories and methods* (5th ed.). Boston, MA: Pearson Education.

Bok, M. (1992). *Civil rights and the social programs of the 1960s: The social justice functions of social policy.* Westport, CT: Praeger Publishers.

Bolman, L. G., & Deal, T. E. (2001). *Leading with soul: An uncommon journey of spirit* (Rev. ed.). San Francisco, CA: Jossey-Bass.

Boyte, H. C. (2008). *The citizen solution: How you can make a difference.* Saint Paul, MN: Minnesota Historical Society Press.

Brookfield, S., & Preskill, S. (2009). *Learning as a way of leading: Lessons from the struggle for social justice.* San Francisco, CA: Jossey-Bass.

Brown vs. Board of Education, 347 U.S. 483 (1954).

Brown, J., & Allen, B. (2009, May 4). Leadership education in the legal academy: Principles, practices, and possibilities. Retrieved from http://www.law.umaryland.edu/programs/initiatives/lead/docs /LeadershipLawSchoolRpt.pdf

Bryant, J. (2009). *Love leadership: The new way to lead in a fear-based world.* San Francisco, CA: Jossey-Bass.

Burd-Sharps, S., Lewis, K., & Martins, B.E. (2008). *A portrait of Mississippi.* American Human Development Project. Retrieved from www.measureofamerica.org

Burns, J. M. (1978). *Leadership.* New York, NY: Harper & Row.

Burns, J. M. (2003). *Transforming leadership.* New York, NY: Atlantic Monthly Press.

Cahn, E. (2004). *No more throw-away people: The co-production imperative.* Washington, DC: Essential Books.

Cahn, E. (2011). *Priceless money: Banking time for changing times.* Washington, DC: Time Banks.

Cahn, E., & Robbins, C. (2009). An offer they can't refuse: Racial disparity in juvenile justice and deliberate indifference meet alternatives that work. *University of the District of Columbia Law Review, 13,* 1–31.

Charisma. (1985). *American heritage dictionary* (p. 260, 2nd ed.). Boston, MA: Houghton Mifflin Company.

Charmaz, K. (2006). *Constructing grounded theory: A practical guide through qualitative analysis.* Thousand Oaks, CA: Sage Publications.

Children's Defense Fund. (2011). Bounced checks from America's bank of opportunity. Retrieved from http://www.childrensdefense.org/ newsroom/child-watch-columns/child-watch-documents/bounced -checks-from-americas-bank-of-opportunity.html

Clinton, H. R. (2006, 12 August). "When you come to a fork in the road": Sen. Hillary Clinton on the importance of a career in public-service law. *Newsweek.* Retrieved from http://www.thedailybeast.com /newsweek/2006/08/12/when-you-come-to-a-fork-in-the-road.html

Cook, N. (2006). Looking for justice on a two-way street. *Washington University Journal of Law & Policy, 20*, 169–200.

Covey, S. R. (1992). *Principle-centered leadership.* New York, NY: Simon & Schuster.

Crosby, B. C., & Bryson, J. M. (2005). *Leadership for the common good: Tackling public problems in a shared-power world* (2nd ed.). San Francisco, CA: Jossey-Bass.

DePree, M. (1989). *Leadership is an art.* New York, NY: Doubleday.

Downton, J.V. (1973). *Rebel leadership: Commitment and charisma in the revolutionary process.* New York, NY: Free Press.

Duncan, J. (2005). *Historical study of the Highlander method: Honing leadership for social justice.* Retrieved from ProQuest Digital Dissertations. (AAT 3164820).

Eckstein, H. (1992). *Regarding politics: Essays on political theory, stability, and change.* Berkeley, CA: University of California Press. Retrieved from http://ark.cdlib.org/ark:/13030/ft0k40037v/

Edelman, M. (2008). *The sea is so wide and my boat is so small: Charting a course for the next generation.* New York: N.Y.: Hyperion.

Ehrlich, E. (1936). *Fundamental principles of the sociology of law.* Cambridge, MA: Harvard University Press. (Original work published 1912).

Enomoto, E., & Kramer, B. H. (2007). *Leading through the quagmire: Ethical foundations, critical methods, and practical applications for school leadership.* Lanham, MD: Rowman & Littlefield Education.

Evans, C. (1998). *Super lawyers: America's courtroom celebrities: 40 top lawyers and the cases that made them famous.* Detroit, MI: Visible Ink Press.

Fairfax, R. A. (1998). Wielding the double-edged sword: Charles Hamilton Houston and judicial activism in the age of legal realism. *Harvard Blackletter Law Journal, 14*, 17–44.

Fesmire, S. (2003). *John Dewey and moral imagination: Pragmatism in ethics.* Bloomington, IN: Indiana University Press.

Fink, A. (2009). *How to conduct surveys.* Thousand Oaks, CA: Sage Publications.

Finkelman, P. (1994). Not only the judges' robes were black: African-American lawyers as social engineers. *Stanford Law Review, 47*, 161–209.

Fleishman, E. A., Mumford, M. D., Zaccaro, S. J., Levin, K. Y., Korotkin, A. L., & Hein, M. B. (1991). Taxonomic efforts in the description of leader behavior: A synthesis and functional interpretation. *Leadership Quarterly, 2*(4), 245–287.

Foucault, M., & Gordon, C. (1980). *Power knowledge: Selected interviews and other writings, 1972–1977*. New York, NY: Pantheon Books.

Freedom Riders. (2011). Freedom Rides Quotes. Retrieved from http://www.uen.org/freedomrides/downloads/Freedom_Rides _Quotes.pdf

Freire, P. (n.d.). BrainyQuote.com. Retrieved from http://www.brainyquote .com/quotes/quotes/p/paulofreir166475.html

Gandhi, M. (n.d.). The quotations page. Retrieved from http://www .quotationspage.com/quote/27184.html

Ganz, M. (2001, August). *The power of story in social movements.* Retrieved from http://www.hks.harvard.edu/organizing/tools/Files /MG%20POWER%20OF%20STORY.pdf

Ganz, M. (2007). Hillel's questions: A call for leadership. *Being Jewish.* Retrieved from http://www.shma.com/2007/01/hillels-questions-a -call-for-leadership/

Ganz, M. (2010). Leading change: Leadership, organization, and social movements. In N. Nohria & R. Khurana (Eds.), *Handbook of Leadership Theory and Practice* (509–550). Boston, MA: Harvard Business School Press.

Gates, B. (2004). Bill Gates Sr. on public service law: Reflections on the value of public service by the private bar. *Newsweek.* Retrieved from http://www.newsweek.com/bill-gates-sr-public-service-law-111947

George, B. (2003). *Authentic leadership: Rediscovering the secrets to creating lasting value*. San Francisco, CA: Jossey-Bass.

Gergen, D. (2009, November 1). The national deficit of leadership. *U.S. News & World Report, 146*(10), 29.

Goethals, G. R., Sorenson, G. J., & Burns, J. M. (2004). *Encyclopedia of leadership*. Thousand Oaks, CA: Sage Publications. Retrieved from http://find.galegroup.com.ezproxy.bethel.edu/gvrl/ infomark. do?type=aboutBook&prodId=GVRL&eisbn=141292538X& version=1.0&userGroupName=clic_bethel&source=gale; http://galenet.galegroup.com/servlet/eBooks?ste=22& docNum=CX3475799999&q=clic_hamline

Goodreads. (2011). *Marian Wright Edelman quotes.* Retrieved from http://www.goodreads.com/author/quotes/73926.Marian_Wright _Edelman

Graham, J. W. (1991). Servant-leadership in organizations: Inspirational and moral. *Leadership Quarterly, 2*(2), 105–119.

Gray, A. (2001). *Stories for the heart: Over 100 stories to encourage your soul.* Sisters, O.R.: Multnomah Publishers, Inc.

Greenleaf, R. K. (1987). *Teacher as servant: A parable.* Newton Centre, MA: Robert K. Greenleaf.

Greenleaf, R. K. (1991). *The servant as leader* (Rev ed.). Indianapolis, IN: Robert K. Greenleaf Center. (Original work published 1970).

Grills, S. (1998). *Doing ethnographic research: Fieldwork settings.* Thousand Oaks, CA: Sage Publications.

Gubrium, J. F. & Holstein, J. A. (2002). *Handbook of interview research.* Thousand Oaks, CA: Sage Publications.

Hallengren, A. (2001). *Nelson Mandela and the rainbow of culture.* Retrieved from http://www.nobelprize.org/nobel_prizes/peace /laureates/1993/mandela-article.html/

Hammargren, L. R. (2007). Servant leadership and women in the law: A new nexus of women, leadership and the legal profession. *University of Saint Thomas Law Journal, 4,* 624–643.

Heineman, B. (2007). Lawyers as leaders. *Yale Law Journal Pocket Part, 116,* 266–271.

Henderson, N. (n.d.). Dictionary quotes. Retrieved from http://www .dictionary-quotes.com/the-true-meaning-of-life-is-to-plant-trees -under-whose-shade-you-do-not-expect-to-sit-nelson-henderson/

Hinmon, A. (2010). Achieving justice through rebellious lawyering: Restructuring systems of law and power for social change. *Modern American, 6*(1), 15–16.

Hoffman, N. V. (2010). *A portrait of Saul Alinsky: Radical.* New York, NY: Nation Books.

Hope Christian Church. (2012). *Quotes from Stride toward freedom: The Montgomery story.* Retrieved from http://www.hopemn.com /MLK.htm

Horton, M. & Freire, P. (1990). *We make the road by walking: Conversations on education and social change.* Philadelphia, PA: Temple University Press.

Horton, M., Kohl, J., & Kohl, H. R. (1991). *The long haul: An autobiography.* New York, NY: Doubleday.

Howard University School of Law. (2004). History. Retrieved from http://www.law.howard.edu/19

Hughes, L. (2011). Let America be America again. Retrieved from http://www.poets.org/viewmedia.php/prmMID/15609. (Original work published 1994).

Hughes, R. L., Ginnett, R. C., & Curphy, G. J. (2002). *Leadership: Enhancing the lessons of experience* (4th ed.). New York: NY: McGraw-Hill Irwin.

Influence. (1985). *American heritage dictionary* (p. 660, 2nd ed.). Boston, MA: Houghton Mifflin Company.

Inspiration without Borders. (2011). Organisational development. Retrieved from http://www.inwibo.com/14.html

Institution. (1985). *American heritage dictionary* (p. 666, 2nd ed.). Boston, MA: Houghton Mifflin Company.

Intrator, S.M., & Scribner, M. (2007). *Leading from within: Poetry that sustains the courage to lead.* San Francisco: CA: Jossey-Bass.

James, R. (2010). *Root and branch: Charles Hamilton Houston, Thurgood Marshall, and the struggle to end segregation.* New York, NY: Bloomsbury Press.

Johnson, S. (n.d.). Thinkexist.com. Retrieved from http://thinkexist.com /quotation/we_must_remember_that_one_determined_person_can /220203.html

Justice. (1985). *American heritage dictionary* (p. 694, 2nd ed.). Boston, MA: Houghton Mifflin Company.

Kenn, D. (2009). *Lawyering from the heart*. Austin, TX: Wolters Kluwer Law & Business.

King, M. L. (1958). *Stride toward freedom: The Montgomery story*. New York, NY: Harper.

King, M. L. (1963). *Strength to love*. Cleveland, Ohio: Augsburg Fortress Publishers.

King, M. L. (1963). I have a dream. Retrieved from http://www .huffingtonpost.com/2011/01/17/i-have-a-dream-speech-text_n _809993.html

King, M. L. (1968). *The drum major instinct*. Retrieved from http://mlk-kpp01.stanford.edu/index.php/encyclopedia /documentsentry/doc_the_drum_major_instinct/

King, M. L. (n.d.). Quotation database. Retrieved from http://www .worldbeyondborders.org/quotes.htm

Kingdon, J. W. (2003). *Agendas, alternatives, and public policies* (2nd ed.). New York, NY: Addison-Wesley Educational Publishers.

Klebanow, D., & Jonas, F. L. (2003). *People's lawyers: Crusaders for justice in American history*. Armonk, NY: M.E. Sharpe.

Kloppenberg, L. A. (2009). Educating problem solving lawyers for our profession and communities. *Rutgers Law Review, 61*(4), 1099–1114.

Kouzes, J. M., & Posner, B. Z. (2003). *The five practices of exemplary leadership*. San Francisco, CA: Pfeiffer.

Kouzes, J. M., & Posner, B. Z. (2003). *The leadership challenge* (3rd ed.). San Francisco, CA: Jossey-Bass.

Leading Edge. (2009). University of Maryland School of Law Leadership, Ethics, and Democracy Initiative. Retrieved from http://www .law.umaryland.edu/programs/initiatives/lead/docs/LEAD_F09 _newsletter.pdf

Legal Services Corporation. (2009, September). Documenting the justice gap in America: The current unmet civil legal needs of low-income Americans. Retrieved from http://www.lsc.gov/pdfs/documenting _the_justice_gap_in_america_2009.pdf

Levy-Pounds, N., & Tyner, A. (2008). The principles of ubuntu: Using the legal clinical model to train agents of social change. *International Journal of Clinical Legal Education, 13*(7), 5–20.

Levy-Pounds, N. (2010). Can these bones live? A look at the impacts of the war on drugs on poor African-American children and families. *Hastings Race and Poverty Law Journal, 7*(2), 353–380.

Levy-Pounds, N., Aba-Onu, F., Salmen, J., & Tyner, A. (2010). Evaluation of gang databases in Minnesota and recommendations for change. *Information & Communications Technology Law, 19*(3), 223–254.

Lopez, G. P. (1984). Lay lawyering. *UCLA Law Review, 32*(1), 1–60.

Lopez, G. P. (1989). The work we know so little about. *Stanford Law Review, 42*(1), 1–13.

Lopez, G.P. (1992). *Rebellious lawyering: One chicano's vision of progressive law practice.* Boulder, CO: Westview Publishing.

Lopez, G. P. (2004). Shaping community problem solving around community knowledge. *New York University Law Review, 79,* 59–114.

Lopez, G. P. (2005). Symposium: Critical race lawyering—Keynote address: Living and lawyering rebelliously. *Fordham Law Review, 73,* 2041–2054.

Maister, D. H., Green, C. H., & Galford, R. M. (2001). *The trusted advisor.* New York, NY: Touchstone.

Mandela, N. (1994). *Long walk to freedom: The autobiography of Nelson Mandela.* Boston, MA: Back Bay Books.

Marshall, C., & Oliva, M. (2006). *Leadership for social justice: Making revolutions in education.* Boston, MA: Pearson/Allyn and Bacon.

Marshall, C., & Rossman, G. B. (2006). *Designing qualitative research* (4th ed.). Thousands Oaks, CA: Sage Publications.

Maslow, A. (2009). Maslow quotes: Wisdom in a nutshell. Retrieved from http://www.abraham-maslow.com/m_motivation/Maslow _Quotes.asp

Maxwell, J. A. (2005). *Qualitative research design: An interactive approach* (2nd ed.). Thousand Oaks, CA: Sage Publications.

McGee-Cooper, A., & Looper, G. (2001). *The essentials of servant-leadership: Principles in practice.* Waltham, MA: Pegasus Communications.

McNeil, G. R. (1983). *Groundwork: Charles Hamilton Houston and the struggle for civil rights.* Philadelphia: University of Pennsylvania Press.

Merriam, S. B. (2009). *Qualitative research: A guide to design and implementation.* San Francisco, CA: Jossey Bass.

Mississippi Access to Justice Commission. (2007). *Report of public hearings on the unmet civil legal needs of low-income Mississippians.* Jackson, MS: Bonnie Allen.

Monroe, L. (1997). *Nothing's impossible: Leadership lessons inside and outside the classroom.* New York, NY: Public Affairs.

Montesquieu, C. (1748). *L'espirit des louis.* Whitefish, MT: Kessinger Publishing, LLC.

Morgan, G. (2006). *Images of organization.* Thousand Oaks, CA: Sage Publications.

NAACP. (1934). *Annual Report.*

Northouse, P. G. (2001). *Leadership: Theory and practice* (2nd ed.). Thousand Oaks, CA: Sage Publications.

Northouse, P. G. (2009). *Introduction to leadership concepts and practice.* Thousand Oaks, CA: Sage Publications.

Northouse, P. G. (2010). *Leadership: Theory and practice* (5th ed.). Thousand Oaks, CA: Sage Publications.

Obama, B. (2011, January). Speech given at McKale Memorial Center, Tucson, AZ. Retrieved from http://www.nytimes.com/2011/01/13/us/politics/13obama-text.html?pagewanted=all

Parks Daloz, L. A., Keen, C. H., Keen, J. P., & Daloz Parks, S. (1996). *Common fire: Leading lives of commitment in a complex world.* Boston, MA: Beacon Press.

Piomelli, A. (2000). Appreciating collaborative lawyering. *Clinical Law Review, 6,* 427–516.

Piomelli, A. (2004). Foucault's approach to power: Its allure and limits for collaborative lawyering. *Utah Law Review, 24*(2), 395–482.

Piomelli, A. (2006). The democratic roots of collaborative lawyering. Clinical *Law Review, 12*(2), 541–614.

Plessy v. Ferguson, 163 U.S. 537 (1896).

powell, j. a. (2003). Lessons from suffering: How social justice informs spirituality. *University of Saint Thomas Law Journal, 1*, 102–127.

powell, j.a. (2010). Re-thinking poverty in a time of crisis. *Forum on Public Policy: A Journal of the Oxford Roundtable*, 1–18.

Quigley, B. (2007). Letter to a student interested in social justice. *DePaul Journal for Social Justice, 1*, 7–28.

Reed, M.W. (1987). The contribution of Charles Hamilton Houston to American jurisprudence. *Howard Law Journal, 30*, 1095–1102.

Richard, L.R. (2002). Herding cats: The lawyer personality revealed. *Report to Legal Management, 29*(11), 1–12. Retrieved from http://www.managingpartnerforum.org/tasks/sites/mpf/assets/image/MPF%20-%20WEBSITE%20-%20ARTICLE%20-%20Herding%20Cats%20-%20Richards1.pdf

Rost, J. C. (1991). *Leadership for the twenty-first century.* Westport, CO: Praeger.

Rubenstein, H., & Rubenstein, H. (2008). *Leadership for lawyers* (2nd ed.). Chicago, IL: American Bar Association.

Shdaimah, C. (2005). *The practice of public interest law: Power, professionalism, and the pursuit of social justice.* Retrieved from ProQuest Digital Dissertations. (AAT 3173573).

Smith, J. C. (1989). Principles supplementing the Houstonian school of jurisprudence: Occasional paper no. 1. *Howard Law Journal, 32*, 493–504.

Smith, R. (2009). The struggles of lawyer-leaders: What they need to know. *NYSBA Journal, 2009*, March/April, 38–40.

Smith v. Allwright. 321 U.S. 649 (1944).

SMRLS. (2010). Southern Minnesota regional legal services: Free legal assistance for low income people on critical legal problems. Retrieved from http://www.smrls.org/

St. Claire, J. (Ed.). (2010). *Hear my voice: A practical guide to advocacy.* Boston, MA: McGraw-Hill.

Staub, R. E. (1996). *The heart of leadership: 12 practices of courageous leaders.* Provo, UT: Executive Excellence Publishing. Retrieved from http://www.netlibrary.com/urlapi.asp?action=summary&v=1 &bookid=6774

Stein, R. (1981). The path of legal education from Edward I to Langdell: A history of insular reaction. *Chicago Kent Law Review, 57,* 429–454.

Stengel, R. (2008, July 9). Mandela: His 8 lessons of leadership. *TIME Magazine.* Retrieved from http://www.time.com/time/magazine/ article/0,9171,1821659,00.html

Stewart, J. (1991). Policy models and equal educational opportunity. *Political Science and Politics, 24*(2), 167–173.

Straub, G. (2010). The missing piece in the empowerment equation: A strategy for delivering personal agency to women in the developing world. Retrieved from http://www.imagineprogram.net/

Stuckey, R. (2007). *Best practices for legal education: A vision and a road map.* New York, NY: Clinical Legal Education Association.

Sullivan, D. R. (2003). *Learning to lead: Effective leadership skills for teachers of young children.* Saint Paul, MN: Redleaf Press.

Sullivan, W. M., & Carnegie Foundation for the Advancement of Teaching. (2007). *Educating lawyers: Preparation for the profession of law.* San Francisco, CA: Jossey-Bass/Wiley.

Susskind, R. (2008). *The end of lawyers? Rethinking the nature of legal services.* Oxford, England: Oxford University Press.

TimeBanks USA. (2011). Mission and values of TimeBanks USA. Retrieved from http://timebanks.org/

Trawally, B. A. (2009). *Nelson Mandela the transformational leader: The struggle for social justice, equality and democratic change in South Africa.* (Master of Arts in Leadership Thesis, Augsburg College, 2009).

Tutu, D. (1994). *The rainbow people of God: The making of a peaceful revolution.* John Allen (Ed.). New York, NY: Doubleday.

Tyner, Artika R., Planting People, Growing Justice: The Tree Pillars of New Social Justice Lawyering (April 12, 2013). Hastings Race and Poverty Law Journal, Vol. 10, p 219, Summer 2013. Available at SSRN: http://ssrn.com/abstract=2302653

Virginia Law. (2012). *Law school life: The layout.* Retrieved from http://www.law.virginia.edu/html/insider/life_layout.htm

Walker, E. L. (2009). *Transcending moments in the lives of leaders.* Retrieved from ProQuest Digital Dissertations. (AAT 2400217).

White, L. (1988). To learn and teach: Lessons from Driefontein on lawyering and power. *Wisconsin Law Review, 1988,* 699–770.

White, L. (1997). The transformative potential of clinical legal education. *Osgoode Hall Law Journal, 35,* 603–612.

Wildman, S. M. (2008). The social justice education student project. Retrieved from http://law.scu.edu/socialjustice/File/Democracy_and _Social_Justice.pdf

Williamson, M. (n.d.). Thinkexist.com. Retrieved from http://thinkexist .com/quotation/in_every_community-there_is_work_to_be_done-in /216307.html

Windley-Daoust, J. (2008). *Living justice and peace: Catholic social teaching in practice.* Winona, MN: Saint Mary's Press.

World Development Report. (2000). *Causes of poverty and a framework for action.* Retrieved from http://siteresources.worldbank.org/ INTPOVERTY/Resources/WDR/English-Full-Text-Report/ch2.pdf

Yin, R. K. (2009). *Case study research: Design and methods* (4th ed.). Los Angeles: Sage Publications.

Zwicker, M. W. (2002). First among equals: How to manage a group of professionals. *Law Practice Management, 28,* 61–64.

About the Author

Dr. Artika R. Tyner is a lawyer and change agent. At the University of St. Thomas School of Law, Dr. Tyner serves as a member of the Clinical Law Faculty and Director of Diversity. She teaches in the Community Justice Project, an award-winning civil rights clinic. The work of the Community Justice Project focuses on training law students to serve as social engineers who create new inroads to justice, freedom, and equality.

Tyner received her B.A. from Hamline University (Major: English; Certificate: Conflict Studies). Due to her passion for advocating for social justice and educational policy reform, she decided to pursue graduate studies at the University of St. Thomas. She began her journey with law school since she recognized that the law is a language of power and sought to become versed in the law. Subsequently, Tyner earned her Master of Public Policy in order to gain tools for effecting social change through policy reform efforts. Later, inspired by the legacy of W.E.B. Dubois, she obtained a Doctorate in Leadership.

Dr. Tyner is committed to empowering others to lead within their respective spheres of influence. She provides leadership development and career coaching for young professionals. She also developed leadership educational materials for K–12 students, college and graduate students, faith communities, and nonprofits. Additionally, Dr. Tyner teaches leadership coursework on ethics, critical reflection, and organizational development. Her research focuses on diversity/inclusion, community development, and civil rights. She has presented her research and conducted leadership training programs both nationally and internationally.

Dr. Tyner leads by example by organizing policy campaigns, fostering restorative justice practices, developing social entrepreneurship initiatives, and promoting assets-based community development. She serves as a global citizen by supporting education, entrepreneurship, and women's leadership initiatives in Africa.

Dr. Artika R. Tyner, J.D., M.P.P., Ed.D.
Dr.ArtikaTyner@gmail.com
Website: www.artikatyner.com